YAQUI WOMEN

Professor of archaeology at the University
of Calgary, Jane Holden Kelley holds degrees from the University of Texas (M.A.,
1951) and Harvard University (Ph.D.,
1966) and studied at the Escuela de An-
tropología in Mexico City. She is coauthor
(with Rosalio Moisés and William Curry
Holden) of *A Yaqui Life: The Personal Chronicle of a Yaqui Indian* (BB 637) and a number
of journal articles.

YAQUI WOMEN

KELLEY, Jane Holden. Yaqui women: contemporary life histories. Nebraska, 1978. 265p ill map bibl 77-14063. 12.50 ISBN 0-8032-0912-6. C.I.P.

CHOICE

Anthropology

Four life histories of Native American women written by an anthropologist who had previously coauthored a similar work on a Yaqui male, *The tall candle: the personal chronicle of a Yaqui Indian* by Rosalio Moises, Jane Kelley, and William Holden (1971). The two works are complementary. The book's lengthy introduction (a discussion of life history methodology and an analysis of cultural and behavioral aspects of Yaqui life) is a much needed addition to the four histories. Life history accounts often neglect these two features. Kelley's personal and intensive association with Yaqui individuals is documented in the introduction; the histories are written with special insight as a result of this association. The volume is a contribution to Native American and women's studies. There is a small bibliography and no index. The book is not especially suitable for researchers. Lower-division and community college readership.

CONTEMPORARY LIFE HISTORIES

By Jane Holden Kelley

Publishers on the Plains

UNP

Library of Congress Cataloging in Publication Data

Kelley, Jane Holden, 1928–
  Yaqui women.

  Bibliography: p. 70
  1. Yaqui Indians—Women. 2. Indians of North America—Arizona—Wom-
en. 3. Yaqui Indians—Social life and customs. I. Title.
E99.Y3K44   970'.004'97   77–14063
ISBN 0–8032–0912–6

CONTENTS

INTRODUCTION

ARIZONA

• Phoenix

NEW
MEXICO

TEXAS

Eloy
• • Marana
Sasabe • Tucson

Nogales

• Hermosillo
• La Colorada
• Guaymas
• Obregón (Cajeme)

San Blas

MEXICO

• Saltillo

• Mazatlán

Marias Islands

• Tepic
Guadalajara

Irapuato
• Celaya

• Mexico

Progreso
• Mérida

Valladolid

Veracruz

• Acapulco

GULF OF CALIFORNIA

BACATETE MTNS.

• Belem
Huirivis

Rahum

Yaqui

• Vicam Station

Potam

• Vicam

• Torim

River

Bacum

Cocorit

Although the main source for anthropological studies is information obtained from individuals, anthropologists normally concern themselves with whole cultures or societies or segments thereof. The individual is seldom the focus of anthropological analysis, nor does he maintain an identity in the final report except in brief case histories, in anthropological life histories, and in what Swallow (1974:55) calls the "participatory literature." There are anthropological problems, however, that respond favorably to narrower and more individualized analytical frameworks. Some topics amenable to this narrower focus are culture change, human mobility, the role of accident and chance, effects of choices, deviance, values, socialization, personality, range of variation in a society, role analysis, friendship, and factors affecting the structuring of interpersonal relationships. As Cronin (1970:12) points out, "anthropologists do indeed need to study individuals: they extract culture from them." This study of life historical information on Yaqui women is predicated on the belief that a focus on individuals as complex entities existing through time can be a useful approach for examining such problems.

Actual and potential uses of anthropological personal documents or life histories have been thoroughly reviewed by Kluckhohn (1945) and Langness (1965). Both concluded that this method was far from being fully exploited as an anthropological tool. The most successful aspect of the life history medium, and

3

its most universal use, has been in projecting cultural understanding and in portraying a particular life way in a personalized, humanized framework. Other usages are underdevel-
oped and poorly represented. For a time, it was felt that culture
and personality studies would result in more direct and real
concern with the individual, but as Spiro (1972:580) and Langness (1965:50) have shown, this has not been the case. The main
reasons for neglecting an extremely valuable level of investiga-
tion are the distrust of subjectivity (and this sort of research is
among the more overtly subjective), the concern for whole
cultures or societies, and deeply entrenched culture-makes-the-
man concepts.

In formulating the research upon which this study is based,
my central concern was with certain aspects of the life history
field as discussed by Kluckhohn (1945) and Langness (1965).
Among other things, they pointed out that: (1) most life
histories have as their subjects stellar personalities; (2) few
societies are represented by more than one personal document;
(3) a few age and sex categories predominate; (4) surprisingly
little analytical use has been made of such documents; (5) the
scarcity of information about collecting conditions limits the
usefulness of many existing documents; and (6) the reader may
be at a loss to know where the subject fits into the society.

Given these considerations, the following goals were set for
this research: (1) informants would be selected on grounds
other than stellar personality, high status, eloquence, or unusually dramatic lives (none of these criteria are undesirable in
an informant, but selection was not to be made on these
grounds); (2) multiple life histories were to be collected; (3)
categories other than older men would be sought; (4) investigator-informant relationships would be described; and (5) the
position of the subjects in their society would be evaluated.

The Research Base and Methodology

The research, supported by the Canada Council, had the dual
objectives of creating life history narratives and exploring the

life history method as a tool for approaching certain anthropological problems. Between 1968 and 1972, I collected life history information from more than twenty-five individuals, most of whom lived in Yaqui communities and barrios in or near Tucson, Arizona (Pascua, Pascua Nueva, and Barrio Libre); Hermosillo, Sonora; and the Sonoran Yaqui Valley villages of Potam, Vicam Switch, and Torim. I spent slightly over six months' time, mostly during the summers, in the company of these informants. In addition, a teen-age Yaqui girl lived in our home for two years. Until a few months before she joined us, she had lived in Pascua and earlier in Torim.

In electing to collect multiple life histories within a limited time, I realized that depth, fullness, and detail would necessarily be sacrificed. The advantages of exploring a range of personalities, life experiences, and roles would, I felt, offset this severe limitation. To achieve a desirable range of variation, potential informants could not be limited to the highly verbal, stellar personalities. As it turned out, two of the women were exceptional informants who could easily have become the subjects of separate books, but most of the others would not have been appropriate subjects of lengthy biographical treatment.

The sizable volume of information collected from informants, along with other observations, was useful for interpretive purposes. Individual life history data provided by the informants were uneven in terms of fullness, content, reliability, and relevance to the analytical orientation. Only nine individuals produced enough information for preliminary narratives. Two were eliminated from inclusion here because they were not Yaqui; one was a Mexican married to a Yaqui and the other a Mayo living with a Yaqui. Some of the remaining narratives, especially those of a mother and her daughters, were extremely repetitive because the subjects' lives had been so thoroughly intertwined. Life history narratives of four women were selected for presentation in this study because these stories have the most content and fullness, a range of life experiences is represented, and repetition is minimal. In the case of Antonia Valenzuela's narrative, the stories obtained from her daughters and a granddaughter have been interwoven to form a composite picture.

The Selection of Informants

Women were chosen as informants because information obtained from or about women is underrepresented in Yaqui ethnographic sources, just as it is in the broader field of life history literature. Initially, it was hoped that a balanced range of roles, ages, and life experiences could be achieved, either through some form of statistical sampling of selected communities, or through defining a series of categories and seeking women who represented those categories. Both ideas were rejected because the sample size, dictated by limitations of time and resources, would be statistically unreliable and prior knowledge of appropriate categories could not be assumed.

For a variety of reasons, I decided to begin the project by working within a single kin unit. Previous life history work with a Yaqui man, Rosalio Moisés (Moisés, Kelley, and Holden, 1971), gave me a substantial amount of personal and genealogical information about members of his kin group. My known association with him also provided a useful introduction to his female relatives. Moreover, I knew they had undergone a wide range of life experiences. Some had been deported to Yucatán early in this century and, as *soldaderas*, had accompanied their soldier husbands or consorts during the Mexican Revolutionary wars; others, born in Sonora, fled to Arizona with their families; and still others were born in Arizona.

While the range of historical life experiences in the group was adequate, other criteria were not so successfully met. The range of roles represented, for example, was not wide. None of Rosalio Moisés's near living relatives were *cantoras* (women who chant prayers and liturgy in religious services), altar women, or *curanderas* (curers); none were monolingual Yaqui speakers. Although the kin group abounded in younger women and children, adequate age representation proved to be difficult because of factors other than selection procedures, such as the willingness of young women to cooperate, their having time to do so, and their getting approval or permission to cooperate from relevant household members, especially husbands. Younger informants felt they "had no history" and were unwilling to talk in group situations.

During the data-collecting phase of the research, circumstances arose that extended the group of informants to include more distant kin groups and unrelated women. Key informants often decided that I needed to talk to a certain person and made arrangements for such meetings. Eventually, two Mexican and two Mayo women living in close association with members of the primary kin group were included.

The goal of working intensively within a single kin group, proved, by and large, to be feasible: most of the women involved in the project were near relatives of Rosalio Moisés. The selection tactics, however, failed to provide certain key roles. It is especially regrettable that younger women did not furnish enough information to produce narratives. Nevertheless, a great deal of information on young women and children has been integrated into the stories presented here of four older women.

The Motivation of Informants

The idea of recording an anthropological life history normally derives from the investigator's culture, not the informant's. Which individuals are motivated to reveal their life story, and how and why they are motivated are therefore important questions in evaluating the information obtained and establishing the position of the subject in his society.

A basic precondition in collecting a life history is that the subject have a pronounced sense of his individuality, a view of his past life as one distinguishable from other lives, and that he perceive his life as worth recording. This syndrome has been called a sense of self, which is probably an unfortunate phrase, since all "normal" individuals presumably have a sense of self. But the sense of self is not evenly expressed around the world because of psychological and cultural factors. Age, sex, personality, role, and status are variables that can cause some individuals to be better subjects for life histories than others in the same society, or that can cause some societies to produce individuals better suited to life history treatment than others. Leslie White, who felt that Pueblo Indians were not good subjects for biographical treatment, said that "the autobiography of a Pueblo Indian is about as personal as the life history of an automobile tire" (White 1943:327). Considering that one of the all-time anthropological life history classics is of a Hopi, one might well question White's conclusion. Nonetheless, his point, which was expanded by Kluckhohn (1945:119–20), contains a kernel of truth.

Yaqui culture definitely produces individuals with a strong enough sense of self for the method to be used. After overcoming their universal initial reaction that mature and older men were the appropriate sources of information about the Yaquis, women were found to possess quite a strong sense of self, individuality, history, and change. The idea that they had a past, a history worth relating, was most strongly developed in mature and older women. The sense of self appeared to be weaker in women who were regarded by others, and who regarded themselves, as marginal Yaquis. Younger people are often described as not knowing and as having no history—a judgment they tend to accept. Although I worked with seven people between the ages of ten and twenty years in interview situations, the results were disappointing, partly because they felt they had no history.

Kluckhohn noted, "There is something to the view that happy individuals, like happy nations, have no histories—at least they feel themselves to have none—it follows—almost on a basis of statistical probability—that the relatively well adjusted person is less likely to be motivated to continue through many long sessions" (1945:117–18). If happy individuals have no history, one might say that all Yaquis have histories. Few, if any, Yaquis escape hardship, disillusionment, disappointments, and violence. The word most commonly used to describe the Yaqui way of life by all the Yaquis with whom I talked was *hard*. Yaqui law is hard; the Yaqui way of raising children is hard; individuals describe their own lives as hard; other people are summed up as hard.

A vital consideration in collecting Yaqui life histories is the intensity of ethnic identity. There appeared to be a relationship between ethnic identity and control of Yaqui cultural content, on the one hand, and strength of the sense of self on the other. Those who were weak in the former areas also seemed to have a weakly developed sense of self and were poor informants for this research. This supposition may be more apparent than real, however; I was, after all, collecting Yaqui life histories, and it is not unreasonable that marginal people would feel they had less to contribute.

The Yaqui identity does not exist in a compact in-group situation, but in a mobile, dispersed population in intimate contact with other ethnic groups. It is a rare and very young Yaqui who does not routinely distinguish Papagos, Mayos, Mexicans, Apaches, "gringos," blacks, Chinese, and Arabs. The deportations and wartime experiences which gave many older Yaquis enforced knowledge of other cultures also heightened their awareness of themselves as Yaquis. This heightened awareness, in turn, is relevant in obtaining life histories.

The idea that the people who are attracted to cooperate in individualized research are the deviants, the ones who feel they have persistently been misunderstood, and the ones who want an audience with a member of the "superior" society (Kluckhohn 1945:117–18) was partially borne out in this study, although there were no obvious deviants. One of the women, convinced that she was persistently misunderstood, poured out her grievances; several of the women, including some of the best informants, were pleased to associate with a member of the "superior" culture; for others, these factors were virtually inoperable. Working primarily within a single kin unit in group situations made it relatively easy to assess these motivational factors.

Sometimes the motivation for cooperation in ethnographic work is the need to acquire an audience from outside the society to be the recipient of information that cannot be released in normal contexts with other members of the person's own society. Secret or privileged information may be conveyed, pent-up hostilities aired, and so on. In this study, the transmission of information not meant for the ears of others in the society did not occur because of the group nature of most of the interview sessions. No woman sought private interviews, and when some were experimentally set up, older women were decidedly uncomfortable in them. Relatively private sessions were necessary for marginal and younger women who were conversationally swamped in groups, but even in those cases, the feeling that they were saying things they did not want others to know was virtually nonexistent.

This situation was in marked contrast to my earlier work with Rosalio Moisés, with whom all interviews were conducted in complete isolation from other Yaquis. He said things that I very much doubt he would have said in the presence of other Yaquis. During my father's ethnographic work with Yaquis in the 1930s and 1950s, a number of men made intricate arrangements and went to extremes to secure secret, private, almost clandestine interviews because of the prevailing military and political situation.

A person seeking information about the Yaquis continues to receive a warm welcome from large segments of Yaqui society. The attitude that anthropologists are exploiters is just beginning to take root among some Arizona men. I did not encounter this potential motive for refusing to cooperate in any of the women with whom I dealt.

Women approached as possible informants considered the proposal seriously and at length. It was made clear that the results of the study would be published and that undoubtedly some of their friends, neighbors, and relatives would read what they had said. Each discussed the fact that, if she cooperated, she would have "to tell the truth." They realized that some of what they would say would not reflect credit to themselves, and that they would have to commit the cardinal sin of talking badly about others. It was interesting to watch each woman arrive at the conclusion that a responsibility for telling the truth, as she saw it, was part of the agreement. They reasoned that there was a difference between talking badly about people in order to cause trouble and in order to be accurate.

Having decided to cooperate, all the women objected to the idea that their names would be changed in the book. If they were going to contribute, they wanted the credit. Some even considered withdrawing from the project if their names were to be changed, although none did so.

Varied, sometimes dramatic, and often unhappy life experiences; the sense of self; the tenacious survival of ethnic identity; the awareness of themselves as Yaquis in a sea of plural societies—all these combined to give the Yaquis, as a group, the necessary cultural and psychological background for this sort of research. Motivation on the part of each individual was, of course, a personal matter, but the high value placed on recording Yaqui history and culture was significant. Most important, however, was my known association with Rosalio Moisés and the relationship in which that association placed me with regard to the women involved. Minor factors were my amusement value—my presence afforded a break in routine— and the resources provided to informants. For some women, my role as listener to grievances and as audience from another culture played a role in their decision to participate.

The Role of the Investigator as Defined by Yaquis

In the structuring of my role as investigator, the most important referent was the long-term relationship between my father and Rosalio Moisés. In fact, I was quite unprepared for the extent to which this association dominated the relationships. When I first met the various women, I explained that I knew Rosalio Moisés and had worked with him on his life story. However, I also stressed that I was an anthropologist from the University of Calgary (Yaquis, especially in the Tucson area, are quite familiar with anthropologists). I had anticipated that my role as a student of Yaqui culture and history would be meaningful, but it was secondary.

The most common explanation of my presence offered by the Yaquis to other Yaquis was that I was the daughter of Rosalio Moisés's *patrón*; at times I was more directly introduced or identified as his *patrona*. A *patrón* (male) or *patrona* (female) can be looked upon as a boss, implying present or past employment of one or more family members. He or she can also be seen as a protector or provider, not just of the employee, but often of whole families. The *patrón* role extends far beyond economic matters, and the relationship may survive long after actual employment has terminated. Had I been choosing role definitions, the *patrona* image is not the one I would have selected. To me it carried connotations of a social hierarchy, of inequality, and of exploitation, all connotations that a middle-class white anthropologist might well feel uncomfortable with.

In common with the Sonoran *patrón* system, I was a non-Yaqui, I provided resources, and, through my father, I represented a long-term relationship. In contrast to normal practices in the *patrón* system, however, my interaction with Yaquis in Arizona and Sonora was on egalitarian footing. The interaction occurred on Yaqui ground rather than in the setting of the *patrón*, and I was asking for information rather than the domestic services that Yaqui women usually offer *patronas*. These differences from traditional *patrona* relationships were appreciated, and it is perhaps fair to say that the women saw me as occupying the fringes of the *patrona* role. The fact that Rosalio Moisés's youngest daughter resided in my household during part of the research period further reinforced this image.

Visiting and hospitality are fairly rigidly circumscribed in Yaqui culture. Fortunately, the *patrona* image placed me within the range of acceptable visitors to women, as did my sex. There is no doubt that the fact that I am a woman expedited this particular research. Yaqui women respond to outside males, and, for that matter, to males in their own society, in a definitely prescribed manner. It is not that a male anthropologist cannot work with Yaqui women—and indeed such work has been done—but a great many potential problems, most of them questions of propriety, were eliminated by the sexual correspondence of investigator and informants. I could be left alone with any woman or with any age range of females without having to give explanations that might have had repercussions for the informant and injured my rapport with other informants.

The range of information we discussed is often considered by the Yaquis to be "women's talk," and much of it "gossip." We discussed people and mundane events more often than religion and politics. It was thought mildly bizarre, especially by young men, that I would be interested in such information, but it was accepted because I, too, was a woman. A male anthropologist would find it more difficult to maintain appropriate male status if he gossiped with women at the kitchen table or interested himself in the same topics.

Upon several occasions I introduced non-Yaqui men into Yaqui households containing primary informants. The Yaqui women became visibly defensive in every case, even when the man involved was my husband. First of all, it was assumed that men should talk to men. If adult Yaqui men were present, they immediately began to talk with the outside man, excluding the Yaqui women. If no Yaqui men were present, the women either became very formal or refused altogether to interact with the outside man by remaining silent, ignoring a proffered hand, or turning their backs. These reactions were most marked in young and middle-aged women. Older women have a great deal more freedom in such matters.

The reaction of Yaqui men to a female investigator is not a mirror image of that of Yaqui women to a male investigator. It has been quite feasible for me to work with Yaqui men on a wide range of subjects and in a wide range of situations. Here, the role of student of Yaqui culture and history becomes much more central. When men were present, they tended to take conversational precedence over women, especially mature men who were household heads or civil or religious leaders. My conversations with such men were usually less egalitarian than conversations with women—more formal and more structured. Men tended to direct and dominate conversations with me in a more forceful manner than did women. They would initiate conversation on a different range of subjects: international politics, the Vietnam war, astronauts, economic affairs, and institutional aspects of Yaqui culture.

Had the project not been defined in terms of women from the beginning, it is doubtful that it would have been as easy to work intensively with them. Outsiders who express an interest in Yaqui culture or history are almost automatically channeled toward older, mature men who can discuss topics such as the Yaqui wars or Yaqui religion. Wherever I went, but especially in the Sonoran Yaqui Valley villages, my hosts systematically provided older men for me to interview. A great deal of continuous and conscious effort was required to maintain a primary focus on women.

My age, marital status, and children were additional referents that actively shaped my role as defined by the Yaquis. Middle-aged and older women accepted me as someone who had lived long enough to know something—a significant factor because the Yaquis closely correlate age and knowledge.

During the first years of research, I was alone or accompanied by a younger female assistant (one in 1970 and another in 1972). The Yaquis persistently interpreted my relationship to them as kin-based. Even after it was explained that we were not relatives, we would be introduced as mother and daughter, sisters, cousins, or aunt and niece.

The fact that my husband would let me go off on this kind of venture was a never ending topic of discussion. For one season, my husband and children accompanied me. This visit removed my stories of husband and children from the realm of possible myth to reality based in the women's own personal experience.

Several aspects of my background further affected my role as defined by the Yaquis and influenced my rapport with them. First, my experiences on farms and ranches in Texas during the 1930s and 1940s, plus such esoteric talents as livestock judging, provided background familiarity and points of intellectual and psychological contact with the life-style in Yaqui Valley villages. Second, two years of my childhood were spent in the total Catholic environment of a convent boarding school. Third, I had lived in Mexico for two years. Of particular significance were the facts that I had visited places in Mexico which figured prominently in some of the life stories, and that I had learned Spanish there. One of the most frequent comments made to and about me was that my Spanish was "Mexican Spanish"—not book or border Spanish. These particular fragments of my personal history would be meaningless in other research contexts, and, had my past been different, other factors would have been called into play in the Yaqui work. None of the factors mentioned was directly relevant to the research, but all were significant in affecting the nature of investigator-informant relationships and in shaping the Yaquis' view of me as the investigator.

The Collecting Conditions

In the Tucson area, I (and whoever accompanied me) lived outside of the Yaqui communities, only occasionally remaining in a Yaqui household overnight. By and large, we called on informants daily, spending most of each day between mid-morning and late afternoon with them. The Sonoran work involved continuous contacts because there we joined households.

Most of the contact with informants occurred in group situations. The size and make-up of the assembled group varied with household size and composition (households varied in size from one to twenty individuals) and time of day. Women preferred to do their housework in the early morning, and often requested that we not arrive until mid- or late morning. On the other hand, early morning was a good time for less public conversations conducted from the kitchen table while the woman went about her housework. Afternoons almost invariably attracted women and children from other households, some drawn by the unusual situation and others engaged in normal visiting.

Men were rarely present in the households of informants until late afternoon. If present during the day, the men occupied a different area. In those households containing men, the return of men from work in the late afternoon usually caused the women's conversational unit to break up.

The household setting and group nature of most visiting and interview sessions meant that any number of distracting activities could be going on at any one time. People came and went, children got hurt and had to be attended to, visitors arrived and normal hospitality took precedence over the life history project, and various crises arose from time to time. In some households, the woman's directives to children were a constant refrain. Despite these interruptions, however, the group situation was valuable for providing verbal stimulation. Subjects forgotten or avoided by primary informants were sometimes introduced by kibbitzers, and the group situation provided one of the best checks on reliability and accuracy.

I found open-ended interviewing methods combined with informal visiting appropriate for eliciting life history data. A bare chronological outline of who, what, when, and where was established early as a framework. Sections of that framework were then explored and informants were allowed to elaborate on topics of particular interest on an individual basis. The informant's personality and the developing state of that person's life history were factors that affected particular interview sessions. With some informants, on occasion, virtually each piece of information was extracted in response to a direct question. At other times, a flow of information might be sustained for hours, with few triggering questions or comments. Sessions allowing profitable lines to develop with minimal direction often alternated with those devoted to clarifications and prepared questions. Occasionally an informant would forcefully direct the discussion, as happened one morning in Pascua. I arrived clutching a list of questions formulated on the basis of previous interviews. As I crossed the threshold, the informant stated that today she would tell me about witches (her sister had discussed witches the previous day), and for three hours she proceeded to do so.

Interviews differed from informal visiting by being arranged ahead of time, by the recording of informants' hours for calculating fees, by open note taking, and, if possible, by tape recording. No notes were taken in visits, and while gifts were sometimes involved, hourly fees were not precisely calculated. Interviews ranged from short sessions to ones of three or five hours. It was difficult to sustain intensive interviewing for longer periods; moreover, all the women had other activities that demanded their time and attention.

Another important part of the research was the daily write-up of observations. I maintained genealogical files, largely in self-defense as a means of keeping straight the hundreds of characters mentioned in the stories. During the two seasons that I had an assistant, we had daily conferences to review our position, check our perceptions, and plan future work. Between field sessions, the main life histories were put into preliminary narrative form, a procedure that inevitably revealed weak sections and new problems needing clarification. These gaps usually became the first priority in the next field season.

Most of the conversation was conducted in Spanish. I know no Yaqui and the majority of Yaquis are now fluent in both Yaqui and Spanish. One monolingual speaker in Torim who would have made an excellent informant, and one whom I desperately wanted to work with, was eliminated because of the frustrations of working through interpreters. Yaqui was often spoken in my presence, and it is unfortunate that I did not understand the language. Sometimes it was deliberately used to prevent my understanding, an easy alternative to leaving the room for a private conversation. Yaqui-language interludes occurred on some of the tape-recorded interviews, and when I later obtained translations, the subject matter was mostly a rehash of the Spanish conversation. In certain visiting situations, especially between older individuals, when Yaqui was considered the appropriate language, translations into Spanish were often rendered for my benefit. The only time that I felt I was being talked about in a derogatory manner, in a way I was not meant to understand, was when I became the subject of *pascola* jokes at a Pascua *cumpleaño* (death anniversary) ceremony. (*Pascolas* are dancers who combine secular jokes and caricatures with animal motifs.) With the exception of the Torim monolingual speaker, Spanish was therefore an adequate tool for the informants selected.

Investigator bias and selectivity most obviously occurred at the time of recording. I took notes in English or a mixture of English and Spanish, using Spanish words or phrases or longer passages when English alone could have been ambiguous, or when I desired the exact wording. A few words or phrases were simply easier to record in Spanish, and terms I could not translate were recorded as I heard them. My notes were not verbatim transcripts—far from it. This discrepancy became extremely apparent when the tape of an interview was compared with my notes of the same session. Many comments extraneous to life history information were not recorded, although cases of confusion and conflicting information were.

The Yaquis wanted almost as much information about me as I wanted about them. Their questions centered on my purpose for being there, my family, and my reactions to their lives. Did my husband get drunk or beat me? Did I own a TV? Could I dance like the hippies? Did I mind using an outhouse? Did I like their food? What were my religious convictions? Urban Arizona Yaquis wanted to know the depth of my knowledge of and experience with drugs, and especially if my children were involved with marijuana, heroin, or pills. In Potam, the women were curious as to why I washed my hair separately from the rest of me, when they wash their hair every time they bathe.

My strongest post-field-work impression is that the Yaquis and Yaqui culture did not seem strange to me. Personal and cultural shocks were so minimal that they can be listed. There was an uncomfortable period in Potam when boys between the ages of five and twelve years discovered they could make my ten-year-old son react in satisfactory ways by hurting an old dog. It was difficult to know that a boy in an adjacent household was dying while the parents refused to seek medical aid. This distress was shared by relatives of the family, who exercised considerable pressure on the parents—to no avail. Similarly, one informant had a baby so malnourished it never cried, although money was available for both food and medical aid, or so I thought, as did her mother and sisters-in-law. The most unpleasant single episode occurred in Empalme when a group of older Mexican boys discovered that the many women and children with me were Yaquis. Within minutes, verbal insults escalated into taunting of the Yaquis (e.g., Yaquis eat horses and burros, are murderers and thieves, and are decidedly inferior beings). I was afraid open violence would result, although the older Yaqui women interpreted the situation more realistically. Nonetheless, the fact that so much feeling could erupt so spontaneously and in such an innocent setting (we had stopped at an ice house on a quiet residential street), made informants' accounts of personal indignities much more vivid.

In Arizona, my assistant or family and I returned each evening to our own private world; in Sonora we did not have that daily respite. Although I was not adversely affected by the omnipresent humanity, perhaps because I live with four children, nearly every other person who accompanied me was, sooner or later. After one of my assistants locked herself in the camper at midday when the interior was like an oven, we took a break in Obregón. My children particularly disliked being continuously observed and touched by other children.

Frustrations arose when informants failed to show up for scheduled interviews or when interviews were a complete waste of time. A few evasive tactics were necessary, as when I was given a bowl of *atole* which I was unable to face. Since refusing it would have been impolite—it was supposed to be good for me in my "unsettled" state—I slipped out in the dead of night in search of the family dog, who was most coopera- tive. Incidents such as dodging a tractor being driven without lights across a dark and crowded plaza in the midst of a fiesta required fancy footwork.

My position as outsider, guest, and *patrona* directly associated with Yaqui women buffered me and those with me from the harsher realities. When unpleasantness threatened or occurred, Yaqui women moved in to protect us. Once in the Potam church during the Fiesta de Trinidad, a drunk man approached my assistant and caused a minor scene by commenting loudly that, since she was so rich, why was she there looking at the poor Yaquis? He insisted that she eat a dry, rather dirty tortilla resurrected from his pocket. Two Yaqui women, one an in- formant and one unknown to me, watched the scene for a few minutes before moving firmly in front of my assistant, telling the man off in no uncertain terms, and giving him a vigorous push that effectively ended the episode.

Another time, in Pascua, a drunk accosted me and my assistant, alternating between being truculent and making passes. As soon as the woman we had accompanied to the fiesta realized what was happening, she delivered a loud lecture on drunkenness, making it clear that we were with her and not to be disturbed. For the rest of the evening, she placed us in chairs next to the retired head of the *matachines* (one of the societies of ceremonial dancers) and isolated us from the drunken element. At a household fiesta in Pascua, a drunk man put his arm around my waist, an act immediately ob- served by the woman of the house, who told him I was her *patrona* and he would be in trouble with her husband as well as my husband, who was present, if he did not afford me the proper respect.

These episodes—the list could be expanded by several other similar examples—demonstrate the protected status I enjoyed. Yaqui women also protected me in other ways, as in safe- guarding possessions of which I was careless and by advising me about which pleas for money or other things were genuine and which would result in one more drinking bout. Once a young man was forced to return something he had stolen from me.

The protected status I enjoyed did not extend equally to everyone who accompanied me. Non-Yaqui men in my company were placed in a completely different category, as were children. To give a minor example, Yaqui children in the Potam household we joined were orally corrected if they touched me, leaned on my chair, handled my possessions, or demonstrated their presence too loudly for adult conversation to be carried on at a normal level. My children, however, were not buffered in this fashion, with the result that they and their possessions were constantly touched. Since my children knew virtually no Spanish, their objections, in English, were not effective. My son's checker game was more or less commandeered, and his frustration at the innovations in rules was acute.

Many facets of Yaqui life, especially violence and harsh punishment of children, would have led to personal and culture shock if I had directly observed them, but I was only told about these things. Ethnographic conditions among the Yaquis in the 1890s and early 1900s would have been quite different from those I experienced. It is just as well that I did not witness the case of child punishment that occurred in Potam during the research period, in which a mother held her son's hands on hot coals for stealing coins worth less than a peso. It would have been traumatic to encounter at first hand the group rape by non-Yaqui men of a Yaqui woman, who was permanently disabled by the final vicious act of having a broken bottle lodged in her vagina with such force that it injured her spine.

The Effects of Providing Payment and Resources to Informants

Langness (1965:40) pointed out that few life history informants appear to have been paid. Perhaps this omission has been the result of what might be called collaborator psychology fostered by the prolonged and intimate contact required between investigator and informant. Direct payment can be construed as inappropriate in relationships characterized as pseudo-kinship or friendship, the terms used in the great majority of life histories in which the investigator-informant relationship has been described (Langness 1965:40). Many, perhaps most, anthropological life histories appear to be the result of a fortuitous pairing of investigator and informant, a factor that might also militate against payment.

Provision for payment of informants (on a scale roughly in line with that in effect in the communities) was built into my research grant from the Canada Council. Unlike the earlier life history work with Rosalio Moisés, for which he was not directly paid, this project was not fortuitous, but was planned. Complications arose in calculating informants' fees because interviews so often attracted relatives, neighbors, and children, sometimes in substantial numbers. These unsolicited individuals stimulated informants and contributed information, but resources were simply not available to pay several times for the same interview hour. Diffuse payment of everyone who contributed information would have resulted in other problems, such as attracting ever larger numbers of spectators. Some arbitrary decisions were therefore made. Visiting was distinguished from interviewing, and fees were formally calculated only for arranged interviews. At other times, resources were given to the hostess to extend such hospitality as she deemed appropriate.

About half of the informants felt uncomfortable about accepting direct cash payment, and several older women refused. Gifts in the form of money, food, or services were acceptable; however, since we were operating within a gift framework, I was given gifts in return. Interestingly enough, the information these older women imparted was not part of the reciprocal gifts. Rather, they gave me hospitality, meals, and things such as pillow cases, lengths of cloth, a Yaqui rosary, and a miniature *pascola* mask. One woman gave me her wedding ring and gold earrings. Gift exchange was not limited to informants but involved other household members as well. None of the women kept their own record of hours; the calculation of fees was left to my discretion. Only one woman approached me to work for money, and while I was willing to work with her, she proved to be a poor informant. Since I did not attempt to gather information without paying informants, it is impossible to say what would have happened in other circumstances. Certainly a number of women would have talked to me freely without payment, but it is doubtful that I would have been so welcome if my presence had been unaccompanied by more visible resources.

One of the resources I provided for some informants was mobility. Aside from a few confirmed stay-at-homes, the women and the children resident in their households enjoyed shopping, trips to the beach, long-distance travel, and visiting in other households. In Sonora, where fewer individuals had vehicles—and I heard of no Yaqui woman who knew how to drive—mobility for women and children was significantly less than for Arizona Yaquis. Women and children were more dependent on men for permission to leave the house and for transportation. The comment was frequently made in the Potam household that what they would miss most when I left would be the trips to Cochorit beach, Obregón, and the other Yaqui villages. When I returned, the first reaction was that now they could take trips again. My trips from Arizona to Sonora were invariably in the company of women, often joined by children who went along for the ride. Even in Arizona, I performed the service of transporting women, fetching ceremonial specialists for fiestas, and so on.

The effects of providing payment or resources varied with the particular informant. All of the Arizona Yaqui informants could be classed as members of the local culture of poverty, but all had some sources of cash income. Resources I provided did not appreciably affect their living on even a temporary basis. Cash seemed to be used primarily to pay outstanding debts or to help finance household fiestas. The situation in Sonora was quite different. Recompense in whatever form definitely affected the recipients' immediate standard of living. Resources meant that they had more meat to eat, a more varied diet, and medical attention they would not otherwise have had.

The effects were most pronounced in the case of Chepa Moreno of Hermosillo. At the time, she was elderly, in poor health, unable to work, and living alone. Every two weeks a Catholic charity organization gave her small amounts of food.

As long as she was physically able, she walked several miles about once a month to see an old *patrona* who gave her five or ten pesos. She had resorted to signing away the title to her small property. Chepa was on a starvation diet, gradually losing the struggle for survival. When I first met her, she said she was dying—it was "the will of God." The resources I provided radically changed her life, temporarily. Her craving for meat was satisfied, her cupboard was no longer bare, she received medical attention, medicine, and much needed eyeglasses. Having resigned herself to approaching death and to accepting the idea that she would not leave her neighborhood again until she was buried, she was suddenly mobile, seeing places she thought she had seen for the last time. It was said she stopped dying. One year she accompanied me to Potam for a month, becoming my constant shadow. Her Potam relatives joked that she would never let me out of her sight.

If the question arose of an informant's cooperating solely for the sake of recompense, it would arise most clearly in the case of Chepa Moreno. The resources I provided changed the quality of her life for a brief time, but I do not think that she invented information to sustain the relationship. By all odds she was the most difficult of the women to work with. Not infrequently she was in a fractious mood, losing her temper when I did not know as much as she thought I should, or if I asked her to repeat something, or if she thought I was writing too slowly. A day of interviewing amid the cats, dogs, pigeons, and chickens in 110° F. heat was often a total write-off. Although I spent seven or eight weeks in her company, the basic content of her life story was obtained in two sessions. She was consistent in her stories, and those portions of her life that could be crosschecked were reliable.

Reliability, Selectivity, Distortion, and Bias

The investigator cannot observe the events, behavior, and beliefs that belong to the past. How is he to know that informants are telling the truth as they perceive it? The subjective nature of life history information is one of the central problems in making the approach of greater analytical value. The subjective element cannot be eliminated, but it can be minimized by the investigator's explicitly setting forth his criteria for evaluating reliability and elucidating investigator-informant relationships.

Life history information is, by its very nature, somewhat idiosyncratic. No person faithfully mirrors ethnographic reality. Chance, historical accidents, position in society, and many other factors temper the expression of culture in individual behavior. Ethnographic accounts are useful background for assessing the reliability of informants, but they will not serve in the detailed checking of reliability. Crosschecking and verification are possible for much information, but even the most diligent checking will leave an unverified residue.

Deliberate falsification is always a possibility, whether for monetary gain, amusement, or sheer cussedness. A peripheral story serves to illustrate this point. As everyone knows, Carlos Castañeda's books have had a tremendous impact on a wide audience, and Castañeda's don Juan is a Yaqui. I would assume that every anthropologist who has worked with the Yaquis has been bombarded with inquiries about Yaqui drug use, sorcery, and what have you. I have received letters from people wanting an introduction to a Yaqui *brujo* (witch or sorcerer), and the subject of my Yaqui research is never mentioned without someone asking me if there really is a don Juan. Do I know him or people like him? Or are all Yaquis like don Juan? To such inquiries, I can only say that I have not encountered don Juan or anyone like him, an admission guaranteed to lower my social value on the spot.

The Yaquis themselves are now approached by outsiders in search of don Juan. A Pascua Nueva Yaqui leader related that no few Volkswagen buses, usually with California license plates, find their way to Pascua Nueva. The inhabitants of the VW buses are described as "long-haired hippies," for the word *hippie* has deeply penetrated Yaqui consciousness with strong negative connotations. The Pascua Nueva leader explained with some delight his tactics for dealing with these unwelcome intrusions. When inquiries begin, he says he has never heard of don Juan. Slowly he shifts to admitting cautiously that there is a don Juan but he must be protected. Finally he weakens and tells the inquirers where don Juan lives. There actually is an old man named don Juan who lives in Pascua Nueva, one said to have considerable ingenuity in spinning tales. Everyone is vastly amused and the hippies are usually good for a little money, cigarettes, beer, and other things before they realize they have been had.

This same Pascua Nueva leader asked how I knew that what I was told was true, adding that Yaquis are extremely good at making up stories. He says he personally never believes half of what he is told because he knows the Yaquis for what they are. He is also extremely critical of published anthropological accounts, saying that Yaquis have been misrepresented. The only suggestion that anthropologists are exploiters—that I encountered—came from this man, who has been a key informant for other anthropologists. How can any anthropologist really understand Yaqui religion, he asks, when he has yet to meet a deeply religious anthropologist.

Rosalio Moisés's life story is now published (Moisés, Kelley, and Holden, 1971). His own son brands the book a pack of lies, even doubting, in his more negative moods, that Rosalio was born at the time and place specified. The response of the son, who is extremely well informed on Yaqui affairs, was encountered quite early in the present research, raising the specter of unreliability in no uncertain terms. One of the things that I did was to crosscheck Rosalio's story whenever possible. Errors essentially fall into two categories. On the one hand, there are untruths about things concerning people so closely associated with Rosalio, or about himself, that they are obviously deliberate. For example, he gave a tragic account of the drowning of a half-brother and his family in a Yaqui Valley flood. That brother lived for many years after the flood, and none of his family was drowned. One woman whose picture he showed me as depicting an Italian girl he bigamously married in California was actually a relative living in Esperanza whom he claimed by name as a daughter by yet another woman. The stories relating to the various women whom he asserted he had lived with are insofar as I can now judge, where deliberate distortion was most likely to occur.

The other category of errors was not, I believe, so deliberate. I have found that names he gave for people at a certain time and place often do not correspond exactly to names for those same people obtained from informants more closely related and therefore presumably better informed about them. Kinship relations he gave for unrelated and distantly related persons have often proved to be wrong in detail. Stories he was told about events in peoples' lives that occurred beyond his personal experience are sometimes incorrect at a detailed level. To illustrate, he gave the name of the place to which Chepa Moreno was deported, and it is wrong, but the overall tone of his remarks about her deportation is sound. Similarly, he said Dominga Ramírez and her mother returned from Yucatán in 1907 and were deported again in 1909. Again, this is untrue, but they were deported originally under circumstances much as he described. Rosalio's style of storytelling demanded minutiae—he had to append names to characters, describe conversations, detail a route he traveled, list the food at a fiesta, and so on. The nature of the minute details was far more significant than the details themselves. Extensive crosschecking of his story has led me to acknowledge that his reliability about any single "fact" was not as high as I had hoped. However, the gross outline has been vindicated, and the details are in no sense un-Yaqui.

Sensitivity to Rosalio's son's criticisms caused a heightened awareness of the problem of reliability in the new project. Evaluation techniques included collecting the same story at intervals and extensive crosschecking with other people. Group interviews proved to be extremely helpful in detecting omissions, deliberate lies, and half-truths. As I broadened my knowledge of Yaqui culture, made extensive genealogical charts, and otherwise gained control of relevant data, I was able to make better assessments of reliability.

Interestingly enough, the main area of prevarication and deliberate untruths found among the women was the same as for Rosalio Moisés—the number and identity of consorts. None of the women admitted to casual affairs with men by whom they had no children, although the probability is high that such affairs occurred. When asked why several men had been omitted from their stories, they invariably said they did not think I would approve of their behavior. The women's style of storytelling was quite different from Rosalio's. None of the women compulsively supplied details—the minutiae—that he seemed to feel essential.

In spite of the precautions, a great deal of information remains that cannot be independently verified. Events experienced by only one informant could not be crosschecked. Deportation experiences were highly idiosyncratic and today none of the deported informants are in contact with other members of their deportation party. Quite by chance, I met members of the Yucatecan Peón family when they were visiting mutual friends in Calgary and was able to verify that the Hacienda Nokak to which Chepa Moreno was deported in Yucatán had been, in fact, owned by the Peón family as she indicated. *Soldadera* experiences were only broadly subject to checking against accounts of the Mexican Revolution.

Basically, I have assumed that informants are unlikely to be able to sustain for any length of time what Langness (1965:38) calls the web of falsehoods; that if an informant proved to be reliable where checks were possible, the chances are good that other information she provided is reliable also. The question of reliability ultimately comes down to an evaluation of each informant, built up over time. Other people's attitudes toward each informant form part of this picture, as do the crosschecks from multiple informants and internal consistency. The quality of the investigator's judgment is vital.

Checking and evaluating reliability in the ways discussed above are separable from issues of selectivity, rosy-hued or distorted memory, and bias. Franz Boas once said of autobiographies and biographies that "they are not facts, but memories and memories distorted by the wishes and thoughts of the moment. The interests of the present determine the selection of data and color the interpretation of the past" (1943:334). That is a perfectly reasonable statement. Without a doubt, this subjectivity is a major reason personal documents have played such a minor role as an anthropological analytical tool. As I see it, the subjective nature of this class of information can be placed in perspective by the investigator, and if that is done, there are problems for which individualized information is eminently suitable. Attitudes toward subjectivity are changing perceptibly in anthropology, and such shifts have great potential for making life history research a more important tool for analytical purposes.

In the present study, the women informants projected rosy-hued memories and let their biases show. I selected and guided, sometimes consciously and sometimes unconsciously. Had these data been collected from the same women by a different investigator, had multiple investigators been involved, had the contact time with each informant been longer or shorter, had the women been made sensitive to different aspects of their past by the use of different trigger mechanisms in the present—somewhat different documents would have resulted. These women have complex personalities and they have had more experiences than can be put in a few pages. One could say that any value this study has is in spite of these subjective factors, but I prefer to say it is because of them that the study has taken its present form.

Representativeness

Unless an anthropologist is seeking to project a cultural statement in a life history framework, as Radin (1920, 1926) and Pozas (1962) have done, it matters not how "typical" the subject is so long as where he or she fits in society is spelled out. Individuals can be selected on the basis of their participation in what the anthropologist perceives to be key systems or institutions, and some individuals more closely approach cultural ideals, but this does not necessarily make them more representative. It was because range, not the "typical," was sought in this study that multiple life histories were used. I would argue that these women are neither atypical nor unrepresentative, but that is not the same as saying they are either typical or representative.

As noted earlier, some rather vital categories were omitted as a result of the selection procedures used in the project. The absence of *cantoras* and altar women, the only formal religious roles open to females, is possibly more significant to anthropologists than to the Yaqui women. The latter tend to see *cantoras,* for example, as Yaqui women who, somewhat by chance, have additional facets to their social personalities. There is an element of chance in who becomes a *cantora.* Recruitment occurs in several ways, but the most common method is in response to a vow, or *manda,* normally made by another person such as a mother or grandmother upon an occasion of illness or stress. Illness can be handled in other ways. Other *mandas* could be made or other curing techniques used. Actually, the determination of who becomes a *cantora* is considerably more complicated because of literacy requirements and the intensive training required. Nonetheless, the fact that no informants occupied these roles does reflect chance elements to some extent. *Cantoras* have about the same number of husbands and consorts as the women selected, live in households of similar composition, perform the same sorts of daily activities, and have experienced much the same range of events.

Since monolingual Yaqui speakers were excluded, since only one woman wore old-style clothes, and because *cantoras* (famous for their extreme conservatism) were not included, the possibility that my informants were marginal to the heart and soul of Yaqui society must be considered. There are women who would refuse to talk to an outsider like me and there are women whose husbands or parents would not allow them to do so. Perhaps the fact that the women I selected talked to me can be taken as a further indication of failure to get at the conservative core.

Monolingual Yaqui speakers are less likely to be marginal than bilingual individuals or monolingual Spanish speakers. Knowing Spanish or even English does not automatically imply marginality, however; some of the more conservative people are, in fact, bilingual as a result of the diverse conditions Yaquis have experienced for over a century. In regard to dress, few or no Arizona Yaqui women habitually wear the old-style dress. A woman wearing the traditional skirt and blouse with a *rebozo* is immediately assumed to be from the Yaqui Valley. In the Yaqui Valley villages, dress is indeed a measure of traditionalism and economic status, but it is not a totally reliable yardstick. Among the informants, the only woman who wore old-style dress was Chepa Moreno of

Hermosillo, and she was effectively living outside of Yaqui society.

Willingness to talk to outsiders is dependent on a number of factors, one of which is conservatism or traditionalism. More significant, however, is personality. Extrovert women can be extremely traditional and still talk to outsiders. One woman, who was not an informant although I knew her, was described by her daughter (who was an informant) as an inveterate talker: "Why, she even talked to people at bus stops." The mother was definitely at the conservative core of Tucson Yaqui society. A Potam informant, a highly respected older woman, was a perpetual embarrassment to her family because of her penchant for talking to strangers. I have seen her initiate conversations with Yaquis and non-Yaquis in innumerable situations. Two women specified that they had previously refused to act as ethnographic informants. That they agreed to do so in this case was due entirely to my position as the *patrona* of Rosalio Moisés with the known thirty-five-year association between Rosalio and my father. Although several of the informants were accustomed to interacting with outsiders, at least one-third of them were not.

As a group, the informants exhibited a wide spread on a traditional-marginal continuum. None was precisely at the conservative heart, but several were close. Others scattered across the scale, and one young woman completely rejected her Yaqui heritage. The relative position of each of the four women whose life histories are included here will be indicated in their stories.

The Interpretive Framework

The basic tenet underlying this exercise in collecting life histories is that individualized data can contribute an important dimension for anthropological problems that may respond more sensitively to analysis on this scale of magnitude. The broad concern guiding the research from the beginning was an

interest in factors affecting the structuring of interpersonal relationships and adaptive strategies in the face of alternatives.
More specific topics for interpretation were generated in the
course of field work and at later stages. In other words, the
methodology was broadly inductive after the initial orientation,
with an ongoing interplay between raw data and interpretive
framework. Consideration of the structuring of interpersonal
relationships and adaptive strategies exercised by each woman
forms the connective tissue for the interpretive treatment of
each woman's story.

Twenty-five informants represent too small a sample to claim
statistical validation for Yaqui society as a whole, and the
processes of selection must be taken into account. No plea is
made that these data are typical or representative of all Yaqui
women or of Yaqui society. This approach is intended primarily to offer insights into some aspects of the lives of these
Yaqui women that are not otherwise available in ethnographic
reports. Comparative data from other sources are used to
evaluate these findings. Selected topics are discussed below as
a background for the life history narratives.

The Household as a Key Element in Structuring
Interpersonal Relationships

The household is now and has been as far back as pertinent
information can be gleaned the most basic unit in Yaqui
society. A single house or group of houses that form a
household will have a seasonally fluid and long-term shifting
body of inhabitants. Its flexibility makes it a highly adaptive
institution, and this adaptability is an important factor in the
tenacious survival of Yaqui society. The household is the basic
economic unit; its members channel the formation of deeper
emotional ties; it is the primary locus of child care; and it
contributes to the recruitment of individuals for ceremonial
society membership, inasmuch as such membership often
results from vows, or *mandas*, made by household members.

Variation in household size and composition has been discussed by Spicer (1940:79–81; 1954:58–60); further cases are

provided by the life histories here. Not only does an individual experience households of varying compositions, for each individual will, in the course of a lifetime, belong to a number of household units, but at any one time there will be a variety of households other than his own to observe. Thus, diachronic and synchronic experiences acquaint individuals with the range of variation and flexibility of this basic unit.

Sexual differentiation of roles and age grading are the two most salient features of household structure, influencing every phase of life within the household. Sexual differentiation is the normal solution for meeting certain basic requirements: economic support, household maintenance, and the care of its members. Men traditionally furnish the economic base and women care for the household and its inhabitants. When a sexual division of labor is not possible, this basic division of roles is nevertheless maintained. In two households consisting of adult men (in both cases brothers) in one Arizona community recently, for example, one man did the cooking, washing, and household chores while the other supplied income by working for wages. There was no intimation of homosexuality. A similar division operates in households where women and children provide some or all of the economic support. Only where economic support is available from sources such as welfare, social security, pensions, and insurance (more common in Arizona than in Mexico) is this basic division of roles seriously warped. Traditionally, the desirability of incorporating a male to provide income and resources has been a major stimulus to the rapid reformulation of households when this role was not filled. Conversely, while men occasionally wash clothes, cook, and maintain the house, it is considered infinitely preferable to have a woman do these tasks. If there are children in the household, a woman's presence becomes almost mandatory.

Except in instances such as single-member households or small neolocal units, the factor of age grading affects the authority structure, distribution of tasks, and allocation of resources. The larger the household, the more obvious these effects are. As one grows older in Yaqui society, one is accorded increased authority and respect. Ideally, the oldest members contributing to household maintenance and welfare exercise the most authority and receive the most respect. For noncontributing older members, authority may diminish but respect should remain.

Not unexpectedly, the sexual differentiation and age grading can be modified by other factors. In larger households, a household core, composed of the more stable members with greater residential continuity, dominate the arrangements; the house may be recognized as theirs. Other influences are the relationship of individuals to the core members of the household, the degree of permanence in terms of affiliation with a household unit, the relative contributions to support and maintenance, and personalities.

Central to the adaptive, flexible nature of household structure is the fact that alternative household affiliation was and is available to most individuals at most times in their life cycle. Infants and small children have no choice, but older children and all adults have some potential of changing households. Boys and men exercise this option more frequently than girls and women, although girls, before marriage, often change their household affiliation. Life stories show that males between the ages of eleven and fourteen often leave the household in which they have been raised. The greater mobility of males through household units is due in part to the practice of taking short-term employment in different localities, but young men also shift to more compatible households within the same community more often than do females. Freedom to shift household affiliation is reduced after marriage.

When autonomy is exercised in selecting another household unit, the outside limits are determined largely by the kinship system and the strength of the attendant interpersonal relationships. The kin relationships of siblings of parents (aunts and uncles) and their children (cousins, or *primos hermanos*) appear to be the most likely to be activated in selecting alternative household arrangements, although siblings, grandparents, the siblings of grandparents, more distant relatives, and ritual kin relationships may serve. Within these limits, those relationships characterized by ongoing contact and active interpersonal relationships will be favored.

Some individuals may lack known relatives at a particular time and place. Disruptions of family and kin ties in Sonora before and after the turn of the century severed some individuals from their kin base. It is unknown to what extent this disruption limited access to household affiliation, but ritual kin relationships counteracted this unfortunate state, and in times of stress the ultimate kinship of being a Yaqui sufficed. As one Yaqui said, "All Yaquis are kin. If we knew enough about our fathers and their fathers in turn, we would know we are all relatives."

In a mobile society such as this one, location is a consideration in selecting households with which to affiliate. Quite often a decision about where one wants to be precedes the decision of which household to join. In circular fashion, knowledge of where there are households to join strongly influences decisions about where to go. Most Yaquis can easily find households to join in the several urban and rural Yaqui communities in Arizona, in Yaqui Valley villages, and even in California.

The relative affluence of household units and personality factors further affect decisions about household affiliation. In the personal accounts, strong, positive personalities attracted people to their household. When such a stellar person presides over a household with a stable and adequate economic base, a large household is almost guaranteed. The death of a dominant household member, on the other hand, often causes the breakup of a household. In very few cases did the household cease to exist as a physical unit, nor was there total discontinuity of members; smaller segments splintered off. The fissioning process occurs constantly, but the splitting of households under the circumstances of the death of a particularly strong and significant member has emotional overtones lacking in other shifts of household affiliation.

The factors considered so far operate from the point of view of an individual exercising choice in the selection of household units. Individuals may also be recruited by members of the household unit or may be sent to a household unit for specific reasons. Children may change residence as a result of being "claimed" by an adult. When aid is needed during an illness or for child care, relatives may be called upon to join a household to help. Grown children especially are expected to heed such requests. Individuals without visible responsibilities in their own household find it hard to evade such requests, and if they refuse, they are sharply criticized. When jobs are locally or seasonally available, individuals or whole families may be sent for. Likewise, when a household breaks up after the death of a dominant member, relatives may send for individuals or family segments for economic reasons or on the grounds that the members will no longer be happy in the household that has lost its solidarity.

Smaller household units (single-member, neolocal, neolocal plus a few other individuals) are now more common in Arizona than in Sonora because of economic and other factors that have fostered differential culture change. We have no way of knowing postmarriage residential patterns before the 1890s, but faint clues suggest some form of residence with or near the husband's relatives. Spicer (1940:75) mentions that in Pascua in the 1930s, the newlywed couple remained temporarily at the boy's family home. Many of the older women who participated in this study resided in households composed of their husband's relatives after their marriage. A trend clearly visible in the life stories is for women to establish neolocal residence, or to become the dominant woman in a larger household unit, at younger ages. A woman who did not move into a dominant household position until she was in her forties had married daughters who lived in neolocal units when they were in their late teens and early twenties. Whether or not there was ever a dominant pattern of patrilocal or related forms of residence, the situation is now one of great variability, with the considerations discussed above taking precedence.

Old age is preferably spent in a large household containing some of one's children. Traditionally, it has been desirable, indeed essential, to have near relatives on whom one can depend in old age—as is demonstrated clearly in the contrast between Chepa Moreno and Dominga González in the following life stories.

Depth of Emotional Bonds

Affective ties are normally weakly developed in Yaqui society. It is tempting to see this emotional shallowness as arising in the disruptive atmosphere of the Yaqui wars, deportation, and persecutions. Personal accounts of individuals living in Sonora around the turn of the century give ample documentation of violent death, forced removal of individuals from family groups, and other disruptive events. Deep affective ties would have been broken at a debilitating rate and the formation of deep ties may have been slowed down by the threat and actual frequency of such events. Weak affective ties provided a useful defense mechanism for personal, cultural, and societal survival in an unstable and frequently violent world. Whatever the origin of this emotional shallowness—and we have no relevant information before the 1890s—it continues to characterize most Yaqui interpersonal relationships, although the personal accounts show that a few deeper emotional ties existed for most of the informants.

This topic is elusive and subjective. The following observations have only a limited basis in direct statements from informants. The interpretation is built upon the overall picture that emerged as informants talked about their relationships with other people. Most of the informants isolated one, two, or three persons as being of great significance in their lives and worthy of respect. These strong emotional bonds cannot be equated with "love" or "friendship" in any simple way. The emotions involved are complex, often ambivalent. People sometimes associated suffering with the relationship and harbored resentment over harsh or unfair treatment.

Deeper emotional attachments most often occur across generational boundaries. As a rule, emotional attachments formed later in life lack the strength of earlier ones. The deepest attachments are most frequently formed in childhood, and women are more often the recipients of deep emotional allegiance than are men.

The primary requisites for the development of deep emotional ties in childhood seem to be proximity and relative continuity in interpersonal relationships during the formative period. Given these conditions, the child's perception of the person as his chief caretaker may be a decisive factor, although other household members may overshadow the person who is, in fact, the chief caretaker, causing the emotional investment to be made in .a person with a more stellar personality. The quality of child care as perceived by the child is also an important consideration.

It is unlikely that a deep emotional investment would be made in anyone not a member of the same household during the critical period of the child's emotional development. Some continuity of interaction is a prerequisite. When people spoke to me of the individual in whom they had the greatest emotional investment, it was often with phrases such as "she raised me," or "how she fought for me." Such a person may be called mother, but this term does not necessarily reflect the actual relationship.

Ideally, the person who raises the child should be the mother. Many informants, both male and female, made it quite explicit that while one could have many consorts, many siblings, and many children, one had only one mother, and one tendered love and respect to one's mother above all others. The number of children raised by other women is quite high, however. The personal accounts provide numerous examples in which the mother died, left the household, or placed the child in another woman's care, or another woman "claimed" a child, and so on. Many women, for many reasons, did not and do not raise their own children. When a mother raises a child through the formative years, when she is not eclipsed by more dominant women, and when the number of children in her care is small, or the particular child feels that he or she can really count on the mother for material and emotional support, it is likely that a strong emotional investment will be made in the mother.

The primary alternative to this pattern is for the emotional investment to be made in another woman within the household, a situation that can develop even when the mother resides in the household and actually cares for the child. Lineal and collateral female relatives of ascending generations living in the household are the most likely candidates. Strong positive personalities will attract more and deeper emotional attachments than passive ones. "Happy" people are more likely to become emotional foci than "sad" people. The age of the women within a household may also be a factor in the development of affective ties on the part of children, inasmuch as age is normally correlated with authority and status. Women with dominant, stellar personalities were invariably found to be mature and older women.

The quality of child care as perceived by the child is not determined by the presence or absence of harsh discipline in any direct sense. Child training is expected to be "hard," and in some measure, a "hard" upbringing can be seen as meaning that the person in charge cares enough to make the effort. As one woman in her seventies, who had the task of raising a young grandson, said, "Raising children the Yaqui way is a lot of work." Many of the older women were, as children, not only threatened but actually punished with a whip which their caretakers owned for the purpose of disciplining the child, and several of these women had themselves used a whip on their children. Other disciplinary measures reported were burning a child or tying him close to a fire, tying girls to metates, tying children to posts or beds, and so on. Women who exercise these techniques may nonetheless receive the primary emotional allegiance of children in their care.

What seems to be more central than the caliber of the discipline is how the child perceives the treatment he receives relative to others in the household, or relative to children in other households. Large households, especially, are likely to contain a number of children who may be full or half-siblings, cousins, more distant kin, or even unrelated. The ideal is for each child to be treated fairly and equitably, in accordance with his age, in regard to discipline, access to food and other goods, and what have you. Differential treatment does, in fact, occur frequently.

Some individuals do not make a deep emotional investment in another person during childhood. A girl in a Yaqui Valley village can be used as an example. She was born as a consequence of an affair the mother had while still living with her husband. Shortly thereafter, the mother left the household to live with yet another man who did not want the woman's children. The woman abandoned her six legitimate children and "gave" the girl in question to her legal husband. The husband soon established a new alliance, and in time six more children were added to his household. Of the many children, this girl, from the beginning, received the least favorable treatment because of the circumstances of her birth. She had less food, poorer clothing, little affection, and erratic discipline. Since punishment was less an attempt to train her in the Yaqui way than an expression of the punisher's aggression, she perceived her treatment to be unfair. She was constantly told that she had no real right to belong to the household and that she should be grateful to have a roof over her head. As a result, she made no childhood emotional investment of a positive sort.

Children apparently make their deep emotional attachments to women because women, as the principal agents of child care, are in more continuous and meaningful contact with them during the critical period. Men are more mobile, changing household affiliation more frequently. Children are more often raised in households containing their biological mothers than in those containing their biological fathers. Most households, however, contain adult males who could serve as potential objects of respect and affection. When a child does create a deep emotional bond to a man, proximity and continuity of contact are prerequisites, as in the case of bonds to women. Attributes characterizing a man who becomes the object of a primary emotional bond are the same as those cited as making a man worthy of respect. Such men provided support and security for a household, were hard workers, and were regarded as knowledgeable and wise. In no case was a chronic drunk or a person who did not provide adequate support named as being respected and emotionally significant to an informant.

Although the emotional attachments formed during childhood appear to be the most intense experienced in a lifetime, other bonds develop as the individual progresses through stages of maturity. Bonds between generational equivalents are normally weaker than those bonds that cross generations. Siblings, *primos hermanos* (cousins), and marriage or alliance partners are considered here as roughly generational equivalents, although there may be wide age and even generational discrepancies in particular instances.

I observed five groups of siblings in some detail and gathered information about a number of other sibling groups. It is my impression that strong affective relationships between siblings are unusual. The only emotionally strong bonds detected were between brothers and sisters who were separated in age by only a year or two and who were raised together. Since nuclear family units tend to be unstable, siblings may be raised in different households in widely separated locations, and may be born years apart (thirty-nine years separated the oldest and youngest living half-siblings produced by one woman). For siblings or half-siblings raised together, competition for the limited resources and affection, as well as differential treatment of children, may militate against the formation of strong emotional bonds between them.

Although siblings seem unlikely to develop deep emotional ties to each other, the sibling kinship bond with its attendant obligations is strong. Symptomatic of this is the stress that the informants placed on sibling ties in describing kin relationships rather than citing common ancestry in their parents' generation. Sibling and *primo hermano* relationships often form the basis of shifting but repeated and long-term associations of families. One pattern is for siblings to remain in loose proximity, although the focus may be, not the siblings, but a parent or other older person. For example, information covering eight decades has been obtained about a Valenzuela family. A group of brothers was repeatedly but not continuously associated in Sonora during the 1890s and early 1900s until external forces caused the family to fragment, and one of the brothers moved to Arizona. As long as this man lived, most of his children lived near him. Although his children moved frequently as they shifted jobs, they gravitated around their father and consequently maintained high interaction rates. Upon the father's death, the cohesion of the family diminished markedly. Two other large family units about which extensive information is available show similar patterns.

The *primo hermano* emotional bond is frequently stronger than the sibling bond for near age equivalents. Except for *primos hermanos* raised in the same household, there is less competition between them for resources and affection. It is often from one's *primos hermanos* that the age-graded groups (sometimes called gangs in Tucson) of boys or girls are drawn for the period between late childhood and marriage. Members of such groups form mutual friendships, have higher interaction rates than with other segments of their society, and are bound together by the common interests arising from their near age equivalence. The tendency to create age-graded groups is much stronger among boys than among girls, especially in Yaqui Valley villages, where girls are much more strictly supervised.

The marriage or alliance bond is typically weak in terms of emotional commitment and durability; marriages or alliances that last a lifetime are the exceptions. Marriages arranged by elders were typical for all the older informants. These marriages began with neutral or negative emotional responses for the simple reason that the couple had never spoken to each other. Many personal accounts stressed passive acceptance of or active opposition to the arrangements. Women often remembered feeling too young for marriage and not wanting to leave their mothers or the household in which they had been raised.

The ideal in Yaqui society is for individuals to marry in the church before their first sexual experience. Girls were theoretically carefully supervised to prevent premarital sexual contacts and, traditionally, were married at an early age. The life stories show that some disregard of the ideal has long occurred, and that once a formal marriage has taken place, subsequent alliances are freely formed. Many alliances and marriages resulted from the necessity of creating a household unit with adult male and female roles filled. A few women entered alliances because they were enamored of a man. The verbs *querer* and *enamorar* were used to describe this state.

The long-term emotional patterns appear to be much the same whether marriages or alliances were arranged, created for pragmatic reasons, or arose as a result of being enamored. Affection sometimes develops, as does alienation. Ultimately, stability and affection seem to depend on how successfully the husband and wife roles are fulfilled. If a man provides adequate support, is not a chronic drunk, and curtails his extra-

marital affairs; and if a woman successfully manages household resources, raises children properly, and runs the house
satisfactorily, the marriage or alliance has some chance of
longevity, and weak affection may well develop. The life
histories reveal how seldom the husband and wife roles are
adequately fulfilled.

The informants' assessments of their own marriages and
alliances and the reasons they gave for terminating these
relationships, illuminate the typically weak nature of the bond.
Only one woman maintained that she respected and was
enamored of her husband in the face of inadequate support
and chronic drunkenness. Other women cited inadequate
support, drunkenness, their husband's or consort's involvement with other women, and physical mistreatment as reasons
for leaving men, or, if the marriage or alliance was maintained,
as reasons for not respecting their husbands, and as a ra-
tionalization for their own failure to conform to the ideal
behavioral patterns for wives. The only other factor cited by
more than one woman as a reason for leaving a man was place
of residence. A number of women elected to separate from
their consorts or husbands rather than live in a particular
location. The woman might not want to leave a place for
economic or other reasons (she might elect to remain near
certain relatives, especially her mother) or she might see the
location to which her husband or consort was moving as
undesirable (several women refused to move to Yaqui Valley
villages for economic reasons; they also saw the quality of life
there as inferior and violent—"those Yaquis kill people").
Termination of a marriage or alliance may be emotional and
stormy but more often is extremely casual.

Emotional bonds formed in adulthood tend to be stronger to
members of descending generations than to roughly equivalent
generational members. The emotional strength of bonds between an adult and a child is asymmetrical in that adults tend
to make less of an emotional investment in the child than the
child makes in the adult. The care of multiple children inclines
the adult to render a somewhat more diffuse emotional commitment. An obvious, overt demonstration of affection toward
older children is sufficiently unusual that it becomes the
subject of pointed jokes.

Yaqui women normally desire a large family (this is truer of older women than younger, and of Sonoran Yaquis than those in Arizona). Infants and small children usually receive a great deal of attention and fondling from many individuals. If there are older girls in the household, they may carry babies about much of the time. Neglect of infants occurs but is the exception. A number of women, especially older ones who had lost children in infancy, specified that it was foolish to become overly attached to infants and small children who might die. The obvious pleasure Yaquis take in infants and small children is somewhat diffuse, more a pleasure in babies in general than a strong emotional attachment to a particular baby. The character of child training normally changes when the child becomes a toddler or another baby is born. Obedience, often enforced with harsh discipline, is demanded by the time a child is between three and five years of age, if the child is being raised in the traditional manner. Strong parent-child bonds are often forged, not when the child is young, but as a result of repeated interaction afterwards. Mothers and daughters who remain in long-term contact seem to develop the strongest emotional ties, the daughter typically making a larger emotional investment in the mother than the reverse. The bond between several informants and their mothers was apparently the strongest the informants experienced in their lifetime. Many women had extremely weak emotional ties with their daughters and stronger ones with their sons. Conversely, men are said to be more attached to their daughters. The differentiation of male and female roles, with women ideally tied closely to their own households after marriage and men more mobile, may be a factor in diminishing contact between mothers and daughters after the daughters marry. Lower interaction rates result in a lack of reinforcement of any emotional bonds that may have existed. The more mobile sons can maintain contact with their mothers, and fathers can more easily visit daughters who live elsewhere.

The interpretation of factors affecting the development of the deeper emotional ties, of which each informant experienced only a few, is based upon their retrospective judgments. Since many of the informants were middle-aged or elderly, their judgments were based on a lifetime of experience. By the time a Yaqui reached adulthood, it is a rare individual who has not internalized a certain amount of caution in making emotional investments.

Ritual Kinship

The Catholic institution of *compadrazgo* is found around the world with variations through time and space (Gudeman, 1972). As Mintz and Wolf (1950) point out, the Yaquis have elaborated the institution to an unusual degree. Possibly this elaboration has been a response to the disruptive conditions that have long characterized Yaqui life. Whether or not that is the case—and other explanations are possible—the Yaqui system provides an expanded number of people to whom an individual is linked in respect, obligation, spiritual, and ritual kin relationships. The system is a major element in structuring interpersonal relationships.

The three sets of relationships established in the *compadrazgo* system are between parents and godparents (the *compadres*), parents and child (a kin link), and godparents and child (called *padrinos* and *ahijado*). These relationships are established upon the occasions of baptism, confirmation, the Yaqui rite of placing a rosary on a child, church marriage, placing of a religious costume or habit upon a person in response to a vow made during an illness, death, or ceremonial sponsorship. As girls' fifteenth birthday celebrations become more common, another occasion may be added. Spicer (1940:110–11) notes that the ceremonial sponsors of churches and images host the appropriate fiestas, and the sponsorship of churches and images is of the same kind as ceremonial sponsorship of humans.

Since people acquire a formal relationship with each of the parties involved on each occasion, it is obvious that they can acquire a sizable number of *compadrazgo* affiliates in a lifetime. The system is further expanded to include actual kin and ritual kin of the affiliates. On occasions when I asked why someone was addressed as *comadre* or *compadre*, the answers were often of this sort: "He baptized my husband's child by his first woman," or "She is the sister of the woman who baptized my son," or "She is a *comadre* of the *comadre* who baptized my grandson."

Considerable variation exists in the actual number of *compadrazgo* affiliates individuals have. Baptism is the only rite universally observed; some differences in the number of relationships therefore occur as a result of the number of other rites the individual passes through. The most significant differences, however, stem from the frequency with which a person is asked to serve as a godparent or sponsor for others. Some people are asked to serve and accept the responsibility repeatedly, while others are seldom asked or refuse when asked. "Happy" individuals are asked more often than "sad" ones, ceremonial leaders more often than others, and those with high status are favored over those with low status. People known to respond positively to such invitations are preferred over those known to dislike the role.

Babies must be baptized. A major effort is made to baptize a baby believed to be dying, and baptism with sponsors (if possible) takes precedence over medical care. Should a baby be born dead, baptism should still occur. Two babies of informants died in Potam in 1972. Both were baptized with holy water by their mothers after their deaths. No baptismal sponsors were involved, although the normal death sponsors were later chosen, including, in one case, a person previously selected as baptismal *madrina*. It is said that in such crises, any baptized person can make the sign of the cross upon the deceased infant's forehead, reciting, "I baptize thee in the name of God, Jesus Christ, and the Holy Ghost," and God will understand. Such cases are rare, and baptismal sponsors are typical.

One of the parents or some other relative—a grandmother, for example—selects one or both baptismal sponsors for a baby. For extremely poor, low-status families, or for individuals or families living in communities where they know few people, finding sponsors can be a chore. A few personal accounts show how desperate a parent can become when there is no one willing to serve as sponsor for a baby.

The Yaqui way of baptismal sponsorship is to have the same set of sponsors—not husband and wife or closely related—

baptize three consecutive children. The Mexican pattern, on the other hand, is to have a different set of sponsors for each child; frequently Mexican-style sponsors are husband and wife or brother and sister. Yaquis who select new sponsors for each child, or who ask husbands and wives to serve, are said to be behaving like Mexicans.

General agreement exists that godparents or sponsors should be selected from beyond the circle of the household and near kin because the primary social reason of forming these relationships is to establish formal relationships to wider segments of society. At times, this ideal is verbalized quite explicitly. Upon one occasion in Potam, the delayed baptism of a child was being discussed by a group of women. The reason for the delay, which was reprehensible in itself, was that the designated *padrino* had not yet found time to come to Potam from Obregón. The *padrino* was a half-brother of the child's father. A sister-in-law of the child's father delivered a lengthy lecture about the futility of asking near relatives to serve as godparents: "The child might as well not have a *padrino*. Gonzalo is already his uncle and as his uncle he has to take care of the child. What good will it do to have a *padrino* in Obregón? You should have chosen a *padrino* from this pueblo who is not a relative."

Direct lineal relatives are never chosen as baptismal sponsors. Near collateral relatives of the parents such as siblings, cousins, aunts, uncles, or great-aunts and -uncles are sometimes selected. In my field work I came across ten cases of selection of a sibling or cousin, one case occurring near the turn of the century in Sonora. Only one of these involved an alliance of a Yaqui with a Mexican (as parents of the child), and none was described as an example of the Mexican pattern rather than the Yaqui. In another case, a mother, aware that she was dying after childbirth and wishing to ensure that her child would be taken into a particular household, asked her great-aunt to be the child's baptismal *madrina*. The only instances of selection of a baptismal sponsor from within the household unit involved dying babies, for whom there was no time to make alternative arrangements. Affinal or marriage relatives, however, are frequently chosen. The following examples are typical: a man baptized and later raised in his own household two children of his wife's sister; a woman's son-in-law confirmed her two sons; a woman served as *chapayeka* (fariseo ceremonial society) *madrina* for her husband's *primo hermano*; a son-in-law baptized a woman's daughter.

No cases are known of marriages or alliances between close *compadrazgo* affiliates. Such a relationship between *padrinos* and *ahijados* would be close to incest, and between *compadres* would be extremely undesirable. The tendency to extend *compadrazgo* affiliations beyond the members of the basic paradigm does not carry the connotation that marriages and alliances cannot be contracted within these larger limits.

The recruitment of sponsors for childhood life-crisis rites and marriage normally is initiated by parents or by other persons with the authority to make these decisions. Dominant older people such as grandmothers may be the decision makers. Ceremonial society members may request that certain individuals serve as their sponsors, or sponsors may be recruited by other ceremonial society members. Relatively few occasions arise on which individuals recruit their own sponsors, but one notable exception may be cited: A Potam informant named her own burial *padrinos* during her terminal illness in the early 1970s, sent for each of them, and made arrangements for their cooperation and for her funeral. This case appears to be unique, constituting an idiosyncratic cultural innovation (see the life story of Dominga Ramírez). Another informant's dying grandmother (in Tucson during the 1930s) sent for her burial *padrinos* and issued full instructions about her burial dress and funeral, but who actually named the burial *padrinos* was not specified.

People selecting sponsors can follow one of two tactics. They may consistently widen the *compadrazgo* network by choosing different sponsors for rites other than baptism (the same sponsors may be used for three consecutive baptisms), or they may reinforce existing bonds by asking individuals who already stand in a *compadrazgo* relationship. Thus, baptismal sponsors may be asked to confirm their *ahijados* or place rosaries on them, or new sponsors may be chosen. If the baptismal sponsors are alive and available at their *ahijado*'s marriage, it is considered appropriate for them to serve as marriage *padrinos*, but different people may be chosen. Marriage sponsors must themselves have been married in the church, a requirement that eliminates some people from assuming this sponsorship role.

The Yaqui system is essentially horizontal in that most *compadrazgo* relationships are to other members of Yaqui society. Preference for ceremonial leaders and high-status individuals introduces very little verticality. Non-Yaquis have become involved in the system, principally through the marriage or alliance of Yaqui's with Mayos, Mexicans, Papagos, and other predominantly Catholic groups, or through their continued interaction with families of such ethnic groups living in the same community. Rarely are *compadrazgo* affiliations arranged that involve vertical social stratification, although a wealthy Mexican woman in Arizona, who acted as the patron of a Catholic church in Pascua, volunteered to serve as confirmation godmother for Yaqui girls. She bought their confirmation dresses and gave a fiesta for her *ahijadas*, but the relationships so established did not remain active.

Sponsors must agree to accept the responsibility of their office, they must be physically present for the ceremony, and they normally provide some economic resources for the ceremony, the amount and kind varying with circumstances and the sponsors' economic status. Lifelong relationships and mutual obligations are theoretically established and require respectful behavior and the use of *compadrazgo* terminology. *Compadre* terms, even today, take precedence over all other forms of reference and address, such as personal names and kinship terms. In my experience, the terms *padrino* and *madrina* are used more as terms of reference than as terms of address, and the term *ahijado* was never used as a term of address in my presence, nor was it used often as a term of reference. A woman would say, "I am her *madrina*" rather than "she is my *ahijada*." *Compadrazgo* affiliates are included in those to whom hospitality is extended and with whom visiting occurs. The failure to respond properly in these respects is a serious breach of obligations.

Spicer's excellent accounts of the *compadrazgo* system in Potam (1954:60–62) and in Pascua (1940:91–116) discuss the nature of other obligations: "It is to one's ritual kin that one goes first to borrow money for, say, a pair of shoes when household members are unable to buy them" (1954:62). *Ahijados* rely on their *padrinos* for assistance, and vice versa. The *padrino* is often given the responsibility of deciding on treatment for a sick child, and the sick child might be moved to his *padrino*'s house and cared for there. Mutual assistance is expected of *compadres* (Spicer 1940:101–3).

Ideally, the system should still operate as Spicer describes it, but in practice, as detailed by my informants, the situation seems to have changed.

Baptismal godparents are supposed to be willing to assume responsibility for the child should the need arise, but they apparently do so only when no real relatives are available. In the accounts that form the basis of this study, only a few instances were recorded of children being raised by godparents. One, from a life story not included here, involved a woman born in Tucson in 1924. Her father died of diptheria when she was one year old, and her mother departed for Vicam shortly thereafter, first giving the child to her deceased husband's mother. The informant was raised by her grandmother, who died when the girl was fifteen, leaving her with no known relatives in the Tucson area. One of the grandmother's *comadres* asked the girl to join her household and later arranged her marriage to a nephew who resided in the household. In due time a son was born. When this marriage broke up, the elderly woman claimed the son and raised him. The *compadrazgo* relationship that was activated in this case was a remote one and all possible kin alternatives had been exploited before its activation.

When I asked informants what they expected to do for their *ahijados* or *compadres*, they did not expect to do much. Should an *ahijado* or *compadre* die, they would attend the death rites if possible. They did not anticipate circumstances that would cause *ahijados* or *compadres* to join their households, saying that would happen only if there were no relatives to provide care and resources. The personal accounts do not indicate the same level of intimate involvement in the lives of *compadrazgo* affiliates as Spicer has described. Why? Most of the cultural changes occurring in the *compadrazgo* system since Spicer's

work have tended toward a lessening of differences between
the Mexican and Yaqui patterns, with urban Arizona Yaquis
the most affected. The complex series of historical events that
must have resulted in emphasizing the importance of ritual
kinship has no counterpart in recent and contemporary Yaqui
society.

Culture change alone cannot account for differences between
Spicer's interpretation and the picture painted here, however.
Many of the informants were alive at the time of Spicer's
original work and lived in the communities he studied, so the
life histories cover that span of time and space. Equally
significant is the nature of the research. My work has emphasized particular cases—how individuals behaved in a particular
situation. Compromises with the ideal in individual circumstances are undoubtedly more visible in this kind of study.
Insofar as I can tell, the ideal has not changed from the time of
Spicer's work.

The system is now and has long been an important institution in Yaqui society. Bonds of ritual kinship can create
bridges to individuals not otherwise linked, or if other linkages
exist, they are reinforced by this further tie. It is one of the
crucial elements in structuring interpersonal relationships and
effecting social solidarity.

*The Upholding of Obligations as a Factor Affecting
the Structuring of Interpersonal Relationships*

Each distinguishable social system (kinship, ritual kinship,
ceremonial, political, and so on) has associated obligations.
Obligations centered in one system may be intermeshed with
those of other systems. Some obligations associated with some
systems can be clearly defined, but some are subject to different interpretations and even the clearly defined sets of obligations are not always upheld. Perceptions about how obligations
have been upheld are one of the most significant factors in the
personal and social evaluation of individuals and in determin-
ing actual interaction patterns. So many situations and actions

are interpreted in terms of this yardstick that one judgment is added to previous ones in a cumulative fashion. The personal and public evaluation of individuals rests heavily on such judgments.

The idea that relatives should share resources, tender aid, extend hospitality, and provide services is deeply ingrained. Although some rather specific obligations can be isolated, such as the duty of parents to teach children who their relatives are, the most basic characteristic of obligations tied to the kinship system is their diffuse nature. Virtually everything offered to or requested by relatives may be construed as forming part of these obligations.

The extent to which kinship obligations are perceived to be upheld is perhaps the largest single factor in understanding interaction between relatives who have the option of interacting. Factionalism and the alienation of relatives is often traceable to perceived breaches of these obligations. Intensive interaction seldom persists if obligations are seen as having been seriously slighted, except in the case of individuals who continue to reside in the same household, and even here, failure to uphold perceived obligations changes the quality of the relationship.

The kinship system is the one most likely to be activated when an individual or family is in need of basic subsistence resources or services such as care of the sick or of children. In selecting a kin-based source of aid, relatives must be available, of course. Availability is not always a matter of proximity, although proximity may be necessary and persons within the household and nearby relatives may be sought. Requests for aid may be sent by mail or word of mouth for considerable distances, and trips of some duration and distance may be undertaken to seek aid or to fulfill kinship obligations.

The nature of the aid offered or elicited, the location of the desired resources, and the previous history of interpersonal relations will further determine who interacts with whom. If a young man seeks a little spending money, near adult female relatives will be the most likely targets, because women normally handle household resources, including cash. Which woman or women are selected (mother, grandmother, sisters, aunts, cousins, or in-laws) depends largely on who has responded favorably to such requests in the past.

The way in which the location of scarce resources can channel requests for aid is demonstrated by an episode that occurred in 1970 in the Tucson area. A group of related women became disturbed that the grave of a male near-relative lacked a cross. It was seen as the duty of the deceased's son to provide the cross, but the consensus was that he was unlikely to do so. A woodworker who was the uncle of one of the concerned women, but who was unrelated to the deceased, was known to have a white wooden cross, which he gave to the niece because of their kin relationship. Had this group of women been seeking more generally distributed resources, they would not have approached this particular man to uphold their kin obligation to the deceased man. Other necessary resources (tools and plastic flowers) were provided by the women themselves.

Persons who perceive themselves to be in great need may call on a wide range of relatives and other people, exercising much less selectivity—a pattern not dissimilar to the *limosnas* (house-to-house solicitations) made by members of the ceremonial societies for contributions. An example from the Tucson area illustrates this behavioral pattern. A man, who believed himself and was believed by others to be bewitched by his father-in-law, became ill and lost his job. Later he went from house to house of relatives, *compadres*, and friends, asking for money for the curing of his witch-caused illness. Another man, also in the Tucson area, was so deeply into the "vices" of marijuana, heroin, alcohol, and violence that he had not held a job in years. His consort received money from welfare, but it was directed to family subsistence. He spent a considerable amount of time and energy making a circuit of his affinal relatives (for he was not from the *barrio* and had no relatives living there), begging small amounts of cash, returnable bottles, and so on to support his "vices."

A life-crisis household ceremony will trigger a flow of resources and services from relatives, ritual kin, and possibly others. Although the main economic burden for household fiestas is on the sponsors, the outlay is shared by relatives and others. Similarly, public ceremonials are financed in part by the kin and ritual kin of the sponsors. As an illustration of the networks that may be involved, a Torim relative of a Potam woman was a blue *fiestero* in Vicam. (*Fiesteros* manage public fiestas and have other duties. Red and blue *fiesteros* are chosen annually.) The Potam woman sent a box of potatoes grown on Huirivis lands worked by her sons, lands that were inherited from the woman's mother's last consort.

News or information is a resource circulated as part of the various systems, and the imparting of certain classes of information is regarded as an obligation. Within the kinship system, the most specific such obligation is concerned with notification of a terminal illness or death of a relative. The most sensitive indicator of the state of relations between relatives is in the pattern of communicating this vital information. Failure to notify relatives or to respond appropriately to such notification is one of the most serious breaches of kin-based obligations. Informants repeatedly judged the social distance between themselves and their relatives in terms of this criterion.

Age is more or less correlated with knowledge. Older people are said to "know" more. Younger people are seldom said to "know," and what they say is often discounted on the basis of their age. Genealogical and associated information is a resource of some significance, controlled most fully by older people. It is an obligation to impart such information within the kinship system in order to prevent incest. Genealogical information is difficult to separate from all the rest of the personal information that goes along with it which merges into gossip. Personal information is of little interest if it cannot be fitted into a genealogical framework. Genealogical information is, then, an important resource in its own right, and it provides the context or vehicle that orders the transmission of personal information which plays a key role in informal social control and in establishing the more public status of individuals and families.

No Yaqui possesses the physical and emotional strength, the time, or the resources to meet all possible obligations. No person can successfully maintain all the potential obligations to the satisfaction of all concerned. No one is above reproach from some quarter. Most members of the ceremonial societies could have more knowledge; few mothers have achieved the ideal in child training; everyone has refused to give aid or has offered less than relatives would have been willing to accept. As more obligations are successfully met, more demands are made and more potential obligations activated—the "Catch 22" of Yaqui life. In one sense, this is merely saying that no one is perfect, a fact of life with which Yaquis are fully familiar. But it is also saying that real limitations are placed upon the total system of obligation maintenance—limitations that carry the seeds of conflict and factionalism.

Decisions are therefore necessary about which potential obligations are to be maintained. Selective mechanisms are most obvious in the following circumstances: definition of the outer boundaries of obligations to be maintained, interpretation of the less clearly defined obligations, rejection or denial of the more clearly defined obligations, and manipulation of the obligation system for a goal.

Because of the almost infinite number of potential obligations, outer boundaries are normally delimited in some fashion. A rough strategy should be recognizable for any individual about whom sufficient information is available, although the boundary vacillates through time in response to specific situations.

Imprecisely formulated obligations are subject to differing expectations and interpretations. It is not entirely clear what obligations are involved when a distant Torim relative one has never heard of arrives at a household in Pascua having entered Arizona illegally and possessing nothing but the clothes he stands in. It is reasonably certain he will be given household affiliation, maintenance, and hospitality, and will become involved in visiting relationships for a few days. He might expect his relatives to arrange a job for him or provide resources of various sorts, either for the duration of his stay or in the form of return transportation, gifts for relatives at home, and so on. These further expectations might be interpreted quite differently by his Pascua hosts, who would be more cognizant of the difficulties of getting jobs for illegal entrants, or who may feel the relationship to be so distant as to merit a minimal interpretation of the obligation.

More clearly defined obligations may not be upheld. Mothers abandon their children or raise them incorrectly in the eyes of some observers. A *fariseo* (member of the *fariseo* ceremonial society) with a lifetime vow may cease to function as a society member for reasons other than those considered to be adequate justification for such behavior. A man responsible for supporting a household may use all or part of his income for his "vices," with the result that other household members suffer deprivation.

The total system of obligation maintenance is subject to manipulation for certain purposes. A man aspiring to civil or religious leadership might enter into more ritual kin relationships, uphold more kin-based obligations, or assume obligations as an intermediary to surrounding non-Yaqui society than he would if he did not have those aspirations.

Reciprocity is potentially involved in all relationships involving obligations, but it is usually asymmetrical at any one time and in some instances it is permanently imbalanced. People regularly involved in visiting and hospitality relationships tend to localize their interaction in one household. Concrete expressions of hospitality in the form of food or gifts are seldom on an equivalent exchange basis. Aid extended to relatives or ritual kin is exchanged for positive evaluation and enhanced status; it also serves as a hedge against one's own possible future need—a form of social banking.

Hospitality and Visiting

All the women interviewed were extremely emphatic about the inner and outer limits of acceptable visitors and appropriate forms of hospitality. Visiting and hospitality are most intensive between relatives, neighbors, and ritual kin. Proximity, personalities, and the history of previous interactional relationships (including the aspect of past obligation maintenance) further affect actual patterning.

Wide personal variation exists in how many visiting and hospitality options are maintained. Lineal kin relationships are most universally accompanied by visiting; the failure of children or grandchildren to visit parents and grandparents as regularly as possible is condemned. Adult siblings may have high interaction rates, assuring, in turn, that their children will be in frequent contact.

The importance attached to visiting of near relatives is seen in the following case. A Potam informant had several children living in the pueblo. Each morning she made a circuit of the five adjacent households containing her lineal descendants and each afternoon a son, and often a stepson who lived farther away, called upon her. Grandchildren and great-grandchildren living on the other side of the pueblo walked or were carried to visit her every few days. A teen-age granddaughter who ordinarily lived in another community came to Potam in 1968, staying with her other (maternal) grandmother, as was customary. The teen-ager exhibited dress and behavior for which she could have been severely criticized. She was at that time addicted to heavy eye make-up, tie-dyed blue jeans, and tight knit shirts, and she loudly criticized Yaqui life as "uncivilized." None of these things bothered her paternal grandmother at all: "She is young and will learn." The problem was that the granddaughter did not call daily. Her absence was endlessly discussed every day, and after her departure to her own home, the comment continued to be made by all the women of the related households that she had failed to visit her grandmother as often as she should.

Women who tend to localize their movements within the physical limits of their own household or its immediate environs may have fewer visiting relationships, but whether they have or not, visiting and hospitality are limited to the territory within which they move. Several women described as *pegada á la casa* (stuck to the house) spent years within their self-defined territory. They never left this territory for reasons other than economic necessity or to attend death-associated rituals. All their visiting was with people who came to see them.

Visiting across sex boundaries is rather narrowly permissible. Men may, of course, call on mothers, grandmothers, sisters, and aunts; fathers may call on daughters; uncles on nieces. Older women may visit more freely than younger ones. Children may enter houses without regard to sex considerations.

Beyond near relatives, older people, and children, it is generally improper for males to call upon or formally visit with females or vice versa.

When errands or business requires a man to call on a household containing only women and children, the business of the call is conducted in neutral territory at the gate, the door, or on the street, preferably in the presence of as many household members as can be mustered. In Potam, the male household head made arrangements for me to interview several men considered to be appropriate sources of information about Yaqui culture. These men usually came singly to the house. Since the household head had given instructions that the men were to talk to me, they had to be admitted to the compound and offered hospitality. Their arrival inevitably resulted in a redefinition of social territory as older girls and younger women withdrew to a different area, leaving only older women and children in the vicinity of my conversation with the outside man.

Segregation into male and female social units normally occurs when visitors of both sexes, such as a couple or family, arrive. Such segregation is noticeable in contexts other than visiting, as in attendance at fiestas by groups of males and females.

A woman calling socially on another woman within acceptable visiting boundaries would expect certain manifestations of hospitality. The hostess should provide a place to sit and take the time to talk. Some form of refreshment should be offered, be it only water or coffee. Older women tend to place a much higher value on protocol associated with visiting and hospitality than young women. An older woman in Potam found it inconceivable that acceptable visitors should receive less than the best she could offer at that moment. She would be seriously disturbed if she missed visitors, knowing that her several daughters-in-law would not have asked the visitor to rest after a long walk or offered them so much as a drink of water.

Near relatives and people with whom the hostess is extremely familiar can force what they regard as the proper form of hospitality by pointed, sharp joking. In one Tucson area household, the hospitality was usually regarded as below par. The woman's sisters exercised a great deal of ingenuity in getting her to offer food or drinks, and if that failed, they helped themselves as a last resort.

Relatives visiting from a distant community can initiate a sequence of hospitality, maintenance, and gift giving that may result in a considerable economic drain upon the hosts. A two-week visit of four relatives from Potam with near relatives in Pascua involved their complete maintenance during their stay plus the following gifts: a new dress for one of the girls, some ten dresses purchased in second-hand stores to be taken to other relatives in Potam, other clothing collected from the hosts, a box of salt which later served as a gift to a Potam *fiestero*, a transistor radio, food for the return trip, and several cash gifts of from one to five dollars. Visitors may arrive almost empty-handed, or they may make a splash with gifts, thereby enhancing their social acceptability.

Too much visiting, visiting beyond acceptable limits, and visiting without sufficient reason are undesirable. The phrase *walking in the houses* is sometimes used to designate this behavior. People who "walk in the houses" are likely to be seen as idlers, malicious gossips, or possible witches. Between 1968 and 1972, informants repeatedly singled out three women in one community as ones who "walked in the houses." Two of the three were suspected of being witches, and numerous tales were told of misfortunes that befell households they visited. The women who "walked in the houses" did not see themselves as lazy or malicious, but as friendly, interested in their neighbors, and helpful. This is another vaguely defined zone subject to different interpretations.

One further example of delimiting the boundaries of acceptable visiting concerns an eighteen-year-old boy in a Potam household who was asked by a girl in an adjacent household to carry water for her mother. The boy went willingly to help, but he was abruptly stopped by the women of his own household, who exclaimed that he was no longer a child and could not "walk in the houses" as he had previously done.

The Individual and Stress

All individuals in all societies experience varying kinds and degrees of stress. Yaquis live with a relatively high level of stress at the present time, and in the past they have been subjected to even higher levels. For Yaquis who personally experienced the persecutions, executions, deportations, military campaigns, and associated hardships in Sonora before and after the turn of the century, this stress zone overshadows all others. Stresses originating more internally within the society are selected and discussed here as a background to individual responses to stress.

The household, although a flexible and fundamental unit, is not free of stress and conflict. Much of the stress experienced by women is localized there, whereas men experience more stress originating outside of this unit. A primary source of household stress is the way in which age- and sex-determined roles are filled.

In large households, older women have authority over younger ones. A particularly sensitive relationship is that of mother-in-law to daughter-in-law, but the way in which household-based authority is wielded affects other relationships as well. Several older women who lived with their mothers-in-law early in their married lives remembered feeling resentment about having been cut off from their own natal households, having less personal freedom relative to other periods in their lives, having to work hard under the direction of their mothers-in-law, and having little control over their own children. Other women had good relationships with their mothers-in-law while residing in the same household. In none of the latter cases was the mother-in-law described as a hard authoritarian or very domineering. Fairness in exercising authority is related to the degree of stress, whether or not social distance is maintained between the authority figure and others.

Household stress may arise from men's failure to provide adequate economic support, their physical mistreatment of women (usually the wife or consort) and children, and the effects of men's "vices." Disputes over adultery, property, and child custody are also often localized or initiated in the household. Informants often said that only fools became embroiled in conflicts over the behavior of children, but children's actions often provided the excuse for controversies within and between households.

Small neolocal households may generate stress because of the lack of adults to share household responsibilities. One informant, for example, abandoned her husband and six children, giving as the main reasons the husband's lack of support and chronic drunkenness. However, she also said she might have acted differently had there been another woman in the household to help her.

The quality of household life has apparently changed in the last two or three decades. Anthropologists who worked with Yaquis years ago, as well as older informants, have said that most modern households are qualitatively different. I can appreciate the changes somewhat because one Arizona household and one Torim household with which I am familiar appear to epitomize the character of the kind of household that formerly dominated Yaqui society, but since I have little first-hand information about the character of more traditional households, the contrast drawn here is undoubtedly imperfect. Ideally, traditional households presented a calm face to the world—exuding a sense of purpose and organization. The noise level was, perhaps, lower: voices were softer and children controlled in a less verbal manner. (My overwhelming impression of two nontraditional households is of nonstop shrill directives to children, just as my impression of the two old-style households is of peace and quiet.) Respect for age and authority was reflected in minute behavioral patterns. Religious observations centering on the yard cross and household altar were enforced. Surviving traditional households tend to maintain some form of the household religious regime.

It is not clear whether traditional households sustained less stress or if stress was merely less visible. The personal accounts of older informants suggest that stress occurred then as now. The tendency, especially in Arizona, to create neolocal units in which women become dominant at younger ages removes much of the source of stress associated with differential authority between adults, particularly women, but it can also introduce stress through failure to provide individuals to share responsibility. Changes in economic patterns, particularly the change from direct production or *patrón* relationships to a full cash economy, have shifted subsistence-related stress. More opportunities arise for dispute when the male provider furnishes cash, because there is more opportunity for cash to be diverted away from household subsistence. It seems fair to say that modern households exhibit more overt signs of stress than did traditional ones, and that the stress zones have shifted somewhat.

The term *vicio* (vice) is used to cover drinking and drunkenness; the use of marijuana, heroin, or other drugs (this primarily in Arizona); murder and violence; and even tattooing. The prevalence of vices is perceived by many Yaquis to be one of the greatest problems facing their society. By and large the vices are seen as falling in the male domain. Although some women drink or use marijuana or play cards or shoot heroin, their behavior is seen as unusual, whereas men are expected to have vices. The vices can be seen both as a source of conflict and as a response to stress. Aside from fights and other disputes that accompany the actual practice of a vice, a great deal of stress generated as a result of the vices is centered in the household unit. Economic deprivation stemming from the dissipation of resources; the physical mistreatment of, usually, the wife or consort or children; and the failure of the men to provide adequate role models are frequent sources of conflict.

Individual responses to stress range from acceptance or endurance of the stress-producing situation through a variety of stress-reducing tactics, to open conflict, confrontation, or violence. To say that a great many stressful situations are tolerated, accepted, or endured is, of course, an oversimplification. Negative affect, lack of cooperation, withdrawal of support, a shift in interaction patterns, and activation of informal social controls may result from stress, and the psychological reactions of those involved are many and complex. The net effect in many situations, however, is that people continue to live with the stress. Women tolerate drunkenness, lack of support, and physical mistreatment—sometimes passively and fatalistically. Wives say that as long as they remain with their husbands, they have to put up with these things. A daughter-in-law under the thumb of a domineering mother-in-law lives with the situation. Ceremonial society members fail to execute their responsibilities, dishonest officials remain in office, and theft and violence are accepted without legal recourse.

Tolerance of stress must, in part, be seen against the basic belief that life for a Yaqui is "hard." Numerous models of living with stress or conflict exist, and an individual's personal experiences reinforce these expectations. Fatalism is a factor, or so I assume. Some of the more positive role categories have a dimension reflecting performance in the presence of stress (a "good" woman does the best she can in the face of odds; women who do not nag their husbands about drunkenness or lack of support are often described as "good"). Tolerance of stress also results from the social or other cost and the potential ineffectiveness of alternatives and from the negative connotations of "talking badly."

Various forms of informal social controls act in part to reduce stress. The word *talking* covers many of these social control mechanisms directed at correcting behavior perceived as undesirable and reinforcing positive Yaqui ideas. Phrases like "how I talked," "he talked for me," or "he talks for the pueblo" are frequently heard. Gossip and the communication of personal information is both a cause of stress (men are prone to comment that a lot of trouble originates with women's gossip) and a form of social control that can act to reduce stress. "Talking badly" is universally condemned. The fine line between being honest and speaking out on issues, and "talking badly" to cause trouble, is subject to differing interpretations. No one I met admitted to "talking badly," but many were accused of it. Gossip is occasionally formally rebutted. Rumors that certain families were not good Yaquis and had "become Mexicans" were answered in at least three cases by the accused going to the accuser and stating that the charge was not so. Rumors about extramarital affairs may also be answered in a confrontation with the person presumed to be the source of the rumor.

The withholding of support in order to effect a behavioral or situational change is a form of social control that Yaqui informants, especially younger urban residents, felt ought to be more effective than it actually is. When a Tucson woman ostentatiously withheld food and money from a nephew in an effort to get him to give up heroin, he simply got support elsewhere. Because it is so easy to restructure personal interrelationships, the withholding of support and ostracism seldom are effective.

Individual stress may be alleviated through the curing system. Curing may be initiated at any time; acceptable explanations of illness and misfortune are given, blame is localized, and the affected individual is given serious and personalized attention. Psychological withdrawal—temporary introversion and refusal to speak or interact normally—is another way an individual can tolerate stress. This was a fairly common response of older children and teenagers in a Potam household. Adults also go into periods of depression accompanied by a decrease in normal speech and activity. That state is described either as sadness (*tristeza*) or as being angry (*enojado*). Physical withdrawal from a stress-producing situation can be accomplished by changing household affiliation or moving to a new locality. The restructuring of interpersonal relationships on a temporary or long-term basis is a common reaction.

Adults and even older children are held responsible for their own actions. Little or no stigma is attached to the wife of a convicted murderer, the offspring of a reputed incestuous alliance, or the immediate families of Yaqui traitors. Coupled with strictures to "mind your own business" and not talk badly, this attitude serves to isolate stress zones through discouraging the involvement of others. It also means that the alternatives of restructuring interpersonal relationships and of physically withdrawing to another area are always feasible.

Yaqui responses to stress that serve to isolate, confine, and contain the stress zone or to sidestep it are well developed. Fewer tactics exist for more positive resolution. Mediation tactics are surprisingly weakly developed, judging from data presently available. When the containing, enduring, and sidestepping tactics fail, retreat into the vices, various forms of violence, open conflict, and legal action can result. The incidence of the vices, including violence, is high.

Behavioral Constellations

Yaquis recognize several behavioral constellations as non-unique, recurrent phenomena constituting an expectable range of behavioral variation in Yaqui society. Some are named, or perhaps it is more accurate to say that certain Spanish terms in common usage are a kind of verbal shorthand for conveying information about an individual's behavior or personality. Other constellations are not denoted with single terms but form, I believe, recognizable categories. Precise definition of the behavioral categories is impossible to achieve—more significant is the flavor. Some characterize temporary conditions, others are summaries of personality types, while still others have as primary referents certain aspects of role and role performance dominating a person's identity. More formalized roles will be ignored here in favor of less obvious categories emphasized by informants.

These categories depict the more clear-cut and extreme forms of patterned behavior. Much more difficulty is encountered in providing a concise summary of the middle ranges of behavior, "normal" and less noteworthy individuals—perhaps the majority of Yaquis—do not fit easily into these verbal cubbyholes. Recognizable behavioral constellations are, in some senses, an expression of basic Yaqui values.

One pair of behavioral categories are seen as polar opposites, which are often defined by contrasting one with the other: the happy (*alegre*) person and the sad (*triste*) one. The sad end of the scale is well defined and the Spanish term is used regularly to depict this state. The happy end is considerably more nebulous, lacking a clear, single-word characterization; in defining the category I relied on the context and content of personal descriptions given by informants about individuals who were called, among other things, happy, and who appeared to share this constellation of behavioral characteristics. I could use the word *happy* in similar contexts and the connotations perceived by informants appeared to be roughly those described here, although the word is often used in other contexts without the implications given here.

Extroversion apears to be a basic element. "Happy" people are positive, talk a lot, and tend to interact with an above-average number of individuals. They may also be described as liking music, fiestas, parties, and dancing. "Happy" people attract more ritual kin affiliates; they may be the people who uphold the largest number of obligations; they may become stellar members of household units; and they tend to be the individuals who attract deep emotional investments on the part of others. Yet a person can joke, be a thoroughgoing extrovert, and maintain a large number of obligations, and still not be placed in this nebulous but real category. "Happy" people cannot be socially or supernaturally dangerous to those who classify them in this way. Suspected witches, people who "talk badly" or people who "walk in the houses" would not be put in this category, or if they were called "happy," the frame of reference would be more limited. Anyone can have his happy moments, but only mature women were described as belonging to this behavioral category. Women so described are among the most admired in Yaqui society—they approximate ideal role fulfillment as closely as it is possible to. The characteristics of the syndrome are basic to women's roles. To express the best in men, a different set of referents would be involved.

A "sad" person tends to be introverted and passive, talks less, maintains fewer interpersonal relationships, and is unlikely to be described as enjoying the more frivolous things, such as radio music or secular dancing; nor are they as likely as others to attend fiestas or attract ritual kin affiliates. *Tristeza* is an illness characterized by extreme depression—a loss of interest in everything—of which people die. People can be a little bit sad, and temporary sadness can occur at any age. A temporary state of sadness is characterized by withdrawal from normal contacts, a decrease in normal activity, and a lower conversational rate or refusal to talk. The "sad" personality seems to be ascribed to adults of either sex.

The "hard" category, like the "sad" one, has fairly specific connotations. Mature people of either sex can be "hard." "Hard" people occupy dominant roles which they fill with authority in traditional ways. They may freely use harsh punishment for children. Such individuals are often at the conservative core of Yaqui society, upholding the Yaqui way, which is itself regarded as "hard."

Surprising parallels exist between the "happy" and "hard" categories. Individuals in both achieve above-average role fulfillment and act out the basic ideals of Yaqui culture in their own lives. The main differences between the two categories seem to be in the degree of emotional warmth and the way in which interpersonal relationships are structured. "Hard" individuals favor vertical stratification with strong dominant-subservient relationships accompanied by firm exercise of authority, while "happy" people opt for more horizontal, egalitarian relationships and less obvious authoritarian procedures.

A person who drinks is a drunk, one who smokes marijuana is a *marijuano,* and there are heroin addicts, murderers, and others who are involved with vices; but a person described as *viciado* is bad through and through—in danger of consigning his immortal soul to hell for the practice of multiple vices on a grand scale. A *viciado* may see himself as no good or in the hands of the devil, and may commit suicide as a result. When a teenage heroin addict hanged himself in a Tucson jail in the early 1970s, it was said "he was so bad, so *viciado,* that he knew he could not live."

Cantineras are, by definition, women who spend a lot of time in cantinas drinking. Furthermore, they drink with men and are likely to "go with any man." Secondarily, they are unlikely to fulfill their sex-based roles adequately in the household, nor do they stay home as they should. *Cantineras* are not necessarily bad, although, like *viciados,* they may be seen as spiritually bankrupt. At times, *cantineras* are seen as not being able to help acting that way; nymphomaniacs or women who "have to have a man" are often similarly regarded. At other times *cantineras* are considered personally irresponsible—out for a good time at the cost of their children, their families, or their households. The latter view places blame on individuals for their own behavior, in keeping with the more generalized Yaqui pattern of imputing personal responsibility for actions. No informant ever interpreted such behavior as a legitimate response to overwhelming problems. So many women facing similar or worse hardships manage to survive without taking this route that becoming a *cantinera* because of the quality of one's personal life is not advanced as a reasonable explanation.

Stay-at-home women (*mujeres pegadas á la casa*) form another loosely recognizable category. Certain women continually make decisions to optimize their being localized in the household. They do not visit much in other homes, or perhaps they do not leave their own houses or compounds at all. They respond much more slowly than other women to economic pressures by seeking outside employment, and they terminate outside employment as soon as possible. They are unlikely to attend public ceremonials, confining themselves to household ceremonies of near relatives. The most confirmed stay-at-home women are likely to have "sad" personalities, although membership in the two categories is not identical.

In some respects stay-at-home women are also close to ideal fulfillment of women's household roles in that they do stay at home and concern themselves almost exclusively with household affairs. Like "happy" and "hard" women, they usually belong to the more traditionally oriented sector of Yaqui society, although their traditional stance is seldom as overt or visible. They practice rather than advocate. Being so firmly and predictably localized, they may become a target for relatives seeking aid, which they make an effort to provide insofar as they do not have to leave home. These circumstances may result in stay-at-home women's upholding a considerable number of, particularly, kin-based obligations. Such women may be noted for their tendency not to gossip and to talk nicely about people and mind their own business. Stay-at-home women are not forced by others to pattern their behavior in this fashion, although there are women whose husbands or fathers curtail their movements. Rather, they have deeply internalized these aspects of the woman's role or they have personalities that make the contained household world the most compatible place for them to be. Diametrically opposed to stay-at-home women are those individuals who "walk in the houses."

A person described as *corajudo* has a short temper and is excitable. Men are said to become *corajudo* when drunk if they become truculent and engage in fights of any sort. Impatience, verbal attacks, and unfair punishment of children by either men or women are also examples of *corajudo* behavior.

Certain women are described as "good" or "bad." Contextual evidence from personal accounts, as well as responses to direct questions about "good" women, delineated a cluster of attributes centering on successful household maintenance and obligation fulfillment. A "good" woman works hard, often in the face of inadequate support and the chronic drunkenness of household males, raises children properly, is fair, performs her household tasks, manages household resources effectively, and behaves appropriately for her age and marital status. Appropriate behavior may involve asking her husband or father for permission to leave the house or to do other things. Fulfillment of ceremonial obligations is not usually cited as a criterion in this evaluation, nor does it matter how many men the woman has lived with, as long as she lives with them one at a time. Illegitimate children and affairs have no great relevance in the assessment of unattached women as "good."

"Good" and "bad" are not mirror images. A woman who does not qualify as a "good" woman may be said to be "not very good." Really promiscuous women and *cantineras*, for example, may be a long way from being "good," but normally they are not seen as "bad" unless their behavior is extreme. "Bad" women are those who "walk in the houses," "talk badly" about people, refuse to uphold kin or other obligations when it is believed they have the resources to do so, or make trouble. Women occasionally single out as "bad" those women with whom their husbands or consorts have affairs, but this is a more limited usage of the term. A woman described emotionally by an Hermosillo informant as "bad, bad, bad" was a troublemaker of *barrio*-wide fame who did not uphold kin-based obligations. She had a *corajudo* temperament that manifested itself in chronic rudeness and unprovoked verbal attacks, a temperament epitomized by her apparently senseless killing of a little dog with a butcher knife one morning.

The categories described do not represent universal judgments about a person's character, behavior, or personality. Only one or a few individuals may describe another person in these terms, or the evaluation may be fairly widespread.

Personal experience and the specific context affect such judgments. An individual abandoned by his mother in middle or late childhood may, for a lifetime, harbor resentment, calling her a bad mother or saying that she was not a good mother. That same woman might be described differently by her age peers who had more knowledge and experience in shifting alliances and who did not suffer emotional trauma at her hands.

References Cited

Boas, Franz. 1943. Recent anthropology. *Science* 98:311–14, 334–37.

Cronin, Constance. 1970. *The sting of change*. Chicago: University of Chicago Press.

Gudeman, Stephen. 1972. The *compadrazgo* as a reflection of the natural and spiritual person. In *Proceedings of the Royal Anthropological Institute of Great Britain and Ireland for 1971*, pp. 45–72. London.

Kluckhohn, Clyde. 1945. The personal document in anthropological science. In *The use of personal documents in history, anthropology, and sociology*, ed. Louis Gottschalk, Clyde Kluckhohn, and Robert Angell, Social Science Research Council Bulletin 53, pp. 78–173. New York.

Langness, L. I. 1965. *The life history in anthropological science*. New York: Holt, Rinehart and Winston.

Mintz, S. W., and E. R. Wolf. 1950. An analysis of ritual co-parenthood (compadrazgo). *Southwest Journal of Anthropology* 6:341–68.

Moisés, Rosalio, Jane Holden Kelley, and William Curry Holden. 1971. *The tall candle: The personal chronicle of a Yaqui Indian*. Lincoln: University of Nebraska Press.

Pozas, Ricardo. 1962. *Juan the Chamula: An ethnological re-creation of the life of a Mexican Indian*. Berkeley: University of California Press.

Radin, Paul. 1920. The autobiography of a Winnebago Indian. *University of California Publications in American Archaeology and Ethnology* 16:381–473.

———. 1926. *Crashing Thunder: The autobiography of an American Indian*. New York: Appleton.

Spicer, Edward. 1940. *Pascua, a Yaqui village in Arizona*. Chicago: University of Chicago Press.

———. 1954. Potam, a Yaqui village in Sonora. *American Anthropological Association Memoir 77*. Menasha, Wis.

Spiro, Melford E. 1972. An overview and a suggested reorientation. In *Psychological anthropology*, ed. Francis L. K. Hsu, new ed., pp. 573–607. Cambridge, Mass.: Schenkman Publishing Co.

Swallow, D. A. 1974. The anthropologist as subject. *Cambridge Anthropology* 1, no. 3, pp. 51–60.

White, Leslie A. 1943. Autobiography of an Acoma Indian. In *New material from Acoma*, Bureau of American Ethnology Bulletin 136, pp. 301–60. Washington, D.C.: Smithsonian Institution.

The Narratives

The four life stories presented here illustrate to some extent the range of historical events in which Yaquis participated from the 1880s to the present. From the 1880s until the end of the Mexican Revolution (1920), more Yaquis lived on Sonoran ranches, in mining towns, and in centers such as Hermosillo than in the eight traditional villages along the lower reaches of the Yaqui River (Belern, Huirivis, Rahum, Potam, Vicam, Torim, Bacum, and Cocorit). Conflict with Mexicans over land and autonomy has a history that goes much farther back in time, but the Yaqui wars of the 1880s and 1890s had enormous impact on Sonora. Symptomatic of the effects of this deep conflict upon Yaqui settlement patterns is the fact that the parents of all four of the women whose stories follow were born in the Yaqui Valley villages but all four women were born elsewhere in Sonora.

Although Dominga Tava was born in 1901, later than the other three, she was the most historically minded of the four women, and she gives family background that covers military actions and the life ways of the Yaquis involved in the Yaqui wars. Members of her father's family served under Cajeme, the famous—or infamous, depending on one's point of view—Yaqui leader who was killed in 1887.

The other three women were born between the early and late 1890s at La Colorada mine, where a sizable Yaqui community existed for many years. Yaqui men there and at other mines were skilled miners, esteemed as reliable, hard workers. Undoubtedly the adult Yaquis in these enclaves were interested and involved in wider Yaqui affairs, but for children born there, such affairs must have been remote. Life was secure and pleasant; a standard of living which compared favorably to that of workers anywhere in Sonora was maintained.

The apparent security of even these enclaves was effectively demolished early in 1900, when the Mexican government mounted a massive military campaign, determined to end Yaqui insurrection. Its goal was a clean sweep of the Bacatete Mountains, which had long served as a base of operations and a retreat for the Yaquis. Dispersed Yaquis were driven into a few mountain sanctuaries, and on January 18, 1900, several Mexican detachments converged on a place called Mazocoba. Although the Yaqui leader, Tetabiate, escaped, several hundred Yaquis were killed, others jumped off cliffs to their death, and approximately one thousand women and children were taken prisoner. Following this event, Yaquis' lives became considerably less stable. The household unit to which Antonia Valenzuela and Chepa Moreno belonged broke up, and they moved to Hermosillo with one part of the fragmented family. A new era began, characterized by a lower standard of living and taunts from Mexicans about their being Yaquis.

Sonora acquired a new governor in 1903, Rafael Izábal (or Isábal, Yzábal), who inaugurated a new program for dealing with the Yaquis: deportation to the haciendas of southern Mexico. From that time until the beginning of the Mexican Revolution in 1910, Yaquis were subject to seizure by the Mexican military, arrest, execution, persecution, and deportation. The threat that one of these actions would affect one's own family was a constant fear, and families were sundered at a debilitating rate. Chepa Moreno, as a young bride, and Dominga Ramírez, as a child, were among the countless Yaquis deported, both being sent to Yucatán. Their accounts, the first to be published of such experiences, are sufficient testimony to the conditions endured by the deported Yaquis.

No few Yaquis elected to remove themselves to the safety of the United States. Such immigration had begun in the 1880s, but it escalated enormously during the deportation era. Antonia Valenzuela portrays this pattern; taken to Arizona by her grandmother, she lived out her life as an Arizona Yaqui, and all of her children were born and have remained there. Still other Yaquis remained in Sonora throughout these turbulent years. Dominga Tava spent her early life in Hermosillo; in 1916 she accompanied her mother to Arizona and thereafter made Tucson her primary residence.

The Mexican Revolution was in many respects extraneous to central Yaqui concerns for their land and autonomy. For individuals, however, it was an all-involving personal experience. Deported Yaqui men in Yucatán joined one or another army when they were freed from what they regarded as slavery. Sonoran Yaqui men joined up as well. Yaqui women became *soldaderas*, as the cases of Chepa Moreno and Dominga Ramírez illustrate.

Following the Revolution, Yaquis began to return to the Yaqui Valley. Soldiers released from the army came, as did people long resident in Arizona, to begin the remarkable reconstruction of Yaqui lifeways in the eight villages. Dominga Ramírez is the only one of the four women who lived in the villages during that time, and her story fails to reflect the highly significant and deliberate reconstitution of Yaqui civil, religious, and military organization into a functioning entity. Dominga Ramírez was, by her own account, more interested in personal matters during those years. One might also infer that she saw nothing unusual in the reweaving of the fabric of Yaqui society, in spite of living to adulthood without participating in a situation in which all Yaqui institutions were operational. Her attitude implicitly points up the widespread attitude that Yaquis might be refugees or displaced persons for years and years, but Yaqui culture and the Yaqui homeland would transcend these temporary events. Slightly more of the enthusiasm and the reality of the reconstruction efforts emerges in Dominga Tava's narrative. Although living in Arizona by this time, she visited her father in Vicam during the construction of the church; since her father was captain of Vicam, she was much closer to the center of the reconstruction efforts, albeit briefly.

The efforts at reconstruction were not problem-free. Of external problems, the resumption of distribution of Yaqui lands to non-Yaquis by Governor Adolfo de la Huerta in 1919 loomed large. In 1926, Alvaro Obregón was in Sonora campaigning for reelection as president of Mexico. Many Yaquis had served under him during the Revolution and some knew him personally. What could be more reasonable, in the Yaqui view, than to talk to Obregón about their deep concerns over Yaqui land? These intentions were misconstrued (again, according to Yaqui views), and when Obregón's train stopped in Vicam Switch, the resulting confrontation initiated the 1926–27 war—the last open hostilities between Mexicans and Yaquis.

Differing perspectives on the 1926–27 war are seen in the four narratives. Dominga Ramírez was among the Potam residents who fled to the mountains. This particular group saw no military action and eventually surrendered, with the result that most of the party were deported or conscripted into the Mexican army, a fate not shared by Dominga Ramírez. Dominga Tava belonged to an Arizona family that was deeply involved in planning and acquiring arms for the Yaqui war effort, and her father played an active military role in Sonora. Chepa Moreno, viewing the war from the vantage point of an Hermosillo washerwoman, reaffirmed her earlier opinion that the Yaquis did nothing but fight. When she heard that the year's harvest had been abandoned in the rush for the Sierra, she decided the Yaquis were more foolish than she had thought possible. The war is not mentioned in Antonia Valenzuela's narrative; although she knew quite a bit about it, she did not include any episodes related to the war in the story of her own life, an indication that it had little impact on her.

After 1927, Yaqui history entered a less dramatic period, unpunctuated by widely memorable events. The four women continued to live where they had settled earlier, one in the Yaqui Valley, one in Hermosillo, and two in Arizona. Differences in their life styles are apparent, but of greater interest is the position of each woman in her social matrices through time and the strategies each employed in defining and maintaining her position. Dominga Ramírez progressed through a series of states to end up a reasonably respected head of family. Chepa Moreno became more and more of a social isolate, deprived of children and near relatives. Antonia Valenzuela devoted her energy almost exclusively to her household and family. Dominga Tava, in contrast, directed her attentions to extra-household affairs.

In the summer of 1975, I took the revised narratives to Arizona and Sonora for final checking with informants, insofar as that was possible. Chepa Moreno's story could not be checked because, upon her death, she left no descendants or near friends or relatives who had relevant information. Little checking was possible in Potam with Dominga Ramírez's descendants, although some points were clarified. Antonia Valenzuela's daughters all survived, and one of them listened to a complete translation of that narrative, as is discussed in the preface to her story. Dominga Tava was meticulous in her review of her own narrative, producing more details she felt needed to be included.

In the following narratives, I have used a few words and phrases translated literally from Spanish. The Yaquis customarily identify people for whom the ancestral town in the Yaqui Valley is known by saying "He (or she) pertains to Torim," or Vicam or Potam, etc. The phrases "to walk with" and "to talk with" are retained because I know of no equivalent translations that cover the range of activities potentially involved. "To walk with" can mean anything from literally walking with a person, to what could be called dating, to sporadic sexual involvement, to long-term alliances. The meaning implied emerges from the context, or in some cases was never made clear. The flexibility of the verb "to walk" is further seen in the phrase "to walk in the houses" with its associated connotations. Some Spanish terms are used; a translation is given when the word first appears. The names have been changed to accord with the pseudonyms used in *The Tall Candle* insofar as the same characters appear in both books.

An air of quiet dignity characterized Dominga Tava's neat appearance and behavior. Although possessing a subtle sense of humor, she did not usually enter into joking relationships or entertain with amusing stories. Widely respected as an older woman who knew a great deal of Yaqui lore and history, she upheld an extensive network of kin and ritual kin obligations. Too serious to be called happy, and hard only in her outspoken condemnation of drunkenness as the source of Yaqui social problems and poverty, happy and hard were, nonetheless, the behavioral constellations she most closely approached. She was not the least sad, timid, or passive. A talented conversationalist in Yaqui and Spanish, she moved easily in the world outside her household, working throughout her mature years in laundries and as a restaurant cook.

Dominga was only remotely and vaguely related to the other women whose stories are included in this work, and her early life experiences were somewhat different. Born in Hermosillo in 1901, she grew up there, remaining in Sonora throughout the years of Yaqui persecution and deportation and through the early critical years of the Mexican Revolution. In 1916 she moved to Arizona.

Dominga's mother, Matilde Yaqui Larga, dominated her life in a way no other informant was dominated by an older woman, as is clearly reflected in the way Matilde Yaqui Larga dominates the first half of the narrative. Dominga's own identity is slow to emerge. Certainly Matilde Yaqui Larga received Dominga's primary allegiance. Dominga made other deep emotional investments in her father and her son. Her father, however, left the family, so that her

78

DOMINGA TAVA

relationship with him, which had stronger affective overtones than that with her mother, lacked continuity. Circumstances deprived her of surviving children. In this respect she resembled Chepa Moreno, although she did not experience the hardships and tragedies that characterized Chepa's life. However, her social position was entirely different. She claimed other women's children to raise and was given still others. After retiring from active employment, she turned her attention to the affairs of the Barrio Libre Yaqui Church, assuming much of the responsibility for the care of the saints and the building, and actively participating in all the organized ritual activity. She actively manipulated information of all sorts, from knowledge about Yaqui culture to casual gossip, to enhance her social standing. These positive actions and the extraordinarily large number of kin and ritual kin obligations she maintained partially compensated for the fact that she did not stand at the apex of a pyramid of descendants. Nonetheless, she realized that the outlook for her final years as a solitary woman without children to support and care for her was, probably, loneliness and hardship.

One of the best informants, Dominga could easily have been the subject of a full-length biography. Accustomed as she was to conversing freely and at length with non-Yaquis, she spoke so easily and with so little need for direction that I received the impression that I was hearing stories often told before. When I asked to review stories after an interval of several days or even weeks, she repeated them almost verbatim. Like other informants, she went to a great deal of trouble to provide independent verification of certain episodes by showing me old

79

letters and other documents and by introducing me to other people who knew about particular events and beliefs. Much of the information about her early experiences in Hermosillo, especially supernatural information, could not be crosschecked and is idiosyncratic in that no other informants mentioned these things, nor is there relevant comparative published information.

Dominga would probably have agreed to act as an informant under most circumstances because the role is compatible with her entire behavior and personality. The informant-investigator relationship was given added depth in this case because I had met her father in Vicam Switch in the early 1950s, when he served as an informant for W. C. Holden and Robert Ravicz. Lengthy tape recordings of those interviews cover some of the same events described by Dominga, providing a useful independent source. Her father, Vicente Tava, asked my father, W. C. Holden, to hand deliver a letter to Dominga. It was symptomatic of the wide range of obligations she maintained that twenty years later I arrived at her door with a message from a Yaqui man in Denver.

Although I only worked with her only during my last data-collecting season, we were together that summer in a wide range of settings. Dominga accompanied me on a trip to the Río Yaqui with visits to relatives in Hermosillo, Potam, Torim, Vicam Switch, and Esperanza. We also visited her comadres in Barrio Libre and Pascua. Much of the formal interviewing occurred in her Barrio Libre home.

During the 1975 checking of the manuscript with informants, Dominga clarified a number of points (mostly about who was where at a particular time), corrected some place names I had misunderstood, and added details (especially to those episodes involving her father). We were traveling together in Sonora during some of the manuscript reading, and our presence at locations mentioned in her life story elicited further clarifications and additional details. She retold many of the stories; these new versions corresponded closely to earlier ones. The largest discrepancy was evident in the story involving her grandfather, a ghost, and buried gold in Hermosillo. Both versions are included here.

I returned to Tucson for Holy Week in 1977, spending most of my time in Dominga's company. Additional information emerged about her first marriage, and of course the continuation of her life had produced changes, of which the most significant had to do with her recent involvement in her grandson's household and the developments

*in the saga of the Barrio Libre church. One major discrepancy arose
with her earlier accounts, however, for which I lack an adequate
explanation. Originally she related that her younger half-brother,
Manuel Mosen, died as an infant in the 1918 influenza epidemic in
Tucson. Throughout the earlier interviews, Dominga consistently
indicated that only two of Matilde Yaqui Larga's children lived to
adulthood: herself and her sister Lola. In 1977, a recently deceased
adult brother suddenly surfaced in the context of a discussion of legal
problems about the title to Matilde Yaqui Larga's house.*

*Dominga had heard that a man in Pascua Nueva was saying
derogatory things about her life story. This man, the same who said
even more derogatory things about Antonia Valenzuela's and her
daughters' life stories (see preface to that narrative), had earlier
approved of my working with Dominga, saying that she was a good
woman who knew things. His relationship to Dominga over the years
had been respectful; they are* compadres, *having baptized together.
Dominga was unhappy with and rather insulted by his change in
attitude. She renewed her efforts to introduce me to people who would
verify a certain story, commenting pointedly that while he might
know a great deal, she was older and knew more: "How would he
know anything about my life in Hermosillo? How would he know
about my father's life in Vicam? He can't know any of that!" After
discussing at some length with me and with her friends the reasons
for his antagonism, she finally decided that the reason was political.
This man is attempting to consolidate the Yaqui identity and presence
in southern Arizona at Pascua Nueva (or New Pascua, or New
Village, as it is also called, but which he calls Pascua Pueblo). Among
other things, he wants the ceremonial structure to become firmly
based in Pascua Nueva. When legal controversies arose over the land
on which the new church stands in Barrio Libre, he supported his
relatives who want the land back; Dominga was fighting to retain the
church.*

Matilde Alvarez, better known as Matilde Yaqui Larga, was
thirteen when she married the slightly older Vicente Tava early
in the 1890s in the cathedral in Hermosillo. Neither wanted to
marry and at first both refused; when their wishes were
ignored, they hid. Even at the church, they refused to give the

correct responses to the priest until their mothers muttered in Yaqui what would happen to them later if they refused to conform. So began the marriage of Dominga Tava's parents.

Matilde belonged to the large Alvarez family headed by her father, Manuel Alvarez, a famous *sabio* or *saurín* (wise man) possessing special powers to protect his family and control witches. Pertaining to the pueblo of Torim, the men of the family had, for several years, worked on an hacienda of Antonio Gandara, but they also had a house in the Hermosillo *barrio* of La Mariachi where Matilde's mother preferred to stay and where Matilde grew up.

Vicente Tava belonged to the extensive Tava family of Vicam pueblo. Vicente, his parents, and his several siblings lived in La Mariachi at the time of Vicente and Matilde's marriage, working on nearby haciendas. Shortly after their wedding, the large Tava family returned to Vicam. Matilde Yaqui Larga, who had felt she was too young to be forced to marry and was now being forced to leave her mother's company, was surrounded in Vicam by her in-laws, who were virtually strangers. Joaquina Tava was a hard mother-in-law.

The Tavas' residence in Vicam was short-lived; as hostilities with the Mexicans intensified, the family fled to the Sierra. All of the men were accustomed to the hardships of the mobile life, since they had all previously served as Yaqui soldiers. Vicente's father and several of his older brothers had fought under Cajeme. Vicente's own stories about Cajeme and the wars, as told to his children and in recorded interviews, make it sound as though he actually served under that Yaqui leader. He told of going through several battles armed only with a bow and arrow against Mexican rifles, and he cited the battle of Capetemayo as the first in which he was equipped with a rifle. That battle occurred in 1882; if his children were correct that he was twenty-six years of age at the time of the 1900 Mazocoba massacre, he would have been a seasoned soldier at the age of eight.

Whether he actually served under Cajeme or was reflecting the stories and attitudes of his father and older brothers, he, and consequently his children, consistently pictured Cajeme as a traitor who betrayed the best interests of the Yaqui tribe. The debacle of Cautorreon in 1887 was described by Vicente as sheer treachery: Cajeme sent all able-bodied men on a make-believe raid, and when they had departed, he lit a bonfire to signal Mexican soldiers waiting in Torocopobampo. Many women, children, and old men were killed and the rest taken as prisoners to Rahum, while Cajeme went to Guaymas a free man.

Vicente firmly distinguished between Mexicans and Spaniards. Spaniards were good and trusted friends of the Yaqui tribe while the Mexicans were the enemy. His grandmother told him the following story of the first meeting between Spaniards and Yaquis at what is now Guaymas. The heads of the eight pueblos met honorably with the Spaniards, exchanging gifts at a fiesta to which both parties contributed food and at which both performed traditional dances and music. The Spaniards, respectfully asking to be allowed to build docks, paid the Yaquis for this privilege, for in those days, tribal land extended from Guaymas far to the south. Cordial relationships continued until the Mexicans expelled the Spaniards from Mexico, at which time the Spaniards entrusted their extensive treasures to their valued allies, the Yaquis, for satekeeping. The Spaniards retained one copy of the inventory; another was held by Yaqui elders. For generations the Yaqui inventory was safe—until it fell into Cajeme's hands. He, however, did not know where the treasure was buried. After he gave or sold the inventory to some Guaymas merchants, they bribed a Mexican general to execute him, and that is why Cajeme was killed in 1887. Vicente's aunt, who walked to Cocorit to see the body of the fallen Cajeme, which had been returned to his own pueblo for burial, also told Vicente these things were true.

Although the Mexicans were never friends of the Yaquis, a delicate balance was maintained, according to Vicente, until the regime (1876–1911) of Porfirio Díaz, whose actions in sending five thousand Mexican soldiers against the tribe initiated the wars in which the Tava father and sons became involved.

Life in the Sierra during the 1890s involved walking countless miles through the rugged mountains, sleeping in the open, and suffering repeated hunger and sickness. Vicente rose rapidly to the rank of *cabo* (corporal), at which time he was placed in command of a group of approximately one hundred Yaqui soldiers and their families. For tactical and subsistence reasons, his followers were dispersed, spending much of their time searching for food and water. Everyone learned the location of even the most minor water sources because the Mexicans, when they came, took over known water holes in an effort to drive the Yaquis out of hiding. One of Vicente's duties as a *cabo* was to lead raiding parties to obtain provisions from isolated Mexican ranches or the Yaqui villages where the "tame" Yaquis lived. Amused at the terrified reaction of the people whom he raided, Vicente, and Dominga also, stressed that his group never killed unnecessarily.

Matilde Yaqui Larga hated every minute of her life in the Sierra, or that is the impression she gave her daughter. Two sons born there died within a few days of their births. Matilde believed they were deliberately killed by her sister-in-law, Josefa Tava, because their light-colored skin and hair led her to announce that the babies could not possibly have been fathered by the dark Vicente, and that Matilde must have been walking with Mexicans. Josefa, who acted as Matilde's *partera* (midwife), cut the babies' cords so short that air entered their bodies, causing them to bloat and die, foaming at the mouth.

In 1900, the Mexicans mounted the massive military sweep of the Bacatete Mountains culminating in the infamous Mazocoba massacre. The Tavas were involved in the fighting at Tatoi-Tacusa but not at Mazocoba. After these battles, they climbed the Cerro del Gallo, trying to find friends and relatives, but no one was there. Near Samahuaca, they encountered a battle from which they escaped by pretending to be Mexicans. A few days later, near Hermosillo, Vicente's father and several brothers and brothers-in-law were taken prisoner. The old *patrones* to whom their wives appealed were able to secure the release of the younger men, but the father was shot.

Vicente and his siblings returned to Hermosillo, much to Matilde's great delight. She vowed never again to go to the Sierra or to live in the Yaqui villages, a vow she kept. The years of hunger and perpetual hardship were over, and best of all, she was reunited with her mother, because it was in the

Alvarez household in La Mariachi that Vicente and Matilde established their residence. Vicente obtained a good job working in a nearby flour mill, and they were quite well off when Dominga was born in 1901, with Matilde's mother, Lucía Alvarez, acting as *partera*. Dominga's coloration was as fair as her dead brothers' had been, but Lucía knew that coloring ran in the family. This time no one suggested that Vicente was not the father. Manuel Alvarez told the family that Dominga would inherit his power to cure and would follow him as the family protector because she was born with the *signo de gracia* (sign of grace) on her forehead.

Matilde's father, Manuel, who was a *blanco* (had fair skin and light hair) like Dominga, and his sons spent their working days at the Hacienda Gandara as they had for more than a decade. Their horses, cows, goats, and chickens were kept at the hacienda. On Saturday they came into Hermosillo on horseback, joining Lucía and the other women and children in La Mariachi. Even when Manuel was elsewhere, he "knew" what was happening to his family because of his power. Upon occasion he foretold events that would affect family members.

When Dominga was a baby, she suddenly became seriously ill. As she was told the story over and over again by her mother, she wanted to nurse but Matilde impatiently refused her. Dominga closed her eyes tightly, and when she opened them, blood ran forth and neither Matilde nor Lucía could stop the flow. In desperation they took Dominga to a *curandera* (curer) living next door. Sucking on the "sign of grace" on Dominga's forehead, the woman sucked out a horned toad. Dominga improved immediately and Matilde and Lucía were pleased. Late that night, an angry Manuel rode in from the hacienda. He had "known" of Dominga's sickness and came as fast as he could to cure her. Although no one told him about the *curandera*, he "knew" about that, too. He said that because his wife and daughter had shown so little faith, they had caused irreparable damage. The *curandera* had stolen Dominga's "sign of grace." Now the powers that should have been Dominga's would belong to that woman. As his wrath lessened, he said sadly that no one would be able to protect the family after he died.

Dominga felt, for the rest of her life, that she had been deprived of something precious. Had she possessed the power, she would have used it only to do good things. Proof of the power was demonstrated by the fact that the *curandera* later became one of the most famous in the Río Yaqui, whereas earlier she had been quite ordinary. Dominga was left with only a pale reflection of what might have been: the ability to dream future events.

Manuel had better luck in protecting his son, José María Alvarez, an inveterate card player. One day José María played with a *brujo* (witch) and won, with the result that the witch retaliated by making him sick. Within a few days he was unable to leave his *petate* (mat, or bed). Once again, Manuel "knew" of the situation, and he came to Hermosillo to save his son. Passing the family house, he rode straight by without looking to the right or the left, going directly to the witch's house. Matilde followed him and saw the whole thing. The witch saw Manuel approaching and, knowing how powerful he was, ran to hide. His wife ran in a different direction, crying, "There comes don Manuel to kill my husband." Calmly dismounting, Manuel called the *brujo* back. Even though the witch did not want to come, such was Manuel's power that he had to return. Manuel directed the *brujo* to dig at the corner of the house until an *olla* (pot) containing cactus spines, nails, "poisons," and a candle was exposed. "Break the *olla* and put out the candle," he was told. "If my son had died, as he would if the candle had burned down, I would kill you. But I will spare your life." Manuel then removed the long leather whip he always wore wrapped around his waist, and doubling it, he beat the witch. It was with this whip that Manuel dominated witches. When Manuel and Matilde returned home, José María was cured.

Yet another account of Dominga's grandfather's power concerned a woman of the *barrio* who was bewitched. Lucía sent for Manuel to come and cure her. Rather than curing the woman directly, he sent for the witch who had caused the harm: "He called her with his *mente* [mind] and she had to come." He directed her to prepare the proper medicine for curing, but she denied knowing how. "I will teach you with

my whip," he threatened, and so she tried. Twice he threw out
the medicine she made. On the third attempt, he took a little
black root from his pocket and added it to the medicine, saying
that now it was ready. He made the witch cure the illness she
had caused.

Dominga was slightly over a year old when she again
became quite ill. Lucía said it was caused by Matilde's not caring
properly for her child. Lucía made a *manda* (vow) that if
Dominga recovered, Matilde would walk from Hermosillo to
Magdalena, carrying Dominga, to atone for her carelessness.
Dominga, of course, remembered nothing of this, but Matilde
retold the story so often that Dominga could repeat each detail.
One of Lucía's brothers, named Layo More, also had a vow to
fulfill; he therefore accompanied Matilde on her pilgrimage,
but he was so old and lame that she had to help him as well as
carry Dominga and the bundle containing a sarape and food
for the six-day trek. Every step made her angrier, since she felt
she had not been careless with Dominga. Matilde's temper rose
to new heights when Lucía waved cheerfully at the trio from
the window of a passing train. Layo said later he thought
Matilde would burst.

Lucía calmly awaited them at the church in Magdalena.
Without giving Matilde time to rest, she insisted they enter the
church immediately and offer Dominga to San Francisco. At
the moment Dominga was held over the reclining life-sized
figure of the saint, diarrhea struck—with disastrous results.
The furious Lucía said that had happened because Matilde
entered the saint's presence filled with *coraje* rather than with a
clean heart. Retiring from the church, Lucía settled Matilde,
Layo, and Dominga by the church wall while she went to buy
medicine. All afternoon she cured Dominga and lectured
Matilde on the importance of having a clean heart. Late in the
afternoon, Lucía decided everyone was in a fit condition to
approach the saint again. Dominga was held up to kiss the
saint, Matilde prayed for forgiveness, and Lucía thanked God
and the saint for Dominga's recovery. Then they went to stay
with relatives who ran a *panaderia* (bakery), having a pleasant
time for several days. Matilde was allowed to take the train
home. In later years as she remembered this incident, she

would say to Dominga, "Cómo me hiciste sufrir" ("How you made me suffer").

Although living in Hermosillo, Vicente was still a Yaqui *cabo*. In 1902, he was sent by a Yaqui general to Arizona to buy guns and ammunition, the first of several such commissions. This meant quitting his job at the flour mill, and because the Yaquis had no money, he had to get a job on the Southern Pacific Railroad in Arizona to earn enough to make the purchase. He walked both ways. Upon his return, he obtained work in a brewery, moving Matilde and Dominga to a little house near his employment, where they remained for several years. It was here that their next two babies were born: Chepa in 1902 and Ramona in 1906. Chepa appeared to be normal when she was born, but when only three days old, she became partly paralyzed, growing "crooked and twisted," with a clawlike hand. Dominga was not fond of the deformed child, remembering her as an evil-tempered little girl who bit people at every opportunity. When Chepa was perhaps two years old, she bit Dominga's hand, causing a painful, deep wound that probably got infected since it took weeks to heal.

Vicente was eager for his children to go to school in order to learn to read and write. Although Matilde said it was a waste of time, Dominga was sent to a private, Catholic school for perhaps a year. This period she recalled with a great deal of pleasure because every evening Vicente would ask her to repeat her lessons. Not only did that give her cherished hours with her beloved father, but it caused her to be at the top of her class. When a new pupil entered, Dominga was given the task of helping the child to catch up. Unfortunately, this caused her to fall behind in her own work, something that infuriated the teacher so much that she hit Dominga on the back of the neck with a heavy whip. As a result, blood ran from her nose for days. Vicente refused to allow Dominga to continue under the tutelage of that *maestra*, transferring her to an inferior school. At the end of the year, Matilde insisted that Dominga was too old to go to school and, saying Dominga knew enough anyway, demanded that she stay home to help care for her little sisters. Vicente was sad, but he had to agree.

Occasionally, Dominga and her sisters were taken to the Hacienda Gandara to visit their grandfather, Manuel, for a few days. The best part of their exciting visits was riding on the loaded wagons in the wagon train that transported the hacienda harvest to Hermosillo. The Hermosillo wagon yard held endless fascination for the children. A male cook who accompanied the Gandara crew on the trip made the biggest wheat tortillas Dominga ever saw. Stretching from his shoulder to his finger tips, they required an enormous *comal* (griddle) for cooking.

Yaquis in Sonora were being deported, killed, imprisoned, and persecuted. Several members of the family thought it would be wise to move to Arizona. Manuel Alvarez, however, refused, saying, "No. I have to die here. But I will tell you one thing. The day I die, they will stop killing Yaquis. I will die, but for my people." One day in 1905, he told his son, Jesús, "Tomorrow the soldiers will hang me," further prophesying that his wife, Lucía, would die three days later. Full instructions regarding inheritance of his property, mainly livestock, were imparted to Jesús. Since Lucía was going to die, the goats and chickens were to be taken to Matilde Yaqui Larga. Again he lamented the fact that Dominga's "sign of grace" had been stolen, because no one would be able to protect the family.

As predicted, Mexican soldiers came to the hacienda, acting on information received from a Yaqui traitor (a *torocoyori*), and Manuel was charged with aiding the Sierra Yaquis, as indeed he had been. The Mexican captain put a rope around his neck, instructing the soldiers to raise and then lower him. "Now you will tell me the truth about the Yaqui." To which Manuel replied, "You want to know the truth? Well, here is the truth. You will not kill any more Yaquis after this," and he spit in the captain's face three times. The infuriated captain ordered Manuel to be hanged on a big mesquite tree. When Manuel was dead, they rounded up fifteen Yaqui men, including the fifteen-year-old Jesús and took them to the gray stone prison in Hermosillo to await deportation.

Manuel's older son, José María, had been elsewhere on the hacienda at the time and was not taken by the Mexicans. He returned to Hermosillo to tell his mother the news, but when he found that she had suffered an attack of *susto* (fright), having already been told her husband was dead, he lied to her, saying Manuel was alive. She said, "In my heart I know he is dead." She died within three days, as Manuel had predicted, without speaking another word.

Although Lucía was dead, Matilde Yaqui Larga decided that the only way to get young Jesús released was to petition his freedom on the grounds that his mother was dying and her deathbed wish was to see her son. Accordingly, she went to Vicente's *patrón*, a señor Cuvillo, with the story. He in turn talked for Jesús to the military authorities and Jesús was released. For the rest of his life, Jesús stayed with his older sister, dying "in her hands" many years later.

It was to Jesús that Lucía appeared in a dream three days after her death. He woke up suddenly and, waking Matilde, asked, "Where is Lucía?" "Lucía is dead." "But she was just here." Matilde asked, "What did she say?" "She said money is buried in that corner and I am to have it when I marry." Immediately they began to dig, and when no gold was found inside in the designated corner, they first tried the other three and then they started digging outside the house. At the corner Lucía had indicated, they found a bucket of gold *cruzeros* (coins). Jesús asked Matilde to keep it for him, and she secretly reburied it for safekeeping.

Shortly thereafter, a *bulto* (apparition) appeared to Matilde several nights in a row. It wanted her to follow, but she was afraid. She told her neighbor and *comadre*, Dominga Cruz (who had named and baptized Dominga), and a Mexican neighbor named Ramona about the *bulto*, and the two women joined Matilde so they could follow it together. That night it again appeared, and the three women and Vicente followed it, spades in hand, around the hill of La Mariachi to a *peñasco* (rocky ridge) where it disappeared. The noise of their digging aroused a *panadero* (baker) across the road who came to see what they were doing. His jealousy caused the gold to appear as bones and ashes. The *panadero* asked if they had found a burial. "No." "Well, what are you doing?" "Just digging." "At midnight?" Giving up, they returned home.

Manuel had found the gold they were searching for years before as he was coming to La Mariachi from the hacienda. A black *bulto* and a *lumbre* (light) appeared to him at the same spot. Before he could investigate, he had to cure his frightened horse by rubbing it with dirt. Then the *bulto* greeted him in a deep voice that sounded as though it were coming from the ground. Manuel asked, "Are you from this world or the other? What do you want?" The *bulto* replied that he was a lost soul. "If you will have a mass said for me, I will show you where my gold is buried." Manuel arranged the mass and was shown the hiding place. Knowing that people would kill him if he suddenly possessed such great wealth, he left it where it was, collecting a few coins whenever he passed. This was the source of the gold buried at the corner of the house. Matilde had been told about it, and she felt Manuel had sent the *bulto* as a reminder. She was afraid to try again, and they never retrieved the gold. In later years when the *peñasco* was dynamited to level the ground for houses, Dominga heard that gold was found there.

During the 1975 checking of the manuscript Dominga gave a second version of this story, which is as follows. A dead person (*defuncto*) stopped Manuel as he rode into La Mariachi one night. Manuel was not afraid, but his horse was, so he first quieted it by rubbing dirt on it. Then he talked to the *defuncto*: "Are you from this world or the other?" The *defuncto* said nothing but led him to a place and disappeared. Manuel dug there with the machete he always carried and found a copper box filled with gold *cruzeros*. He took some, then he reburied it exactly as it was. When he got home, he gave Matilde some gold and told her to prepare a fiesta, "because I am going to hold a wake tonight. But first I must go to the church." So he went to the church and gave the priest some money. By the time he returned, Matilde had summoned *pascolas* and had women cooking food, and the fiesta was ready to begin. They invited all their friends and neighbors. People they didn't know heard the fiesta and came. All were fed. Manuel gave money to his sister, Angela Alvarez. She buried her money in the kitchen in a hollow place under the *pretil* (fireplace). She never dug it up, but long after she died, her son and a granddaughter tore down the old kitchen to build a new one. They found the gold. It wasn't much, but it paid for their new kitchen with a bit left over.

After Manuel Alvarez's protection was removed, bad things began to happen to the family, to their near relatives, and even to their *compadres*. In 1907, Dominga's *padrinos de pila* (baptismal godparents) Dominga Cruz, and her son, José Juan Cruz, were taken for deportation. The young Dominga, who felt she had been partially raised by her *madrina*, pleaded with Matilde Yaqui Larga to ask *patrones* to intercede on their behalf, but Matilde sadly said it would be futile. Both mother and son died in Yucatán.

For a number of years, Manuela More, one of Vicente's cousins, had been part of the household. She had been visiting Matilde Yaqui Larga when her parents and siblings had been deported from the Gandara hacienda of Topahue, and thereafter Matilde cared for her. Manuela married Rosario Romero from Matilde's house. Although they often stayed at Topahue, where Rosario also worked, they always returned to Matilde's house when in Hermosillo. They were living there during much of 1907, when their two small sons, Filberto and José María, died within a short time of each other. These two boys had been the favorites of little Chepa, who was otherwise an unhappy child. Although Chepa could not talk, she made signs asking for her playmates, searching endlessly for them. When the five-year-old Chepa died, it was said that she died of *tristeza* for her two friends.

José María Alvarez was among the last of the Yaquis taken by soldiers. His capture occurred after the Revolution had begun elsewhere, but while Federal soldiers still occupied Hermosillo. Matilde tried frantically to secure his release, appealing both to former *patrones* and directly to the military authorities, only to be told that José María was scheduled to be shot in three days. "Don't waste your food," the soldiers said when she took him beans and tortillas in the old gray stone prison.

Just at that time, General Bule, a Yaqui who had earlier served with Vicente and other Tavas in the Sierra Yaqui army and who had subsequently joined the Mexican Federal Army, entered Hermosillo. Hearing of his arrival, Matilde immediately went to see him. He ordered José María's release. Matilde thanked him and went to the cathedral to give her thanks to God.

Vicente decided to accompany his mother and numerous siblings to Vicam. Matilde, pregnant at the time, reminded him that she had made a vow never again to live in the Yaqui pueblos or go back to the Sierra. As Dominga said, "Each of them had a road." His departure marked the end of their marriage.

Soon caught up in fighting in the Yaqui villages, Vicente and a cousin were wounded in a skirmish near Torim. Vicente's foot injury healed and he was able to continue as a Yaqui soldier, but he was never again able to perform the intricate steps of the *matachine* dancers. As soon as the Revolutionary Army was organized in Sonora, Vicente joined, spending the next four years as a soldier. Most of the time he was assigned to Alvaro Obregón's Sonoran battalions, but for a time he was with Pancho Villa's famous División del Norte.

At one point he was stationed in Nogales, where he met Ignacia Yoimere of Barrio Anita in Tucson, who was looking for a member of the Tava family because she had a baby fathered by Guadalupe Tava, Vicente's brother, who had been in Tucson. When her pregnancy became obvious, her mother had thrown her out, calling her a whore and saying she would never receive the baby. A kind *patrona* allowed Ignacia to stay at her house and have the baby. Although she thought her mother would relent, she was wrong. Ignacia had decided to give the baby to the Tavas, and, accompanied by an old aunt, she had come to Nogales to look for a member of that family. Vicente escorted Ignacia and her aunt to Hermosillo, where they delivered the baby to Dominga. Why Vicente did not give the baby to Matilde was not clear, but Dominga was, repeatedly, quite specific: "Vicente gave the baby to me." Ignacia returned to Tucson with her aunt; her mother then allowed her to return home.

Without Vicente, Matilde's household was now very poor, although her two unmarried brothers provided support. The young baby needed milk every day, but milk was beyond their means. Matilde therefore sent Dominga, the younger Ramona, and the baby to her uncle (Lucía's brother), Domingo More, a truly good man who worked on a hacienda near Sacatón, Sonora. There, Dominga was taught to milk a goat and given full responsibility for the baby.

After the battle of Hermosillo (in November 1916), in which Pancho Villa failed to take the city from Plutarco Calles's troops, Calles's soldiers came to Sacatón, ostensibly looking for deserters (to capture) and dead soldiers (to cremate), but in reality, they came to loot. Many hacienda workers, including Domingo and his family, piled into wagons and fled to Topahue, about thirty miles away. Those who remained watched the soldiers sack the houses and round up all the livestock. One of Domingo's cows was slaughtered. The soldiers ordered an old crippled man who had been unable to escape to cook the cow for them. This man could not walk. He used two stools, sitting on one while moving the other, then sliding onto it. In leap-frog fashion, he was able to move around slowly. The rough soldiers pushed him with rifle butts, causing him to fall off his stool, to the accompaniment of their raucous laughter. Considerably battered, he managed to do as they demanded before collapsing of exhaustion. Dominga described the desolate scene that greeted the people returning from Topahue: looted houses; scattered, worthless possessions; rotting animals; and the old man, exhausted but alive. Domingo's milk goats had been senselessly killed, along with the rest of the livestock. Without milk, the baby, Ignacio, sickened and died.

Matilde had given birth to Vicente's last child in 1910, several months after his departure from the household. The baby girl was named María Luisa. When she was perhaps a year old, Matilde formed an alliance with Lorenzo Mosen, who lived next door to the La Mariachi house that Matilde took over when Lucía died. Lorenzo was living in Dominga Cruz's old house and was, in fact, a nephew of José Juan Cruz, Dominga's *padrino de pila*, in whose company he had often visited the household to talk to Vicente. At the time he moved in with Matilde, he was a Federal soldier and, some said, a *torocoyori* (Yaqui informer). When the Revolution broke out, he joined the División del Norte. Matilde's first child by Lorenzo was born about 1911 or 1912.

She now had most of the responsibility for supporting the household. Her first work was as a washerwoman in a red-light house, but this meant that her baby was sometimes alone because Dominga and the others were in Sacatón with the baby Ignacio. Another way she tried to make money was to catch rattlesnakes in the *monte* (brush)—which she did by setting out a glass of milk to attract them to where she was waiting with an ax—for sale to bullfighters, who believed they would be lithe and supple if they ate the meat. Then she sold tortillas in the markets. A *comadre* suggested that she could make more money by feeding soldiers at home. Soon she had a clientele of about twenty soldiers who came to her house every day for their main meal. They joked with her and called her "Madre."

Just before the battle of Hermosillo, the soldiers came as usual. "Madre, today we go to fight Pancho Villa in Zamora. But we won't have to fight much because it is said he doesn't have many men—and only thirty 'Yakas' [as they called the Yaquis]. All we have to do is round them up and put them in the *corralón* [big corral]." But at first Villa fought well, taking the plaza in Hermosillo. To encourage the troops, a captain called out that there were lots of girls in Hermosillo they could have if they won the battle. The thirty Yaquis with Villa, all from Hermosillo, thought about their own wives, daughters, and sisters. The Yaqui captain told the Yaqui drummer to beat retreat—"Por atrás, por atrás." Villa then saw that the battle was going badly; most of his Chihuahuan forces were dead and the Yaquis were unwilling to continue fighting. He told the Yaqui captain, "You men are of this city. Your families are here. Go home." Slipping away, the Yaquis hid their guns in trees or along the river and went home to their families. And so Lorenzo Mosen rejoined the family, seeing his baby, Lorenzo, for the first time. However, since Lorenzo was afraid to show himself in Hermosillo because he was known as both a *torocoyori* and a Villista, Matilde sent him to join Dominga and Domingo More in Sacatón and he was there when the hacienda was sacked.

After Ignacio's death, there was no reason to stay in Sacatón, so Dominga, Ramona, and Lorenzo returned to Matilde in La Mariachi. Having lost his enthisiasm for soldiering, Lorenzo elected to work in Hermosillo. As the days lengthened into weeks, it became apparent to Matilde and her older children that Lorenzo was a poor substitute for Vicente. Not a particularly hard worker, he drank regularly and heavily, beating Matilde and the children when he staggered home late at night. Once he attacked Matilde with a butcher knife, but Matilde (whose size fitted her name of Yaqui Larga) easily wrestled the knife from his hand, broke it over a dog's head, and tossed the pieces into the street. Depositing him bodily on the bed, she held him down while Dominga ran next door to rouse her aunts, crying, "Lorenzo is killing my mother." The women came with stout sticks. A somewhat sober Lorenzo asked with what dignity he could muster, "What are you doing here?" "We have come to beat you." Lorenzo got away from Matilde and ran out of the house to hide.

Another time Lorenzo came home, drunk, to find Matilde ironing by the light of a kerosene lamp and the children asleep. Without a word, he hurled the burning lamp toward the children's bed. Fortunately, his aim was bad and the lamp exploded on the dirt floor, awakening Dominga, who ran screaming to get her aunts to come and beat Lorenzo with their sticks. Hastened on his way by the iron lamp base, which Matilde threw at him, he did not wait for the aunts.

Dominga was now old enough to perform household chores. She regularly helped with the corn grinding, tortilla making, and cooking, but her main tasks were running errands and carrying the water for the household. Water was obtained about a block away, and to get it, Dominga had to pass a house where three Mexican girls lived. They often made comments about the "uncivilized Yaqui" as she passed, and one day they knocked her bucket of water off her head with a rock. Dominga retaliated in a rock-throwing, hair-pulling fist fight.

When Matilde Yaqui Larga returned from selling tortillas at the central market to discover that Dominga had been fighting, she punished Dominga and lectured her about the evils of fighting. It would have ended there except that the Mexican girls' mother came to harangue Matilde about Dominga's behavior, saying that Matilde was responsible for the fight because she had not raised her daughter properly. The woman grabbed one of Matilde's *rebozos*, taking it home and burning it. Matilde then went to her house to ask why she had burned the *rebozo*. A *pleito* (dispute) resulted, causing neighbors to call the police, who arrested both women. The judge agreed that the woman had no right to burn up Matilde's *rebozo* and Matilde was released.

Trouble with the three Mexican girls continued. One of the girls, approaching the soldiers that Matilde regularly fed, asked, "Muchachos, ¿dónde está la Yaqui?" ("Boys, where is the Yaqui?") Dominga went out to confront her, saying, "Aquí está la Yaqui" ("Here is the Yaqui"), and they had a hair-pulling fight in the street for which Dominga was again punished. The next day as Dominga returned home from the shop with bread for the family and salt for the pigs, the same girl was lying in ambush with a thick wire she attempted to use as a whip. Wrestling the wire from her hand, Dominga said, "Three of you attacked me the first time, but now you are alone. Now we will see who wins." Dominga hit her in the face, grabbed her hair, knocked her down, kicked her in the stomach, and bit her hand before Matilde, who was going on an errand, stopped the fight. "Dominga, what are you doing to Carmelita? Fighting again!" Dominga defended herself, and a woman who had seen the whole episode told Matilde that Carmelita had started it. Carmelita said, "Yaqui desgraciada, me la va a pagar" ("Wretched Yaqui, you are going to pay me"). Diverted by this new declaration of war, Dominga said, "¿Cuánto te debo? To lo voy a pagar ahora" ("How much do I owe you? I am going to pay you now"), and the two were fighting again. Matilde hit Dominga with the bucket she was carrying and dragged her home.

Carmelita's grandmother brought the girl to Matilde's house, saying, "Look at Carmelita's face. Dominga did this." Matilde lost her temper, berating Dominga as "one of those bad women who fight in the streets." Dominga again defended her actions, saying that in every instance she had been attacked first. The grandmother, who was much more reasonable than the girl's mother, said that she felt Dominga was right. Earlier in the day she had seen Carmelita with a heavy wire. "I did not come here to blame Dominga, but to ask you to cure Carmelita." Matilde, who was a *curandera*, did as she asked.

No sooner had everyone relaxed than the girl's mother appeared, wanting to fight Matilde. She had been "filling up with *coraje*" since the judge had told her it was wrong to burn Matilde's *rebozo*. Now she said many bad things about Matilde and about Yaquis. Matilde listened and said, "I do not want to fight with you." Finally the woman went home, leaving Matilde furious with Dominga for causing all the trouble.

The next day when Dominga returned from fetching water, Matilde decided she had been fighting again, although she had not. Feeling that more drastic action was required to deter Dominga from becoming a bad woman, she got out the heavy leather whip. A Mayo soldier named Nacho took the whip from Matilde, saying, "Madre, listen. We are soldiers. If the enemy attacks us, we win or we lose. That happened to Dominga. She was attacked and she won. Let there be an end to this."

A sad episode in 1912 involved Angel Castillo, a relative of Matilde's, and his wife and her sister, all of whom were living in the household. They had come from Torres after the mother of the two women had died. Angel's wife had a baby, with Matilde serving as *partera*. Both mother and baby were ill, and it appeared certain that the baby would die. Angel, concerned that the baby be baptized, frantically searched for a man to serve as a *padrino*, while Matilde designated the eleven-year-old Dominga as *madrina*. The three to take part in the baptism ran with the baby all the way to the cathedral, where a priest began the rites. The baby died before the ceremony was completed, but the priest said the baby was innocent and would go to heaven. Since Dominga was the *madrina de pila*, she was also involved in the death rites. Two days later, Angel's wife died also.

Further tragedy was in store for the household in 1912. María Luisa died. It was believed that Dominga inadvertently caused her death by wetting her *mollera* (fontanel) while playing with her in the canal. Dominga had not known of the danger and no one blamed her, but the family was very sad. Some said the accident was the result of witchcraft. Of Matilde's seven children, only three remained alive.

A virulent smallpox epidemic swept through Hermosillo in 1913, killing people by the hundreds. Soldiers patrolled the streets searching for people with the disease. Houses harboring smallpox victims were marked with a red flag on the door to keep others away until the men from El Polvorín came to get them. El Polvorín, next door to a brickyard, was nothing but a few houses run by a handful of nurses. Wagons collected the dead from this smallpox center once a day and carted them off to a mass grave.

When Dominga contracted smallpox, the soldiers made Matilde take her to El Polvorín. Jesús Tava, whose daughter had just died there, saw them arrive with Dominga in an unconscious state, blood running from her nose. Jesús fainted because that was the way her own daughter had arrived. Matilde saw where Dominga was laid on the floor of one of the houses before rushing back to help revive Jesús. When Jesús was able to walk, they both went to care for Dominga whose fever had broken. As consciousness returned, Dominga saw that the five or six other victims on *petates* were naked, coated all over with a white pomade. A girl seemed to be calling, so Dominga crawled to her side, only to discover that the unconscious girl was breathing laboriously. Dominga was sitting up with Matilde and Jesús when a nurse came by with medicine. Jesús whispered to Matilde that the drops were poison and her daughter had died after having taken them. "Tell the nurse we will give Dominga the medicine in a little while." Jesús then fed the drops to a passing dog, which died two hours later. The verdict of poison was confirmed. Dominga believed that because most of the victims were going to die anyway, and because the nurses were so overworked, it was better if the victims did not die slowly. Only about one in twenty of the patients survived.

Patients had to stay at El Polvorín until the scabs dried, usually about a month. Bulk food was supplied by the government but each patient had to be cared for by relatives. Almost none of those without relatives survived; since so many of the soldiers were from elsewhere in Mexico, they were probably the segment of the population that suffered the highest mortality rate. Matilde Yaqui Larga, who had contracted smallpox as a child, nursed Dominga during her long stay, making a medicine from civeri, a small cholla, to reduce the itching and dry the scabs.

No sooner was Dominga released than the baby Lorenzo was taken to El Polvorín. Less lucky than Dominga, he died almost immediately. Matilde now had only two surviving children, Dominga, who was now twelve, and Ramona, who was seven. As the family continued to experience tragedies and troubles, Matilde often thought of Dominga's lost power and the protection Manuel Alvarez had provided for them.

The next incident was Matilde's illness caused by witchcraft. Angela Tava, one of Vicente's aunts, asked Matilde for a *rebozo* that caught her eye. Matilde politely said she had only the one *rebozo*, but she would buy Angela one just like it the next time she went to the central market. Angela was something of a witch. Annoyed by Matilde's refusal, she began to harm her, causing her to "become crooked—bent over as though her arms were tied to her knees." Her head drooped over her shoulders. When Luis Flores and his wife, Carlota, came to visit, they immediately noted Matilde's altered appearance. "Come to my house late this afternoon and I will cure you," Luis said. Afraid to leave her two daughters alone lest the witchcraft affect them, too, Matilde took them with her to see the Floreses, who rubbed a medicine all over Matilde's body. "Go home and go to bed, but rise when Lucero [the morning star] rises and grind the *nixtamal* [corn softened by soaking with lime from which the masa for tortillas is prepared]." Early the next morning, Carlota Flores entered their house, calling softly, "Matilde, ya se levantó el Lucero. Levántate a moler" ("Matilde, the Lucero has risen. Get up to grind"). Matilde stood up straight, all crookedness gone, and began to grind the corn.

A number of people, including Luis Flores, told Matilde that powerful witchcraft was directed against her family. Recalling all the tragedies, they advised Matilde to move away from the source of harm. Matilde said that she would stay where she was, because where else would they go? Three events changed her mind. First, Dominga, whose supernatural powers were now limited to dreaming the future, had a dream in which she was walking through the *carrizal* (canebrake) by the river. A man tried to grab her. Every time he lunged at her, she flew out of his reach; then, there he was, trying to grab her again. As the family and neighbors agreed, the dream was clearly an omen of further danger. Second, Matilde dreamed that Angela Tava was poking burning sticks into her eyes; soon her eyes began to water and hurt all the time, and it was feared she was going blind. Third, Ramona died after large butterflies heralded the death of someone in the family. Jesús Tava killed one of the butterflies, which Matilde said was the *chichal* of a witch.

Matilde decided that if they stayed where they were, they would all die. She was especially concerned about the fate of Dominga, her only surviving child. Sadly telling Domingo More good-by, for he refused to go with them, Matilde, Dominga, Lorenzo Mosen, **Jesús Alvarez**, and Manuela More and her husband, Rosario Romero, left on the train for Arizona in 1915 or 1916. Fighting at Santa Ana had destroyed the bridges. Advised by the soldiers to return to Hermosillo on the train that had brought them, Matilde said it shamed her to turn back. Walking across the river, they climbed on a troop train that would take them north. However, a second bridge was out. Matilde built a fire and made coffee. A passing soldier asked if he could buy a cup, which gave Matilde the idea of setting up a kitchen to feed the soldiers. From their stock of provisions, she put Dominga to making tortillas while she cooked beans. They did a brisk business and and sold all their food before they had to go back to Hermosillo, where everyone was surprised to see them. As soon as the bridges were repaired, they set out again, crossing the border March 14, 1916. They went immediately to José María Alvarez's home in Nogales, Arizona. He and his family had moved earlier, and he had a good job on the railroad.

One of the first people they met after they got to Arizona was Pedro Alvarez, Matilde's cousin who had been married to Chepa Moreno (whose life story appears later) before they were deported to Yucatán. A deserter from the Mexican army, he had settled in Tucson. After greetings were exchanged, he said, "Matilde, you have been harmed by a witch but I can cure you." Pedro was a good *curandero* and, some said, a witch. Within a short time he had cured Matilde's eyes.

The best jobs for Yaquis in Arizona at the time were at the Sasco Smelter, so they moved there. Lorenzo and Jesús went to work in the smelter, and Matilde and Dominga began cooking and washing for a man named Baldenegro. Many Yaquis they had known in Hermosillo were there, and both Matilde and Dominga were asked to baptize babies. For a time, it was the most carefree and affluent period the family had known for many years.

Lorenzo spent so much time in the cantina that they saw him very little. Soon he got sick, probably from drinking too much, and lost his job. Matilde went to an old friend of her father's, an elderly man living with his daughter, Guadalupe, and her husband, Juan Kutah Maesto, a *maestro* (member of one of the men's ceremonial societies which perform certain religious tasks), and told him Lorenzo was no longer able to work. The old man asked Matilde to come and help care for himself and his wife, arranging for them to live in a house next door. Matilde and Dominga no longer worked for Baldenegro but made tortillas and sold them house to house, in addition to caring for Matilde's father's old friend.

Juan Kutah Maesto figured prominently in a dream Dominga had in 1917. A number of men were playing cards, but one man was sitting apart. Three large dogs attacked her. The man seated apart took off his belt, which was really a leather whip, and handed it to her. With this, she hit the dogs and they ran off. Then came three enormous wolves, and they, too, ran off when faced with the *chicote* (whip). Last came Juan Kutah Maesto, screaming that she was very bad and for that reason the dogs and wolves had attacked her. Dominga responded, "Aye, you are the one who sent them. Now you will see. I will hit you, too," but he backed away. Dominga knew that her grandfather, Manuel Alvarez, had protected her by giving her the whip with which he dominated witches. Matilde agreed with this interpretation. When Dominga went to borrow some lard from Guadalupe the next morning, she found Juan Kutah Maesto lying on his bed, his face tied up in a cloth. Dominga asked, "Did you wake up sick?" "You made me like this because you are bad. I don't want to play with you any more." Dominga replied, "And I don't want to play with you any more," adding, "I didn't know you were a dog! I hit at dogs and wolves, but I did not touch you." He remained silent.

That afternoon, Juan Kutah Maesto told his father-in-law that Dominga had made him sick, "but I was only playing." The father-in-law laughed and said he had picked a dangerous person to play with. "Don't you know who her grandfather was? He was Manuel Alvarez, and he knew much," and he began to tell of Manuel's powers. Juan Kutah Maesto never tried to play with Dominga again. She said of the episode, "That time, I won." In succeeding years, Dominga baptized many babies, but most of them died. She believed Juan Kutah Maesto caused their deaths because he never forgave her for beating him, but when she asked him, years later, if he was harming her *ahijados*, he said, "Oh, no, I am not that bad." Dominga shrugged and said, "¿Quién sabe?" ("Who knows?").

Matilde moved her household to Tucson, acquiring a house south of the modern *barrio* of Pascua on Thirteenth Street. One of their neighbors, old don Nicho García, a Mexican, called on Matilde every day and she gave him coffee which he said was the best in the world.

Lorenzo, whose health had improved, got a job in the railroad yards and Jesús got a job on a nearby farm, returning to the household each weekend. Although both men earned good wages, little money reached Matilde because they drank it up. They did not drink together, however, because Lorenzo was a mean drunk, always wanting to fight. Matilde said it was a miracle he never killed anyone. Jesús, on the other hand, drank himself quietly into oblivion. Matilde and Dominga augmented their income by selling tortillas. Dominga decided it would be better if she got a real job. First she worked in Jacome's store, but her old-fashioned dress and the fact that she could not speak English made her self-conscious, so she changed to a laundry where Spanish was spoken.

Matilde gave birth to her eighth child in 1918, a boy named Manuel Mosen. Giving birth had always been easy for her, and this time she simply went into the back room, had the baby in a squatting position, caught it, and wrapped it up. A few minutes later she came out and went back to her chores. Both Matilde and Dominga were happy to have a baby in the house, but Spanish influenza swept Tucson late in the year, claiming many Yaquis, including the baby, Manuel. Many families were unable to hold *velorios* (wakes) and *novenas* (second funeral ceremonies held nine days later) for the dead, but Matilde insisted that her little boy be buried properly. Dominga also contracted the disease, and for a time Matilde was afraid she would die, too, but she recovered.

The following year, Matilde had another child, Lola Mosen, who lived. Manuela More also had a baby about this time. The little girl, named for and christened by Dominga, lived only a few weeks. This was also the year that José María Alvarez's wife came to Tucson looking for Matilde to tell her that her brother, José María; Vicente Tava; and his mother, Joaquina Tava, were in Nogales waiting to see her. Dominga was overjoyed. Perhaps now her mother would leave Lorenzo and return to Vicente. Matilde, however, said she had vowed never to return to Mexico and sent Dominga with José María's wife. Dominga's reunion with her father was one of the more emotional experiences of her life. Vicente was a good man whom Dominga loved and respected. When he asked in detail about Matilde, Dominga tried to persuade him to go to Tucson, sure that if he asked Matilde to live with him again, she would agree, because she often compared Vicente's good qualities with Lorenzo's bad ones. But Vicente responded, "I like your mother and respect her. I would like to live with her again, but it is not possible. I have taken my road and she has taken hers. My road is in the Yaqui pueblos, and I am now captain of Vicam pueblo. Matilde has said she will never return to the pueblos. We must live apart."

Saddened that she could not reunite her parents, Dominga nonetheless listened eagerly as her father recounted his experiences since he left the family in 1910 to return to Vicam. After joining the Revolutionary Army, he had walked with Villa for a time before joining Obregón's forces. He had reached Mexico City just as Francisco Madero was shot, and he went to see the place while the blood was still wet. By 1914, he was back in the Yaqui villages. On December 31, 1915, he and thirty-eight other Yaqui men were sent by the Yaqui generals and pueblo officials to Guaymas to negotiate with the Mexicans. When Vicente was told of the mission, he said he would go, but he would not name the men to accompany him because he thought the mission would probably end in disaster. The elders, therefore, had to name the other men. One of the men they sent was Vicente's brother, Guadalupe Tava.

Arriving in Guaymas, all of the men except Guadalupe went to a little market to eat, stacking their rifles to one side. Soldiers arrested the group and confiscated their arms. In vain Vicente protested that this was a peace party come to negotiate on behalf of the eight pueblos. Without obtaining a hearing, the thirty-eight men were deported to the Islas Marías, arriving on January 9, 1916, after a four-day boat trip. The prison commander met the men to explain that their crime was in having claimed the lands of the Yaqui Valley which now belonged to the government. A further charge was that they had stolen cattle. They were put to work in the prison fields, or chopping wood, or in the prison shops, or hunting in the mountains. Guadalupe, who had escaped arrest, returned to the Sierra with the news of what had happened.

Accounts of subsequent events have been obtained from Vicente himself in the early 1950 interviews, from his son in Vicam Switch, and from Dominga. Since the three accounts vary in their sequence and in some details, Vicente's own version is used here, although both Dominga and her half-brother were well informed. For reasons that are unclear, an American on the Islas Marías posing as a German hunter and photographer got in contact with the Yaqui party, saying he was a representative of the United States government trying to achieve justice for the Yaqui tribe. After writing down all their complaints, he said he would send an American warship to free them, and he left the island.

In June 1916, the thirty-eight men were placed below deck on a small Mexican cutter armed with two guns, bound for

Mazatlán. An American warship of about twenty guns did indeed appear. An American officer questioned the Mexican captain about his ship's cargo and destination while the Yaquis below deck laughed and joked, sure they were to be saved. To their bitter disappointment, the captain convinced the Americans that the Mexican ship was taking part in normal troop movements, and the ship proceeded, heading for Manzanillo rather than Mazatlán.

Vicente had boarded the ship with two possessions acquired in the Islas Marías: a little white chicken and a small dog he named Otelo. The chicken amused everyone by wandering drunkenly over the ship. Otelo proved to be a good sailor.

In Manzanillo, the company was placed in jail under heavy guard. They were allowed to build fires and cook the provisions they had brought from the island, before being shipped east the next day in a boxcar. The guard was reduced at Colima, and after that they seemed to be free to get off the train at stops. Believing they were being taken to Mexico City to be killed, Vicente wondered what to do with Otelo. At a stop in Jalisco, he took the little dog and gave it to a woman, saying, "We know where we are going and what will happen to us. I would like Otelo to have a good home. Won't you take him and we will see if he doesn't bring you luck." In Guadalajara, a group of women who liked the looks of the Yaqui men asked if they could go along. "Well, let's see what kind of tortillas you can make," the men replied. The women's tortillas were no better than those the men made, so they refused to take the women.

In Mexico City, they were placed in a Yaqui battalion, where they found many old friends. A few days later, the thirty-eight were scattered among the various companies so they would not be together, and they were issued rifles. Vicente was highly amused that the Mexicans went to so much trouble over thirty-eight Yaquis on a peace mission. He believed the Mexicans hoped none would survive the Revolution to return to the Yaqui pueblos to fight again for their land. Only seven of the thirty-eight did survive.

Vicente was released from the army in 1919 through the good offices of General Méndez, a half Yaqui–half Mayo, who sent Vicente home to Vicam with all his back pay. He collected his mother and they went to Hermosillo to locate relatives. From there they went to Nogales, where Dominga met them. Vicente announced that they must all go to the Día de San Francisco fiesta in Magdalena, and the five set off in high spirits. They encountered more friends and relatives, including Vicente's *primo hermano*, a *maestro* named Miguel Tava, and his wife, Epifania. Vicente had given his bag of money (all of his army pay) to his mother. Epifania, however, had other ideas when she discovered how rich he was. She produced a niece, Loreta, and suggested that Vicente form an alliance with her. Vicente at first refused, saying he already had a wife. Epifania swept aside his answer, pointing out that Matilde had been living with another man for some years, and even if that had not been the case, Matilde would never live in Vicam. Epifania was persuasive, and Loreta was young, pretty, and eager. Vicente agreed. To seal the bargain, he took the bag of money from Joaquina and gave it to Epifania. Dominga watched the transaction with a sad heart because she had not given up hope her mother and father would live together again. Vicente later regretted giving his money to Epifania because he never saw a single centavo of it again.

Vicente, with Loreta now firmly attached to him, insisted that Dominga go with him to Vicam to know her pueblo and her Tava relatives. Leaving José María Alvarez and his wife in Hermosillo, the party went home by train. This was the first time Dominga had seen the Yaqui pueblos. She renewed her acquaintance with the relatives she had known in Hermosillo and met many more. Vicente wanted her to stay with him, but she said her mother needed her and returned to Arizona.

Jesús Alvarez died in 1919 or 1920 with blood coming from his mouth. Matilde, who had withstood so many tragedies, seemed to crumple under this last one. Now she was *triste* all the time. For days she cried, remembering how she had saved her little brother in 1905, caring for him as though he were her son. "He was a good man. Poor Jesús. He never married. He never got the bucket of gold."

The household composition changed often in the next year or two. First, Rosario Romero decided to return to the Río

Yaqui. Manuela More refused to go, preferring to stay with Matilde. Shortly after Rosario's departure, Manuela began walking with Simon Medinas, and soon he moved in. Then they bought a lot in Barrio Libre, and as soon as their house was built, they moved there.

About 1920, José María Alvarez, his wife, Juana, and their son Juan rejoined Matilde Yaqui Larga's household, having last been a part of it in Hermosillo. Juan was only two months younger than Dominga. As age mates who had grown up together, the only surviving children of the Hermosillo years (for José María and Juana had lost several sons), they were very close, and Dominga was delighted to have this portion of the family reunited. Even Matilde Yaqui Larga was somewhat more cheerful with a brother again in her household. José María began building an enormous bread oven back of Matilde's house in preparation for resuming his trade as a baker. The plan was that Juan would help him. The oven was never finished, however, because José María died in 1921, bringing new sadness to the household. Juan refused to become a baker, preferring to work in the railroad yards.

In 1921, Vicente wrote, asking Dominga to come to Vicam. Matilde thought about it, finally saying, "He is your father and you ought to go to him." Dominga was secretly glad to go, not only because she would see her father, but because Lorenzo had been making explicit suggestions that he was very attracted to her, would like to go to bed with her, and would even consider running off with her. This bothered Dominga a great deal and increased her dislike of her stepfather, but she did not want to tell Matilde. In Vicam, the construction of the new church occasioned tremendous activity and excitement. Dominga joined the women cooking for the workers and it was like having a fiesta every day.

While this was going on, an old woman was sentenced by the Vicam authorities to die by burning for the crime of witchcraft. The condemned witch was confined in a rough cage of poles while green wood was piled up. The cage was perched on top of the pile and the fire set. The execution occurred some distance from the new church because "she did not pertain to the church." As the flames licked higher, she screamed *maldiciones* (curses) at the people who had condemned her, crossing and recrossing her wrists. As the captain of Vicam, Vicente played an active role in this affair.

When Dominga returned to Tucson, Matilde greeted her with the news that Ignacio (Nacho) Flores had asked to marry Dominga. Dominga was somewhat surprised, because she had previously heard that Nacho was promised to another girl. Matilde dismissed that information as gossip, just as she swept aside Dominga's lack of enthusiasm for any marriage plans. Matilde pointed out that Nacho was the nephew of doña Carlota and don Luis Flores, who had cured her of Angela Tava's witchcraft in Hermosillo some years before.

Nacho was born on an hacienda near Guaymas. After his mother died in 1912, his father, Guadalupe Flores, moved to Hermosillo to live with his brother Luis. They and others of the family later moved to Tucson. Matilde respected Guadalupe Flores as a good man and he returned her respect. These two made the arrangements, over the opposition of Nacho's consort and doña Carlota. Dominga requested that the wedding be postponed so that she and Nacho could be *novios* (sweethearts). The elders agreed. Nacho called daily, but mostly he talked to Matilde, whom he treated with respect and affection. Dominga usually said little to him beyond "Good day," and she never accompanied him anywhere. One day, however, her curiosity triumphed, and she asked if he had really been *novios* with Pancha González. At first she thought he wasn't going to answer, and then he said: "it is right that you know the truth." Doña Carlota and his stepmother had wanted him to marry Pancha; he had agreed and the arrangements were made. However, after he found her in the back seat of a car with a Mexican milkman, he decided he didn't want to marry her. Since that time, he had learned that she had walked with other men, and he felt it was a good thing he had broken with her, because she seemed to be a woman who had to have a man.

Shortly after this conversation, Dominga and Matilde were involuntarily brought into the problems surrounding Pancha González. It seems she was walking with another Mexican, this one a garbage collector. She apparently believed they were *novios* and would be married. He was already married, however, and his wife found out about Pancha. One day the wife appeared in Pascua, looking for Pancha, calling on Matilde and Dominga, among others, saying she wanted to kill Pancha. Matilde naturally said they had never heard of Pancha González. A few years later, the man was shot by an irate husband.

During the period that Dominga and Nacho were *novios*, her stepfather again became ill. His chronic drinking was probably responsible for his final illness. After he lost his job, Dominga returned to work in the laundry, adopting the modern-style dress that she retained for the rest of her life. Matilde sold tortillas, as she always had in times of economic stress. Lorenzo's death late in 1921 was observed with the proper Yaqui rites. Matilde was left pregnant with her last child. The household now consisted of Matilde, Dominga, Lola, Juana and Juan Alvarez, and Lorenzo's brother, who had lived with them for some time. Dominga's marriage was scheduled early in 1922. She asked to have it postponed until Lorenzo's *cumpleaño* (fiesta held one year after a person's death) had been held, since it would not be proper to be married during the mourning period, but Matilde insisted that the wedding take place as planned.

Dominga had little to recount about her wedding; instead she emphasized that it meant leaving Matilde, for Nacho refused to join Matilde's household, electing to live with his own family. When Nacho and several of his brothers and cousins decided to go to Chandler, Arizona, to work on cotton farms, Dominga of course had to go along, which meant real separation from her mother—a separation she felt more acutely than the separations in Hermosillo. She was sad to leave Matilde alone and pregnant with the care of the household, because Lola was too small to help. However, Dominga seemed to cheer up in Chandler, taking more pleasure in Nacho's company.

About June, 1922, Dominga received word that Matilde had been seriously injured. Asking Nacho for permission to go to Tucson and care for her, Dominga left Chandler. She found that Matilde, who had been delivering lunch to Lorenzo's brother, had been thrown from the wagon when the horse bolted at the sight of a train on the Calle Anita crossing. Matilde's heavy skirts caught on the wagon and she was dragged for some distance before her skirts tore loose. A shopkeeper caught the horse and called a doctor. The accident induced labor, and the baby, named Juan, was born a few days later. Although the doctor wanted to operate, Matilde refused, saying she knew that if they operated, she would die, but if they did not, she would live a long time. While Dominga ran the household, Matilde made her own medicines for sickness of the *matrices* (the womb or female organs) and slowly cured herself. The baby died within a month. After the death rites, Dominga sadly returned to Nacho in Chandler, at Matilde's request. Juana Alvarez died shortly thereafter, and Dominga made a hurried trip to Tucson for her death rites, again returning to Nacho.

Friends who worked on the same farm decided to get married at the fiesta de San Francisco in Magdalena, Sonora. They asked Dominga to be their *madrina de boda* (wedding godmother). Nacho went along, and the trip was a great success, the highlight of their marriage.

Matilde Yaqui Larga, now feeling better, and little Lola joined the Floreses in Chandler for the cotton-picking season, leaving their house in the care of the other household members. Dominga by this time was in an advanced stage of pregnancy, and Matilde wanted to be with her. When cotton picking started, they camped in the fields and every man, woman, and child worked.

At dusk on a cold October day in 1923, Dominga's baby was born in the cotton field with Matilde as *partera*. Dominga, who had picked cotton all day, collapsed. About daylight, the baby began to cry. Nacho was frantically looking for a car he could borrow to take Dominga and the baby to a doctor in Chandler when the baby died of the cold. The nightmare of that night is Dominga's worst memory of her lifetime.

Nacho decided they would be better off in Tucson, and this time he agreed to live with Matilde. The next two or three years were perhaps the happiest period in Dominga's life. Nacho got good jobs and his wages supported the household so that the women did not have to go out to work. No tragedies occurred. Dominga and Matilde baptized several babies, cooked at household fiestas, received guests, and otherwise led a pleasant life. Dominga's second child, Vicente, was born fat and healthy in 1925.

Shortly after Vicente's birth, Dominga was given another baby to raise. This came about because Matilde's cousin, Juan More, left his consort with Matilde when he went to Hermosillo to see his dying father. Since his immigration papers were not in order, he could not return to Arizona, and his consort, Francisca Ibarra, bore her baby with Matilde acting as *partera*. Francisca did not recover from the difficult childbirth of María More, and when she was dying, she gave the baby to Dominga, saying, ''You have cared for her since she was born. Now you will be her mother.''

Dominga, Nacho, and Matilde were deeply involved in the 1926 Yaqui uprising in a number of ways. They regularly received Sierra Yaqui refugees, meeting them at Mesquital. For perhaps a year, a succession of Sierra Yaqui refugees formed part of their household, staying until they located relatives and then moving on, to be replaced by a new group.

Vicente Tava was even more intimately involved in the war, having been present at the incident in Vicam Switch that set it off. One of Dominga's accounts of the beginning of the war is given here. Juana Tava Martínez, Vicente's sister, lived in Nogales at the time Obregón was there campaigning, before the Vicam Switch episode. Juana went to see him, as did countless others. While walking with the crowd, she overheard someone saying that Obregón was going to Cajeme (the town renamed Obregón) to sell something to some Americans. Fearing that the something was Yaqui land, she decided to go to Vicam Switch on the same train as Obregón to warn Vicente.

Meanwhile, Obregón received a telegram that the Yaquis planned to attack the train. In order to foil such a plan, he telegraphed orders for the Yaqui soldiers at Vicam to proceed to Hermosillo (on a wild goose chase), and for the Mexican detachment from Potam to go to Vicam Switch. When the train reached Vicam Switch, Vicente and the only three Yaqui soldiers left in town stopped the train with lanterns. There were no soldiers on the train with Obregón, and Vicente talked to Obregón. "Why didn't you bring the Yaqui soldiers from Hermosillo?" he asked. Suddenly the Mexican soldiers from Potam arrived, shooting. Vicente told Obregón to get inside the train or he would be hit by a Mexican bullet. Then the Yaqui soldiers arrived on a second train, having exchanged shots with the Mexicans since Oros (north of Vicam), where Juan Rivera was killed. Just before Vicente left the train, he asked Obregón why the Mexicans were fighting the Yaquis again. Outside he located his sister Juana, listened to her warning, and urged her to continue on the train to Cajeme, feeling that the Yaqui villages would soon be a dangerous place to be.

Shortly thereafter he led his soldiers to the Sierra, where they carried out raids on the Mexicans. From there he wrote to Dominga and Matilde, and they in turn served as a clearing house for letters and information from a number of Yaqui leaders about arms and other matters.

Adolfo de la Huerta came secretly to Tucson from his place of exile in California to meet with Yaqui leaders. As governor of Sonora from 1919 to 1923, he had gained some Yaqui support because of his aid in rebuilding the Yaqui churches, although he had also resumed the distribution of Yaqui land. Now he was interested in the war as a means of reestablishing his own position, for he had been ousted as governor. Among the Yaqui leaders who came to confer with him was Vicente Tava, who walked from the Bacatete Mountains. The details were all arranged through Dominga, Nacho, and Matilde.

When Vicente arrived, he conversed politely with Matilde, and Dominga once again tried to effect a reconciliation between her parents. Vicente said that he was now captain of Vicam and his place was there with his second family. He asked Dominga to take him to the hotel where Adolfo de la Huerta was staying, and she was present for their lengthy interview. The two men began their discussion by reminiscing about their childhood in Sonora, for they were the same age and Vicente had been born on the de la Huerta hacienda, where his father worked. As boys they had played together. They recalled the day that don Adolfo's father came upon the two boys, asking each, "Muchacho, ¿qué piensa hacer?" ("Boy, what do you plan to be?"), to which don Adolfo replied, "When I grow up, I am going to be a big man and talk for the nation." Vicente responded, "I, too, will be a big man, and I will talk for the Yaqui people." The elder de la Huerta laughed at Vicente, saying it would be better to be a good man.

Vicente told de la Huerta about the abortive peace mission of 1915–16, saying perhaps it would have been better if the thirty-nine men had fought. Don Adolfo said it was better they had not, because they would surely have been killed: "Now you are still alive to help your people. We are both fighting for our people. For the moment we have had to run away because of bad people, but we will win."

They then turned to discussing the current crisis and their plans to triumph over the bad people. Although don Adolfo was, himself, practically destitute, since he and his wife had been obliged to leave Sonora hurriedly with only the clothes on their backs, he had friends in California who were raising money to buy arms which would be shipped to Tucson and walked down the trails to the Bacatete Mountains.

After the interview, Vicente walked back to the Sierra and don Adolfo returned to California. Dominga, Matilde, and Nacho became more deeply involved in the American side of the preparations. The code name for de la Huerta in the numerous communiques was *nuestro abuelo* (our grandfather), because they knew the letters would sometimes be read by Mexicans or *torocoyoris*.

A load of arms from California was brought to Tucson by Francisco Feriz and a man named Luis, who stayed at Matilde Yaqui Larga's house. Federal officers came to the house, arresting the two men, Nacho, and Matilde. Nacho and Matilde said they had nothing to do with the arms shipment, and Matilde was released. Nacho was detained and then he and Matilde were both sent to California for trial. Don Adolfo talked for them, and it turned out that the arms were not destined for the Yaquis, but for their opponents. When they were released, Matilde returned to Tucson at once, but Nacho stayed with don Adolfo, working for the cause until the end of the 1926–27 war.

After Nacho returned to Tucson, he began to act differently. Whereas before he had worked hard and stayed at home, he now came home late at night, and occasionally didn't come home at all. Acquaintances soon informed Dominga of the reason for his changed behavior: a woman named Pancha Papaga who sold bootleg liquor in Barrio Libre. Her house was more or less like a cantina and many men went there, but Nacho stayed with her. After several weeks, Nacho's father, Guadalupe Flores, came to Dominga one Monday at noon. Father and son worked together, and for the first time Nacho had not showed up for work. Guadalupe asked, "Where is Nacho?" Dominga replied that she wasn't sure. Guadalupe said, "We know where he is. Go get him and tell him I said for him to come to work." Guadalupe further arranged for his nephew to drive Dominga to Barrio Libre. So she went to Pancha Papaga's house, where she asked a boy in the kitchen if Nacho was there. "Yes, but he is asleep." "That is why I am here," said Dominga; "I will wake him up." The boy again said that Nacho was asleep. Undaunted, Dominga walked into the bedroom, where Nacho and the Papaga were still asleep. Dominga pulled the covers off their naked bodies, which of course awakened them. Nacho was furious. The Papaga protested that Dominga's and Nacho's marital problems had nothing to do with her, to which Dominga answered, "No, but you always sleep with him." Dominga then delivered Guadalupe's message, saying, "El padre manda mas que la mujer" ("The father commands more than the woman"). Nacho got up, dressed, and returned silently to Pascua and his job. Dominga felt that Guadalupe must have talked to Nacho, because for a while he came home. Their own relationship did not improve appreciably, however.

Within a few weeks, the Flores extended family moved to the farms near Marana to pick cotton. Pancha Papaga was among the many laborers so engaged, and Nacho was often to be found picking near the Papaga. They decided they would leave together on the next payday. Pancha told several

people she had "won" over Dominga, confiding their plans of
going to Phoenix. These people told Dominga, and she
decided to make a final effort to hold him. On payday she
enlisted the aid of several relatives to let the air out of the
tires on Nacho's car. An angry Nacho set about pumping
them up again, but before he had finished, Pancha Papaga
came by with her father. In the ensuing scene, Pancha said
that if she couldn't have Nacho, neither could Dominga.
Nacho stayed.

Soon thereafter, Nacho developed a cough and his health
began to fail. They returned to Tucson, where Dominga began
working in a laundry again, because Nacho could no longer
hold a job. Matilde cared for the children. A doctor could find
nothing wrong with him, but he got progressively worse. His
illness lasted nine months.

A friend at the laundry asked Dominga about Nacho. "He
is very bad. The doctors say there is nothing wrong with him,
but I have already lost him in my dreams," she replied. The
friend said, "Take him to my mother. She is a very good
curandera." Nacho refused to go, but Dominga went in a last
effort to save Nacho. The woman had a crystal ball which she
placed on the table. In a moment she called Dominga to come
and see if she recognized the woman who appeared in it. It
was Nacha Félix, the wife of Nacho's *primo hermano*. That
figure faded and a second woman appeared—Nacho's aunt
and Nacha's mother-in-law, Francisca Flores. "These two
women are harming Nacho. I will try to help him, but the
harm is far advanced and he may die," said the *curandera*.

Nacho's condition worsened, and Dominga decided she
could not leave him. When Chepa Alvarez came, Dominga
pleaded with her to stay: "The witchcraft is very strong."
Francisca Flores approached the house, causing Nacho's condition to worsen. He told Dominga, "Don't let her in the
house. Talk to her outside. I can hardly breathe now." When
Dominga refused to allow doña Francisca in to see her
nephew, she became angry, and the harm intensified. Nacho
died late in 1928. Nacha Félix's death shortly afterward was
attributed to the harm she had caused Nacho.

Other people had contrary explanations about who caused Nacho's death by witchcraft, some suggesting that Dominga was responsible because she felt Nacho drank too much and she resented his involvement with Pancha Papaga. Although Dominga admitted both these things were true, she said, "I did not harm him. I tried to save him." In retrospect, she saw Nacho as a good man, deeply involved in Yaqui affairs, worthy of her respect and affection, as demonstrated by her correct behavior as a Yaqui wife. His drinking and affairs could have been tolerated.

Only a few months later, Angel Vásquez asked Dominga to live with him. He had come to the house to see one of Lorenzo's cousins, Elijio Tecu, who joined the household after a long absence in California. Indeed, many men came to see Elijio. Angel, of Barrio Libre, had worked with Elijio in years gone by, and after he noticed the young, attractive widow, he came quite often, finally, as he left one day, handing her a letter containing the vital question. He had, of course, never spoken to her. On the next visit, he asked if she had read the letter. "Yes." "Well, will you?" She said she had not made up her mind: "I know what it is to have a bad stepfather, and I don't want Vicente and María to have the same bad experiences." Angel promised to be a good stepfather and said that his job was good enough that Dominga would not have to work. Finally she agreed, moving to the house in Barrio Libre where Angel lived with his mother, Lorenza Medinas, after a civil wedding ceremony.

Dominga was encouraged to take this step because of ugly rumors spreading through Pascua. "Everywhere I went, I saw people whispering bad things about me. My comadres passed me without speaking." Soon people were saying she walked with a lot of men. One woman in particular seemed to be responsible for most of the rumors. This woman, doña Josefa met Dominga on the street one day, opening a public confrontation by observing that although Dominga said she worked in a laundry, she obviously did no such thing or else her hands would be white from the strong soap. Dominga replied that of course she worked in a laundry, and the reason her hands were not white was because she ironed. Doña Josefa continued, in good voice, "If you don't work in a laundry, then what do you do all day? You go with men!"

Feeling completely helpless in the face of what she described as unmerited attacks, Dominga discussed the situation with Matilde.After more women turned against her, Matilde said, "You had better move to Barrio Libre. Once you are settled with a man, the talk will stop." They discussed the propriety of Dominga's forming a new alliance before Nacho's *cumpleaño*, but decided the seriousness of the situation merited such action.

Dominga took Vicente with her, leaving María More with Matilde. If there was any period of happiness with Angel, Dominga retained no memory of it. In spite of his promises, he turned out to be like Lorenzo Mosen—drunk much of the time and mean when drunk. Dominga liked and respected his mother, Lorenza Medinas, and the two women became allies against Angel's drunkenness and the women he went with. For his part, he complained that there was hardly any point in coming home to two women who yelled at him. Dominga soon had to go back to work at the laundry, leaving Vicente with Lorenza. Mother and daughter-in-law really ran the household for many years, Dominga furnishing the financial support and Lorenza managing the household.

For the next two decades, Dominga's life seems to have been unpunctuated by major dramatic events. She told few stories about this period. Most of those she told dealt with Angel's drinking, his many women, and his lack of support. Twice he attacked her with a knife, but she had learned from her mother how to handle that sort of attack. The most noteworthy change in her life was leaving laundry work, because the steam was causing her to go blind, and becoming a restaurant cook. With the owners of the restaurants she worked in, she established long-term *patrona* relationships that survived long after her employment ceased. She believed that "it is far better to find a good *patrona* and stick with her than to take another job for higher pay, because if you have been faithful to your *patrona*, she will take care of you when you are old and sick."

In the early 1940s, Dominga claimed two children left orphaned when a Barrio Libre woman drank poison and died in agony in front of them, having just prepared their breakfast. Vicente was now in his late teens, and Dominga was glad to have small children to raise. It was a matter of some concern to her that she had borne only two children, and none by Angel. The children she claimed had no relatives or *padrinos* who could take them, and Dominga "took pity." Both called her "mother" and married from her house.

Dominga acquired two more children to raise, perhaps a decade later. Matilde Yaqui Larga felt that Lola, her younger surviving daughter, was improvident and simply did not look after her children. Unlike Dominga, Lola was not a good housekeeper. When there was no food in the house, she would sit and cry rather than get a job. Matilde had helped Lola as much as she could, but when Lola decided to go with a new man who did not want her children from an earlier alliance, Matilde felt she was too old to take on the raising of two young children. Matilde herself was supported by the now grown María More, whom she had raised. María, who had turned out to be a good, hard-working woman, did not earn enough to feed two more. Matilde, therefore, brought the two children to Dominga in Barrio Libre and gave them to her.

In 1958, Matilde came to Dominga in order to die "in her hands." None of the many relatives who had lived with Matilde came to see her when she was dying, not even Lola, nor did they help with the *velorio* or *novena*. Only María More came. Dominga, always faithful to such obligations, felt their behavior was inexcusable, especially when the death rites concerned someone as good as her mother. Lola, however, was quick to appear with a lawyer to claim Matilde's house and three lots which Matilde, on her deathbed, had given to Dominga. Dominga wanted María More to have the property, but the lawyer said if Dominga did not want it, Lola would have next claim. The lawyer's fees were probably more than the property was worth, and María and Lola ended up living there, although the legal title remained in Dominga's name.

Dominga had corresponded regularly with her father, but she had not seen him since 1926. Now he wrote that he was in Nogales and wished to see her. She found him destitute and sick. After several unsuccessful attempts to arrange his papers so she could care for him in Barrio Libre, she established a schedule of working all week and going to Nogales each weekend to feed and nurse him. Since her hours in the restaurant were long and she often did not get home until the early morning, she spent several months with only minimal sleep. One weekend she found that Vicente had left Nogales— he had become bored and returned to Vicam Switch.

Vicente's home life had not been successful for many years. He and Loreta had three children in the early days of their alliance. During the 1926–27 war, Loreta was one of many Vicam women and children rounded up and taken to Potam, where she attracted the attention of one of the Mexican soldiers, Juan Gutiérrez. Soon they were living together. Vicente took his three young children and his mother to the Sierra. As old as she was, doña Joaquina cared for the children as the group moved around, often having to camp without shelter, a familiar way of life to doña Joaquina. Vicente's youngest daughter fell on the rocks, cutting her head badly. This injury, plus the other hardships and the amount of hard work she had to do at such a young age, was believed to have weakened the child so much that, shortly after they returned to Vicam in 1926, she caught a cold and died within twenty-four hours. While still in the Sierra, Vicente started walking with a young woman named Vicenta, who, with her mother, was among the Vicam residents under Vicente's command.

At the end of the war, Vicenta was pregnant. Both she and Vicente rather assumed that his alliance with Loreta was over, especially when they found out about Juan Gutiérrez and the new baby he had fathered. Loreta, however, had other ideas. After moving back into Vicente's house with her baby, she threatened to kill Vicenta. Fearing that this was no idle threat,

Vicenta and her mother left Vicam without telling anyone where they were going.

Loreta asked Vicente if she could give her baby the family name of Tava, and he agreed. Although Loreta and Vicente continued to live in the same house, Loreta walked for several more years with Juan Gutiérrez. Vicente reluctantly agreed to the bestowal of the Tava name on two more Gutiérrez babies. When Loreta attempted to give Vicente's name to yet another child by yet another man, he told her to go to her lover and use his name. She left, but the three Gutiérrez children stayed with Vicente and he raised them. By the late 1950s, Vicente presided over a full house, but there was no adult woman to care for him. Simona, his surviving daughter by Loreta, was a good woman, but she was in Mexico City training to be a nurse.

At Christmas of 1959, the child Vicente had never seen came to live with him. He had never known whether Vicenta had had a son or a daughter, or even if the child lived. Now he learned that he had a daughter named Marcela. She wrote him from Obregón, asking if she could come to Vicam Switch. Vicenta, on her deathbed, had said to Marcela, "You will be all alone. Go to your father. He is a good man." Vicente was overwhelmed; "You are my daughter," he said, admitting her to the family and giving her a place in the household. Marcela did much to make Vicente's last months more comfortable.

Dominga found Vicente's lengthy illness to be a financial drain, taking her carefully hoarded savings. For a time she picked cotton during the day and worked in a restaurant at night in order to support her own household and to have money for Vicente. She went to Vicam as often as possible; and while these trips added to the physical strain of the time, she enjoyed reforging her many Tava kin ties in Vicam, entering fully into *pepinando* (gleaning leftover crops in the field) with the women, cooking for the household, and visiting.

When Vicente died in 1960, the family sent for Dominga. Receiving the message at work, she rushed home to prepare to go, only to find her house in flames and Lola's two children burned to death. She had to arrange their *velorio* and burial before she could go to her father. In Vicam Switch, relatives felt that Vicente's two daughters should see his body, but Dominga was delayed and Simona had to come from Mexico City. For two days they packed his body in ice. When that was only moderately successful in delaying decomposition, they decided to bury the coffin, but they inserted a piece of glass over the face so he could be disinterred when his daughters arrived. The daughters, however, felt such action was not necessary: "Ya tiene su lugar ("He has his place now").

This was the first time Dominga and met her half-sister, Marcela. They liked each other, each deciding that the other was a good woman. In subsequent years, Dominga became Marcela's champion in the family disputes that developed. Some of the friction centered on Marcela's right to reside in the household, with her sister-in-law insisting that Marcela had no right to remain there because she had been raised elsewhere. "She doesn't even speak Yaqui, and who knows if she really is Vicente's daughter?" Dominga maintained that Vicente had received Marcela as a daughter and that gave her the right to live in the house and share in the property. The property was another center of controversy, especially after Vicente's son sold a lot without splitting the proceeds with his sisters.

The same year that Vicente died, Dominga dreamed that her son, Vicente, would die. There seemed to be no reason for such a prediction, as he had returned from the army, married a pretty girl who had borne him three healthy children, and held a good job at the airport. Dominga did not tell him of the dream, but she believed he had a premonition of his own death because he had a lawyer establish Dominga's title to the Barrio Libre house, which had been left to him when Lorenza Medinas died, even though Angel Vásquez (Lorenza's son and Dominga's husband) was still alive; Vicente also named Dominga as the beneficiary of his veteran's insurance. Bringing her the papers, he said, "Mama, if something happens to me, I want these to be yours. There are those who would take it from you." A few days later he complained to a fellow worker at the airport that he was cold. The man gave him his coat, but still he shivered. That night he died.

Strangely enough, Dominga had few stories that centered on her son, and he appears only incidentally in this narrative—probably because nothing particularly dramatic happened to him. Her devotion to him was matched only by her devotion to her mother and father. The loss of all three people she loved deeply within three years deprived her of her strongest emotional contacts. The death of her son was the final and most severe blow because she had confidently expected that he would bury her properly and she would have him near at hand until that day.

As Vicente had foreseen, there were people who wanted to deprive Dominga of the security he had arranged—namely, his own widow, who felt she was entitled to the pension. The ensuing arguments and legal problems alienated Dominga's daughter-in-law, who "took the children away" by refusing to let them visit Dominga. After the daughter-in-law remarried, the family "became Mexican."

With the pension, Dominga "retired." She no longer had to work long, regular hours, but she did not stop working, because to Dominga work as a way of life was good and idleness was bad. Rather, she shifted the pattern of her work. Relationships to her old *patronas* were intensified as she worked for them in their homes. A regular clientele developed for her homemade tortillas, gorditas, buñuelos, tamales, carne machado, and other specialties. She ran a stand at fiestas in downtown Tucson, priding herself on her stream-lined techniques that allowed her to sell four hundred tacos an hour while the neighboring *puestos* (stands) sold only fifty. She firmly accepted the idea that mass production and a competitive price yield a greater profit.

Dominga's "retirement" gave her more time to devote to visiting relatives in the *barrio*, elsewhere in Arizona, and in Sonora, with the result that she became much more mobile. On a trip to Vicam to visit her half-brother, she discovered that he was going to Mexico City, so she went along. The other change in her life was that she moved fully into the

ceremonial life of Barrio Libre. Always deeply religious, she
had been collecting *santos* and religious pictures for years.
Now, with an altar woman, she assumed a large part of the
responsibility for the Barrio Libre Church and its *santos*. When
the new San Martín Church was built, she was one of the
women who played an active role in cooking for the laborers
and making large amounts of *tesquine* (an alcoholic beverage
made from parched corn) for their refreshment. She attended
every service when she was in town and cooked for every
household fiesta.

After Dominga acquired the title to her house, she moved
Angel out completely into a small shack to one side, ending
thirty-two years of living together. It is possible that the early
years of their alliance were more normal and traditional than
her account indicates, and she may have been generalizing
the dissatisfactions of the later years to the whole of their
relationship. Certainly it had deteriorated by the late 1930s,
when he first attacked her with a knife, and it is clear that he
either never had or did not long retain her respect and
affection. Because she did not respect Angel, their alliance
developed along very different lines from her marriage to
Ignacio. She became more independent and self-sufficient,
never asking Angel's permission to do anything. His position
in the female-dominated household became more and more
peripheral until he was pushed out completely.

"Things" were important to Dominga. Her five-room
house, rebuilt after the fire, was cluttered with several bedroom sets, a sofa, at least two refrigerators, kitchen stoves, an
impressive saints' corner, radios, a television set, and so on.
Oil paintings (one a portrait of Dominga done by a school
teacher; another a romantic Aztec scene with palm trees,
painted by her half-sister in Mexico City), photographs, and
religious pictures covered the walls. Mementos of many years
were wrapped in plastic or stored in boxes throughout the
house or stacked high in the lean-to kitchen and enclosed
area at the back of the house. She bemoaned the loss of items
burned in the 1960 fire, especially the collection of letters
dealing with the 1926–27 war. If material was needed to dress
a saint, if a rhinestone bracelet was needed to create a crown

for the figure of a Virgin, if paper flowers or glass jars were needed, "Ask Dominga," said everyone in the *barrio*.

Many Yaqui women exhibited a passive acceptance of drinking and drunkenness. Not Dominga. Drinking was bad, not because it was sinful, but because men's drinking caused their families to suffer deprivation. Among her culinary accomplishments was making *tesquine*, and she fully approved of its public consumption upon certain occasions. Other drinking was, by comparison, seen by Dominga as private and not beneficial to the community. Men who were habitual drunks could not be respected, for they were usually mean and certainly were wasting money that their families needed for food. She showed open contempt for any drunk. Rather than pass a drunk quietly, she would usually make a few audible remarks about their poor, hungry families. Should one beg for money or food, she would launch into a more detailed lecture on the evils of his behavior, willingly keeping up her end until the unfortunate drunk disappeared—without a handout. Often she said she knew how to run off (*correr*) drunks. At public fiestas, Dominga found other respectable, sober, older people and together they decried the the drunkenness they observed.

In her seventies at the time of the interviews, Dominga was constantly and efficiently in action, deeply involved in a large and far-flung network of kinship and ritual kin relationships, with their attendant obligations, and with her ceremonial work. Although essentially optimistic, she was deeply disappointed in her solitary existence after a lifetime of belonging to large and active households and worried about who would care for her in her terminal illness and bury her properly.

Although always identified by others and identifying herself as a Yaqui, this woman became separated from functioning, meaningful segments of Yaqui society through a series of historical events. Her story is a case history in deculturation or culture loss occasioned by the loss of her societal matrix.

During the eighty-odd years of Chepa Moreno's life, the face of Mexico changed. The pressures that affected the Yaquis in Sonora and swept them into broader events shaping the nation are reflected in her story. Born into a locally secure Yaqui environment about 1890, she spent the first ten years of her life remote from persecution and hardship. The 1900 Mazocoba massacre shattered the peace of her world and scattered her family. The next several years were spent in the markedly different social environs of Hermosillo, where the Yaquis were under considerable pressure. Shortly after her arranged marriage, she was deported with her husband and baby. The deportation itself, the hardships she endured, her life as a "slave" in Yucatán, the deaths of her seven babies, and the dissolution of her marriage, which left her alone in war-torn Yucatán, were bitter memories. Caught up in the Revolution, she became a soldadera with her second consort, traversing Mexico in the wake of the armies. After separating from her second consort at the end of the Revolution, she made her way to Hermosillo and established herself in a kinsman's household, carving out an economic niche as a washerwoman.

126

CHEPA MORENO

Historical accidents deprived her of vital kinship and ritual kin ties, with the result that in the latter part of her life she often lacked the security that such ties bring. After the death of her third and last consort, and as her few older friends, relatives, and ritual kin affiliates died, she became more solitary. Finally, when she became too old and sick to work, hardship and deprivation were again her lot.

Chepa's life after she left Yucatán was essentially that of a Yaqui living outside of Yaqui society. To a certain extent this isolation was a conscious decision, although the influencing factors were complex. After the Revolution she could have joined her second consort's mother's household in the Mayo area (Huatabampo) or she could have returned to the Río Yaqui villages. As a solitary adult woman she elected to return to a known community, for she had never lived in the Yaqui villages or even visited them as a child, and she gave priority to the economic realities of making her own living. To survive as a washerwoman, she needed clients. To get clients, she had to go to a place that had more affluent people who could pay for this service. Stripped of effective kin ties, she activated old patrona relationships dating from her earlier residence in Hermosillo. Patrona relationships remained of central concern until her death. The adaptive strategy controlling all her decisions after her return to Sonora was that of economic self-sufficiency.

Chepa's old-style dress, her preference for the Yaqui language, and her carrizo-fronted house proclaimed her Indian identity to all. It was never said of her that she became Mexican. In the last years of her life when her older associates were dying off and the trend for Yaquis to become Mexicanized was pronounced, Chepa was perhaps the most visible Yaqui in the two adjacent barrios.

During the research period, Chepa lived alone in the carrizo and rock house built by her last consort in the Hermosillo barrio of Las Pilas, a barrio that grew out of the older, adjacent barrio of La Matanza. Many Yaquis live here and have since at least the 1890s, but the barrios have never been Yaqui communities. Rather they are low-class Mexican barrios in which Yaquis are concentrated. The intermarriage rate with Mexicans is high and ritual kin relationships are formed to Mexicans at a higher rate than in other Yaqui communities. Yaqui ceremonialism is weak at the present time, although Yaqui Easter observances held elsewhere in Hermosillo attract Yaquis from the entire urban area. Household ceremonial observances tend toward related Mexican patterns.

As an informant about Yaqui culture, Chepa had definite limitations. Because she seldom lived in a fully functioning Yaqui community, she knew little about the formal Yaqui institutions.

Her recall of events in her own life was fairly good, although names sometimes eluded her. Her knowledge of family relationships was somewhat limited by her long loss of contact. She maintained a correspondence with some relatives by dictating letters to a literate person and getting the replies read to her, for she could not read or write. In this way, she was relatively well informed on births, deaths, the whereabouts of certain relatives, and important events in their lives.

Like other informants, Chepa was reluctant to discuss her multiple alliances with men. For many weeks, her legal husband was the only male she admitted to having lived with. The identity of her second man was revealed by another woman after I had struggled with inconsistencies and obvious gaps in the story of the Revolutionary years. She successfully obscured the existence of the third man in her life for even more weeks, until his identity was disclosed by another informant, who was greatly amused that Chepa could talk around this man for so long.

Chepa placed me in a more pronounced patrona role than did other informants for the obvious reason that she was more accustomed to dealing with outsiders in this particular framework. In keeping with the patrona image, I set the schedule, decided on our activities, and provided resources, which she accepted without comment. Inside of these outer parameters, the age-dominance factor dominated. She was an elder instructing a younger woman. She often led the conversation, was impatient with my slow note taking, and on the days when she felt worse than usual, she was less than cooperative. Not infrequently she instructed me in correct behavior; one day she made me return to a household we had been visiting to shake hands properly with our host. It seems probable that her occasional fractiousness was generated by the long period of social isolation that preceded our contact. She had so few interpersonal contacts that there was virtually no one at whom her frustrations could be directed. Had she told off the Mexican woman across the street who interacted with her more than anyone else, the cost would have been too high. She used me as an audience for her bottled-up feelings, and that often meant unproductive interview hours.

Chepa enjoyed our association. She had become one of the most low-status individuals in the barrio, not because she was an old-style Indian, but because of her poverty and her social isolation. The research enhanced her status, improved her standard of living, gave her mobility, and allowed her to reforge kin ties in Potam. She was exceptionally pleased to have someone interested in listening to her, who made her an important social person; and for the listener to be an outsider more affluent than her neighbors, and to supply much needed resources, was even better.

Chepa experienced very few deep emotional attachments to other people. Her strongest childhood tie was to the woman who raised her: her father's half-brother's wife. The death of her children prevented the development of strong or long-term attachments to them. Her emotional investments in her husband and two consorts were not great. After she returned to Sonora, some distant kin and friendship ties provided a weak social matrix. Friendship with a fellow washerwoman in Hermosillo was one of the most significant emotional attachments of her life. Chepa had an appreciation of kin-based obligations and the niceties of visiting and hospitality, but her opportunities for participation were often extremely curtailed.

Most people who knew Chepa placed her in the "sad" behavioral category, describing her as sad, passive, serious, and timid. Her wit, imitative abilities, joking, and free-flowing repartee apparently surfaced in only a few situations in her life; normally they were submerged in the daily grind. Fortunately, these facets of her

*personality were occasionally visible in our relationship, although
her sense of humor does not carry through into her life story. She
was humorous about contemporary situations and affairs, and indeed
people present at our interviews often commented that they had
never seen her so lively. She recalled her past life, however, as serious
and tragic.*

*All the informants demonstrated fatalism at some point, but Chepa
was the most fatalistic of all the women. The overall pattern of her
life, with its periods of great hardship, was strongly shaped by
chance and historical accident. Her life shows clearly what happens
when kin and ritual kin ties are weakened and no meaningful
replacements occur. Chepa lived much of her life beyond or at the
margins of Yaqui society, but she lived and died a Yaqui.*

Josefa (Chepa) Moreno was born at La Colorada Mine, So-
nora, about 1889 or 1890. Her father, Francisco, son of Rosario
Moreno and Juana Sewa, was from the Río Yaqui pueblo of
Torim, where, the old ones said, they had owned many cows
and many horses. When he came to La Colorada, Francisco
brought with him his wife, a Torim woman named Carmen
Domínguez, by whom he had three legitimate daughters:
Eulalia, Jesús, and María. When Carmen died, Francisco
moved his family into the household of his half-brother,
Abelardo Cochemea. Soon Francisco, the *blanco* "with a big red
mustache" (his coloring made everyone believe he had been
fathered by a Spaniard, probably old Rosario's *patrón*), began
living with Antonia Sasueta, whom her daughter, Chepa,
believed to be part Pima. Antonia died before Chepa was a
year old and Eulalia, Chepa's oldest half-sister, died about the
same time.

Chepa's earliest memories were of living in relative comfort
in the household of Abelardo Cochemea. Of Abelardo's wife,
María Valencia Palos, she said, "This is the woman who
raised me." Their son, Miguel Palos, and his wife and children; their daughter Camilda and her husband and children;
and Chepa, her father, Francisco, and his old mother, Juana
Sewa, completed the household. Chepa looked after Miguel's

and Camilda's children, all of them younger than she. Two of Miguel's children were Rosalio Moisés, whose story has been told in *The Tall Candle* (1971), and Antonia Valenzuela, whose life story appears later. She saw little of her surviving half-sisters, who were older and already married.

Until about 1900, when Chepa was ten or eleven, the extended family was a comfortable social unit, free from want and persecution. After 1900, the several nuclear families were splintered in the aftermath of the Mazocoba massacre and subsequent tightening of governmental control of Yaquis. Chepa's father, Francisco, her half-sister María, and María's husband, José Yomaiza, moved to Princhera, another gold mine; Miguel Palos, also a miner by profession, took his wife and baby to a different mine, leaving his older children, Rosalio and Antonia, with his mother, María, at La Colorada Mine. Camilda's husband was killed by Mexicans. Abelardo, María, Camilda, Chepa, and the other children soon moved to Hermosillo, where Abelardo got a job at an orchard called La Playita. They lived there five years.

In Hermosillo, the quality of their lives changed dramatically. María, who in La Colorada had been somewhat aloof from the children's lives, but kind and gentle, firmly assumed the position of dominant authority in the household, and she exercised that authority freely. She became a hard woman. As Chepa said, "María never hit anyone in La Colorada, but in Hermosillo, she hit all the children on the slightest excuse." Even her grown daughter, Camilda, was not exempt. If María thought Camilda had been speaking to men on her trips into town to sell tortillas, Camilda was beaten like a child. Camilda's children could not look to their mother for protection; María ran their lives. Chepa had had to do little in La Colorada beyond looking after the younger children, but in Hermosillo everyone had to work to survive. She began helping Camilda make tortillas to sell, as well as helping María wash for *patronas*.

When Chepa was fourteen or fifteen, Pedro Alvarez asked his uncle to arrange a marriage with her. María managed the negotiations, and Abelardo gave his consent. They never asked Chepa, who was strongly opposed to the marriage. She threatened to hang herself rather than marry Pedro, but María just replied that that was all right, as she would hang Chepa herself if she did not go through with it.

For the wedding in the big cathedral, María made Chepa a dress out of a length of white material and bought her a blue *rebozo* and a pair of black high-topped lace-up shoes. María, Abelardo, and Camilda represented Chepa's family at the wedding, and Pedro's uncle, Domingo Alvarez, and his wife, Josefa Aldama, represented Pedro's family. Domingo and Josefa, who were from Torim, had also been in La Colorada, and Josefa's mother was a Valencia relative of María's. After the wedding, everyone returned to La Playita. María had prepared a wedding meal, but a Yaqui wedding fiesta was impossible because the government prohibited gatherings of Yaquis. Chepa remembered her wedding dinner as a poor affair.

Pedro lived in another of the laborers' houses at La Playita with his uncle, who, like Abelardo, worked in the orchard. Accordingly, he took Chepa there on her wedding night. "Qué miedo" ("what fear"), she remembered. Since she was still living at La Playita, she was able to visit María and the old household every day, and apparently continued her subsistence activities there. Pedro did not work in the orchard but for Augustín León at a farm called Llano.

For a short time after she married, Chepa lost her initial fear of her husband and became "enamored" of him: "Había un rato cuando quería mucho a mi esposo" ("There was a short time when I liked my husband very much"). At least ten years older than she and already a heavy drinker, Pedro was nonetheless good-looking and charming, and he made a good living. Like a lot of other Yaqui men, he went into Hermosillo on Saturday and did not come home until Sunday night, having spent his money on mescal and "bad" Yaqui women. Chepa made quite a point of the fact that she had never personally known a Yaqui woman who "would go with anyone" and had never talked to the likes of them. Nevertheless, she knew quite a lot about two women, Isidora and Civilagua, with one of whom Pedro often greeted the Sunday dawn. Chepa was sure that the women Pedro went with every Saturday night were always Yaquis, never Mexicans. Although Chepa repeatedly described Pedro's women as "bad," she did not regard them as full-fledged prostitutes. His alliances with Isidora and Civilagua seem to have been fairly stable, as he was rather consistently involved with them over several years, having initiated the relationships well before his marriage. The two probably also "went with other men," who, like Pedro, regularly gave them money.

Chepa was pregnant within a year of her marriage. Although she viewed pregnancy itself with a certain fatalism— "Así es la vida" ("That's life")—she seems to have been remarkably uninformed on the actual process of childbirth, in spite of the fact that Camilda had produced one and possibly two children while Chepa was in the Cochemea household and old enough to be aware of what was happening. When the baby came she was staying with María, as she sometimes did, rather than at the Alvarez house. Her description of her first childbirth was as follows:

I didn't know I was having a child. I had had pains in my stomach. All night I wandered around the yard feeling like I needed to urinate. Finally, about daylight, the pains got so bad that I hung on to a post and the baby came out on the ground. I didn't know what had happened. María was in the kitchen ramada. She saw the baby on the ground and came out and washed it in water and wrapped it up. When the afterbirth came out, María put it in an *olla* and buried it. Then she told me to go to bed. I stayed in bed five days, then I got up and started helping Camilda make tortillas again.

This son was named Carlos. His *madrina de pila* was Candelaria Buitimea, who lived at Ranchito; her husband, José, was the baptismal *padrino*. Neither Candelaria nor José was a relative. The wife of Pedro's *patrón*, who gave them milk for the baby, was remembered as a good woman.

Within a few months of Carlos's birth, soldiers came for Abelardo, and María could do nothing to effect his release. All Yaquis were subject to arrest and deportation. Although the *patrones* were fined heavily if they did not turn in their

Yaqui laborers, they did not want to do so because Yaquis were good workers. Many a crop was left to ruin in the field because a *patrón* lost his Yaqui laborers.

Not long after Abelardo was deported, Pedro was taken to the same prison that Abelardo had been in to await deportation. The soldiers asked Pedro if he had a woman, and he foolishly said yes. If he had kept quiet, Chepa believed, they would never have come after her. Most Yaqui men said nothing when asked about their wives, but Pedro said yes, and so they came after her, too. She was allowed to collect a change of clothing for herself and for Carlos, but nothing else.

The month before a trainload of Yaquis was collected for deportation was a grim one for Chepa, already pregnant again, and her infant son. Of course, no one could come to see them, or they would be imprisoned too. Prison food was cooked by men, and poor cooks they were, buying bread—which Carlos did not like and would not eat—instead of making tortillas. Carlos was accustomed to milk and wheat tortillas, and neither was available. The men made *pozole* (a hominy stew) that was little more than water, as well as watery rice and beans, but there was never enough. This was the first drastic hunger that Chepa had endured. They were crushed into a small cell in the second tier of cells with a number of other Yaquis. There was not room for everyone in the cell to lie down at the same time. Everyone had to eat and perform the necessities in this cell, which was cleaned out infrequently. Once a day they were allowed fifteen minutes of exercise time in the courtyard. The baby soon got sick.

When over three hundred Yaquis had been rounded up, they were herded into railroad cars—"just stuffed in like goats." At Guaymas they were packed into a small boat for San Blas, and everyone was put below deck in crowded rooms. Since no fires could be built for cooking, the food was aging cold beans and tortillas. Both Chepa and the baby were very sick. She could do nothing but lie down, for no one was allowed up on deck.

From San Blas, the Yaquis were marched to Tepic, where men and women were separated and kept in different parts of the *cuartel* (army post). There Carlos died of hunger and thirst, and a soldier went to tell Pedro, but they would not let him come to Chepa. A soldier walked her to a hospital about half an hour away, where he made her leave the baby, wrapped in her *rebozo*, on a white table. She begged to be allowed to bury her baby, but they dragged her out and at bayonet point forced her to return to the army post, crying all the way. She was convinced that they threw the baby to the dogs since they would not let her bury him.

After a sad month in Tepic, the Yaquis, men and women together again, were escorted to San Marcos, the nearest railhead. Here they entrained for Guadalajara, where they rested for two days in a *cuartel*. For the first time since they were imprisoned, each person received a small ration of soap. Next they went by train to Mexico City, crowded into cattle cars as usual. There the soldiers became more efficient. Instead of loosely herding the Yaquis from one enclosure to another, as had been their wont, they formed a solid "human corral" to conduct the Yaquis to Cuartel Alfonso, where the men were quartered. The women were billeted in nearby houses.

Chepa was assigned to a house some two blocks from the *cuartel* with four other women, one of whom had a small child. They were each given ten centavos a day to pay for their room, and fifty centavos a day to buy food for themselves, their children, if any, and their husbands in prison. Every day at noon the women lined up for their meager dole. Then they went to the small market nearby, called Mercadito Mixcalco, where they bought coffee, beans, and tortillas, saving enough to take to their men night and morning. Chepa was lucky. She was feeding only herself and her *viejo* (old man); she felt sorry for the women who were feeding children as well.

The Yaqui women, who had come from the hot lowlands and possessed only cotton clothing, felt the cold of Mexico City keenly. One of Chepa's two *rebozos* had been left with baby Carlos in Tepic. The Mexicans issued no sarapes, no warm clothing. They did not even have a *petate* to sleep on, but slept on the cold dirt floor. Chepa wondered that she was not sick—what with the cold climate, the constant hunger, and being pregnant—but somehow she was not.

The Yaqui women were free to move around the city. Sometimes Chepa and her four fellow lodgers would walk downtown. Once they went to a place that had a lot of old guns and other weapons. Each Sunday they attended a nearby church.

One day when she took Pedro his food, he said their names had been called; they were to leave for Yucatán. ("The Yaquis were sold like so many goats.") The Yucatecan *patrones* would come to Mexico City and "buy" the number of *peones* they needed—usually three, four, or six men with their wives and children. The man who "bought" Pedro was called Manuel Peón "for *peones* he kept." He took six men and their families on this trip: Pedro and Chepa; Miguel Irrabas and his wife, Alvina; Luciano Angulo and his wife, Chepa de Angulo, and their two sons, Alvino Luciano and José (who were old enough to work and counted as two men); and an old man named José who had no family with him. They went to Vera Cruz by train and on to Progreso by boat, passing through Mérida on their way to the Hacienda Nokak.

At the hacienda all the men were put in the henequen fields. Chepa did not have to work in the fields, but for several months she was employed in the communal kitchen where black beans and corn tortillas were prepared for the workers who did not have women to cook for them. Most of her hours were devoted to grinding a "mountain" of corn masa and making tortillas.

After they had been there about a month, she and Pedro left without permission to visit some Yaquis on another hacienda. They were caught and publicly punished. Pedro was given fifty lashes across the lower back, and she (now in an advanced stage of pregnancy) was given twenty-five. As additional punishment, they were separated for some time. They continued to work, but at night Chepa was locked up in the foreman's house and Pedro in a small hut that served as the hacienda jail.

After this period of punishment was over, Pedro and Chepa were assigned their own thatched-roof house plastered with *cal* (lime plaster). Taking the hammocks they had been given on arrival, they set up housekeeping. Pedro was paid two pesos a week and given a ration of corn and beans by the *patrón* each Saturday at the *despacho* (office). Chepa was never paid a centavo for her work in the laborers' kitchen, but about the time they were given their own house, she was relieved of that duty, thence having only to keep house for Pedro.

On Christmas Day, Chepa's second baby was born. He was named Nicolás because of the saint's day on which he was born. When she was near delivery, the *patrón* sent a Yucatecan *partera* who helped her by rubbing her belly, but who had no medicines. The *partera* cut the cord, bathed the baby, and took the afterbirth away. Chepa had no idea if the afterbirth was buried properly. Nicolás's baptismal *madrina* was Cruz Buitimea, a Torim woman whom Chepa had known at La Colorada Mine. She and her husband, Luis Coyote, had been deported earlier and were already at the hacienda when Chepa and Pedro arrived.

The baptismal godfather was a local Yucatecan *peón* named Luciano Ek, a "very good person." According to Chepa, the Yaquis had a great deal of liking and respect for the Yucatecan Mayas, as witnessed by Chepa and Pedro's preferring a Mayan godfather over several resident Yaqui men. Mayan men always spoke when they passed a Yaqui woman, whether they knew her or not, saying "*adiós chum*," which is a respectful greeting. Chepa picked up a number of Mayan words, including greetings and basic food terms.

After Nicolás was born, the *patrón* added a can of condensed milk to their weekly ration. Chepa was therefore surprised when the baby sickened. When he was in the *agonía* (death throes), they lit candles all around his body, "so that he would die with candles." After he died, they bathed him, put two Yaqui rosaries around his neck and dressed him in an *hábito* (burial robe). A small private *velorio* was attended only by Chepa, Pedro, and the godparents and their spouses. There was no priest and no *maestro*, but they recited. Chepa and Cruz gathered wild flowers to place on the tiny body. Nokak had no cemetery, although there was a small church. The *patrón* arranged for the mourning party to go to the nearest cemetery, at Suetunte, by way of a little flatcar pulled down the railway for two *leguas* (leagues) by two mules. The godparents performed the burial while Chepa and Pedro crouched behind a *panteón* (cemetery) wall so they would not see the actual interment.

Chepa bore seven children, all of whom died as infants. Only the first four were baptized and named—Carlos, Nicolás, Luis, and Eulalia. The births and deaths at Hacienda Nokak became part of a blurred, repetitive picture, and Chepa had difficulty in distinguishing one tragic episode from another in her recollections. Perhaps if Pedro had drunk less mescal one of the babies could have lived. He could not go with other women, and so he spent nearly all his money getting drunk, leaving little for extra food or other necessities. Mescal was always available on weekends for only twelve centavos a half-bottle—enough for a good drunk. Once, when he was drunk, Pedro tried to knock Chepa around. She grabbed a shovel and hit him soundly. He never tried to hit her again. "There are women who run when their man wants to fight. That is wrong," Chepa maintained. "It is much better to grab them—and bam!"

In time, word came to the hacienda that the Yaquis' slavery was ended and they were free to leave if they chose. All of them but Chepa and Pedro left immediately. Chepa was near the end of her seventh and final pregnancy. A week after the general exodus, Pedro decided they would start toward Mérida. After walking a day and a half, they stopped at the Hacienda Techo, for Chepa was experiencing the pains of childbirth. There was no midwife; a resident woman helped, and, for the first time, so did Pedro. Chepa hemorrhaged and was unable to rise from her hammock. The baby, who lived a week, was buried in the cemetery at Techo, with Chepa too ill to attend. Because of her illness, Pedro stayed at Techo, working on the hacienda. Now that slave labor was abolished, the haciendas paid a better daily wage. Pedro made seventy-five centavos a day at Techo, but no provisions were furnished, so they were really no better off.

After three months they went on to Mérida, where they found hordes of freed "slaves" and little work. The swarms of displaced laborers waiting for jobs were kept at the large *cuartel* of La Mejorada, where the *cabecera* (boss) with contracts from the haciendas came to get *peones* for cutting henequen. For perhaps another three months Pedro went out on short jobs in the work gangs formed by the *cabecera*, so this time was spent mostly at haciendas near Mérida.

With the *Libertad* (Revolution), Yaquis were beginning to perform their dances again. Chepa and Pedro saw the first Yaqui ritual since their deportation when some *pascolas* performed at La Mejorada. The *patrones* at the Hacienda Nokak had forbidden the Yaqui rites as heathenish, and had ordered the local priest to baptize the Yaquis. This indignity annoyed Chepa very much; like all the Yaquis born at La Colorada Mine, she had been properly baptized at San José de Pima.

While Pedro was working at the Hacienda Xochil, he deserted Chepa for another Yaqui woman. Chepa had long ceased to be fond of her husband, but his desertion meant that for the first time in her life she had to support herself. She walked back to La Mejorada and signed on for cutting henequen, which cut the flesh like a knife, but her raw hands were eventually toughened. Several months or longer must have passed while she cut henequen with the labor parties, returning to La Mejorada between jobs. She worked with Luz Bakasewa, who had been at Nokak with her daughter, Nacha Bakasewa; her daughter's husband, Juan Flores; and their son Manuel, who was old enough to work on the hacienda. When the *Libertad* came, Juan had joined the Federal Army, taking Nacha and Manuel with him and leaving Luz in Mérida. Luz, much older than Chepa, was also newly self-dependent.

Chepa and Luz were working at the Hacienda Muchaché when they were told everyone was to be shipped to Veracruz. Chepa never knew why they were being moved around, but economic conditions in northern Yucatán were so miserable because of the vast numbers of unemployed Yaquis and Mayas that she thought leaving the area was a good idea. After returning to Mérida, they walked to Progreso and boarded a boat that took a day and a night to reach Veracruz, where they were moved directly from the boat to a train for Mexico City.

Here Chepa and Luz took a small adobe house near the
Escuela de Tiro. Luz's son-in-law, Juan Flores, was transferred
to Mexico City, and he and his family soon joined the household. There was once again a stable income, but one soldier's
pay was not enough to support five adults. At first, Chepa and
Luz begged on the streets and washed dishes for street
vendors in the hope of receiving a taco. Soon it became clear
that they did better by catering to soldiers who had no women
to cook for them, so they began to feed men in their adobe
house and to peddle tortillas.

Shortly afterward, Chepa became ill. She had daily chills and
fever and was dizzy and too weak to move, an ailment she
diagnosed as *paludismo*. They could not afford even a sarape or
an extra *rebozo*. For some months Luz fed them as best she
could. Lying helpless in a strange place, in a cold climate,
completely dependent on a friend who was, however, a
comadre (they had baptized babies together in Yucatán), Chepa
passed through the worst period in her life—"Allí me pasé
hambres y hambres y enfermedades" ("How hungry and sick I
was").

After some months, Chepa became well enough to work
again. Their hand-to-mouth existence continued for perhaps
two years. When the Federal soldiers abandoned Mexico City
and the Revolutionary Army entered from the north, Chepa
and Luz garnered a new crop of boarders, many of them from
Sonora. One of the men who came to eat at their adobe house
was Salvador Muñoz, a Mayo Indian from Huatabampo, a Carrancista, and a member of the Sixty-seventh Battalion under
General Chito Cruz. The general and most of his battalion
were Mayos.

Soon Chepa formed an alliance with Salvador (*me junté con
él*). Her most vivid memories were of her life as a *soldadera*.
Much has been written of the hard life of the Mexican *soldaderas*, and it was, on many occasions, very hard indeed, but
for Chepa the period was a tremendous improvement over the
years with Pedro in Yucatán and the worse years that came
after. Although she maintained her identity as a Yaqui
throughout her life, during her *soldadera* years, it seems, Chepa
enjoyed a role in which her being a Yaqui was not the key

factor in other people's reactions to her. Furthermore, Salvador was a better provider than Pedro had been—and he did not drink nearly so much.

The Revolutionary years with Salvador divide somewhat unevenly into three periods. Before the Revolutionary movement fragmented, Salvador was assigned for six months to Puebla (which was much colder than Mexico City), to Pachuco, and to various places in Veracruz (Orizaba and Córdova). A picture of Chepa and Salvador taken in Orizaba shows her as a vigorous, attractive young woman in a nice white lace blouse. Her face does not reveal how many tragedies and how much hardship she had already seen.

After Pancho Villa left the Revolutionary fold and fell back to the north, many battalions gave chase, including the Sixty-seventh. Salvador was stationed for a month in Irapuato, where the troops were concentrating. One day as Chepa was walking through the large encampment, she saw a man who resembled her father, Francisco Moreno, but, being timid, she was not sure enough to approach him. He, however, recognized and spoke to her. Someone had told him she was alive and with one of the battalions and he had been looking for her. He was alone, with no woman to cook for him, so he came and ate with her as long as they stayed in Irapuato.

Chepa discovered that although her father had been arrested along with his daughter, María, and her husband, José Yomaiza, from the Princhera gold mine, he had never been deported. While they were in the big gray stone prison in Hermosillo awaiting deportation, an officer had come to the prison, looked over the prisoners, and asked, "What is that man doing here? He isn't a Yaqui," because Francisco looked like a Spaniard. Of course, María and José Yomaiza did not say a word, and the authorities let him go. María and her husband were deported and never heard of again. Francisco had then gone to La Playita orchard, where he got Abelardo Cochemea's old job working for Jesús Terelli. There he stayed until he joined the Twenty-second (Yaqui) Battalion commanded by General Lino Morales, a Yaqui from Huirivis.

Pedro Alvarez, Chepa's former husband, was also in Irapuato with the Twenty-second Battalion. She, of course, did not speak to him or to his woman. He had joined (or been forced to join) the Federal forces in Yucatán, where he and his new woman had stayed after the *gente* (Yaquis) were removed to Mexico City. At some point he left the Federal Army for the Revolutionary Army, and here he was waiting to chase Pancho Villa. Irapuato was the last place Chepa saw either her father or Pedro Alvarez, as her father was killed in a subsequent battle and Pedro jumped a troop train in Tucson, minus the new woman, and remained in Arizona for the rest of his life.

This northern swing after Pancho Villa was for Chepa the bloodiest part of the Revolution. She saw the aftermath of many battles, but the worst were the battles of Aguascalientes, Zacatecas, and Celaya in Guanajuato. Chepa's version of the battle of Celaya does not agree entirely with historical accounts. According to her, the Villistas held the town when the Carrancistas arrived. After a long battle, the Villistas withdrew from the town and bottled the Carrancistas inside when they rushed in. Ordinarily, the women were kept behind the lines of battle, but at Celaya such detachment was not possible. Casualties were high. The two armies did not bury their dead, but left the bloated bodies to be disposed of by the townspeople after they moved on. For the first time Chepa actually saw people die violently, and she did not like it. The carnage of Celaya was one of Chepa's few black memories of the Revolutionary years, which were, for the most part, relatively secure and exciting.

Following the operations against Villa, Salvador's battalion was sent first to Mazatlán (a port on the west coast in Carrancista hands) then to Manzanillo, where they were to be shipped to Acapulco (also in Carrancista hands) to take part in military operations against Emiliano Zapata. They were given several days in Manzanillo to get ready for the five-day boat trip, inasmuch as the *soldaderas* had to prepare all the food their families would need on the trip. When they arrived at Acapulco, food was scarce, for the Zapata forces had cleaned out the town as they withdrew. Chepa described the Acapulco of Revolutionary days as a small, ugly, hot, stinking town. The Carrancistas had to eat what was available, mostly green mangoes.

Most of the women accompanying the soldiers of the Mayo battalion were from northern Mexico. The hunger and the foreign southern environment demoralized them thoroughly; most of the women cried a lot and were convinced they would die in Guerrero. This feeling was heightened when the troops went on an extended six-week chase of Zapata, leaving the women to fend for themselves in the small town of San Gerónimo. Chepa did not succumb to the general hopelessness and depression, but said, "If I die, I die," and managed as best she could.

After the Zapata campaign, which also took them for brief periods to Coyuca, Catalán, and Umgarabato, Salvador's battalion was again posted to Mexico City to the Cuartel Alfonso. Life there was relatively easy. Chepa was able to stay warm and well fed, and many Yaquis from Yucatán and other people she had known were there, so it was a time of visiting and reunions. Of her four stays in Mexico City, this was definitely the most pleasant, and possibly the best interlude in her life.

Throughout the revolutionary years, Chepa had cooked from time to time for one of the battalion leaders, General Alfredo Martínez. Without his wife, who preferred living in Sonora to following the army, the general was dependent upon a soldier assigned to cook for him, inasmuch as there was no organized mess. He much preferred Chepa's cooking, and not infrequently she was called upon. He was especially fond of her coffee, *menudo*, and *pozole*, requesting them frequently. Chepa was quite proud that her culinary skill had been so highly regarded by a general. There is every reason to believe Chepa's statement that she observed all the major figures of the Revolution except Francisco Madero and Emiliano Zapata. She saw Pancho Villa, Venuestiano Carranza, Álvaro Obregón, and Plutarco Calles—either in Mexico City or as a *soldadera*. By this time the military campaigns of the Revolution were effectively over. For perhaps a year, Salvador's battalion was given routine assignments to different stations. They spent some months in Baja California, and then returned to Mexico City for the last time. There the Mayo battalion was either disbanded or many of the men, including Salvador, were simply released from duty.

At this point, Salvador left her for another woman. Chepa stayed on with his mother, Sylvana Bachomo, who was stranded in Mexico City with two of her younger children. Chepa had met Salvador's father, Mariano Muñoz, who belonged to the Fourth Battalion, in the massive gathering of troops at the main camp in Irapuato. Apparently Mariano had been released earlier and had already returned home to Huatabampo, Sonora. In any event, Chepa and Sylvana's family requested train passage home from President Obregón, and their request was granted. They traveled together to Navojoa. From there, Sylvana and her children went home to Huatabampo and Chepa continued alone to Hermosillo.

Chepa was in a town she had not seen for some years, and once again without means of support. Her closest relatives were scattered or dead. Chepa's first task was to locate a relative with whom she could live. She soon found Micaela Amarillas, whom she called *tía* (aunt). Micaela's mother, Jesús, was an older half-sister of Chepa's father, Francisco Moreno, by the same mother but a different father. Micaela's marriage to Gregorio Wickoi was unusually stable. They had lived at La Colorada Mine in the late 1890s, and their oldest daughter, Angela, was born there. Deported to Yucatán as a family, they had all survived. After the *Libertad* Gregorio ended up in the Twenty-second Battalion. Their son, Luis, was born in Colima during the Revolutionary years. Gregorio and Micaela had returned to Hermosillo only shortly before Chepa. Chepa's relationship with this family represented one of the few lasting sets of interpersonal contacts during her Hermosillo years. She moved into their house on the steep side of the Cerro de la Campana in the *barrio* of La Matanza. What is today the *barrio* of Las Pilas at the foot of the Cerro was not built up at that time.

After finding a place to live, Chepa quickly reestablished contact with the *patrones* for whom her family had previously worked. She turned first to the Terelli family on Cerdán Street. Even though old Jesús Terelli, who had managed La Playita orchard when Abelardo Cochemea and later Francisco Moreno worked there, was now dead, the daughter, Luisa Terelli, immediately accepted Chepa as a washerwoman. Chepa searched for other households for which she could wash, and soon had six. She purchased a flatiron so she could iron as well as wash and thus make a better living.

Chepa's routine revolved around the washing. She collected the clothes from her *patronas*, carried them to Micaela's house, washed them in the river below, ironed them, and returned them. She tried to handle the clothes of two families at a time, keeping the clothes two days, with one day for all-day washing in the river, and one day for ironing and delivery of that batch and collection of the next. For decades she walked at least five miles on her rounds of collection and delivery. Washing in the river meant standing in shallow water, bending over and rubbing the clothes on rocks, then drying them on the bushes. Chepa believed that prolonged washing in the river contributes to arthritis and rheumatism, as it probably does. Her routine was interrupted through the years by the river's annual flooding, when it became too muddy for washing, and by periods of illness—unwelcome interruptions, for no work meant no income.

Chepa sank, rather gratefully it seems, into the life of a *soltera*, or unmarried woman. After Pedro and Salvador, she had absolutely no interest in men for several years, or so she maintained. Instead, her interpersonal relations centered on Micaela's household and on her companion washerwomen at the river. In paticular, she became friends with Victoria Soto. From what Chepa said, as well as from fuller reports obtained from Victoria's two daughters, this was one of the closest emotional ties Chepa ever experienced. Unlike her other relationships, nothing disastrous happened to terminate it. The friendship, which lasted until Victoria's death about 1967, was reinforced by many factors: they washed side by side for over forty years; they spoke Yaqui together; they were relatives (although neither knew exactly what the relationship was, they agreed that Chepa's mother, Antonia Sasueta, was kin to Victoria's mother, Lina Soto); and both were born at La Colorada Mine, where they knew each other as children. Furthermore, their personalities seemed to complement each other. Chepa could be taciturn for indefinite periods of time, and was frequently described as sad or a loner. She had, however, a lively sense of humor that surfaced in certain circumstances. Victoria's daughters described the two women as constantly talking, joking, laughing, and giggling, and both could perform devastating imitations of other people, something they did only at the river or in their own homes.

Victoria Soto and her mother, Lina, had moved from La Colorada Mine to Hermosillo at the time of the Yaqui roundups and deportations. In the *barrio* of La Matanza they became friends with Antonio Wong, a Chinese who ran a little shop. Throughout the years of Yaqui persecution, Victoria and Lina would hide in a secret basement room in Antonio's shops when the Mexican soldiers were searching for Yaquis to deport. Eventually Victoria began living with Antonio, and they had three children. It is not known whether they were formally married, but probably not.

About 1930 the Chinese in Sonora were "rounded up and deported to China." According to Mariana Wong, a daughter of Victoria Soto and Antonio Wong, "people were afraid of them," because the Chinese were taking over the small businesses. Antonio Wong was among the "deported," and he was never heard of again. Victoria was able to support herself and her small children by washing, and, like Chepa, felt no desire to search out another man.

About 1933, a chair maker named Antonio Mesa came to Micaela and "spoke" for Chepa. Chepa had never spoken to him, but she had seen him around the *barrio* in the years since her return. He was a Mayo, born in Alaseo, living with his mother in the adjacent new *barrio* of Las Pilas. Micaela relayed Antonio's wish to Chepa, who was pleased to accept "because he was so respectable." He moved into Micaela's household during the month it took to have a house built on the lot he had bought in Las Pilas. Then he and Chepa moved into their own one-room Mayo- or Yaqui-style home made of carrizo cane and rock.

Shortly after Chepa moved out of the house on the hill, Micaela died. Her husband, Gregorio, who had worked in the cement plant, had died in the late 1920s, and Micaela had had to support herself and Luis by washing. Now young Luis, who was perhaps twelve, was left alone. Micaela had owned the property, so there was no reason for Luis to give up the house, and he preferred living alone to moving in with Chepa and Antonio, who asked him to join their household. Enriqueta Oruno fed him. Enriqueta was a *yori* (a Mexican, in this case) who had been a friend of Micaela's, but she was not a god-parent or a relative. Chepa explained Enriqueta's assumption of this responsibility simply by saying, "She was a good woman." Luis got a job at the cement plant when he was fifteen, lived alone until he was about forty, then married Catalina, a *yori* widow with five children; they subsequently had three more. Luis and Catalina, like Micaela, were kind to Chepa through the years.

Antonio Mesa was somewhat older than Chepa; she described him as tall, fat, dark (*prieto* or *moreno*), pleasant, and respectable. He occasionally worked at chair making and for a short time held a job at the cement plant, but by and large Chepa supported them both by her washing. Other informants stressed how hard Chepa had to work to support him. They emphasized his kept status, and said Chepa almost seemed to regard him as an ornament. She made certain that he appeared in a spotless white shirt, ironed pants, and store-bought shoes every day. Each morning after she went to wash, he moved his chair out to the front of the house right by the road. There he sat and willingly talked to anyone who passed. He was an entertaining and constant talker. After lunch he made a daily trip to the center of town to see what was happening.

Chepa laughingly agreed that Antonio did not work much, but she had no regrets about having lived with and supported him. She was proud that he was such a substantial, respectable man. An amusing companion, he never got drunk, he could read and write, and he cared for her when she was sick. During one illness her legs became so swollen that she could not walk. Antonio carried her and "did everything" for her, including preparing her meals. After this illness had gone on for some time, Antonio went next door for a *curandera* named Cruz, who cured Chepa by rubbing her all over with an herbal medicine for four days. Antonio paid the woman a nice fee for this service, but he never told Chepa how much it was.

In comparing the three men she lived with, Chepa said she was most "enamored" of Salvador and went through the Revolution with him; Pedro was a drunkard and brought her only misery; but Antonio was pleasant, did not get drunk, and lived with her until he died.

During the years that she lived with Antonio, Chepa often visited with his mother, until her death, and his three sisters. Her relations with the three Mesa sisters, always cordial, were terminated only by their deaths many years later. Chepa was disappointed that their children, even two whom she baptized, never spoke to her or helped her after their mothers died.

Chepa performed what she saw as her wifely duties to Antonio well. She always asked permission to do anything other than her normal economic activities, and if he said no, then she refrained. He gave her permission on several occasions to go to Huatabampo to see Salvador's mother. Antonio never accompanied her, and he never returned to his own home in the Río Mayo in the years she knew him. He had been brought to Hermosillo as a young child, retained no memory of the Río Mayo, and had no desire to see it. She enjoyed attending the Yaqui Fiesta de Gloria, and did so when Antonio gave permission. He seldom went, and had little interest in any religious activities, although he once acted as a *padrino* for a Yaqui *fariseo* named Luis Valencia. During the three years of his *carga*, or obligation, thus incurred, he attended the fiestas at El Río and performed the necessary duties. He also baptized two boys of a Yaqui couple who lived in La Matanza.

During the years Chepa lived with Antonio she had a bad fight with another woman. Carmen Muñoz believed—wrongly, according to Chepa—that her husband, José Valenzuela, was going around with Chepa. Carmen chased Chepa down the street, caught her, and beat her with a piece of firewood. Carmen's niece called the police, who took both women to the gray stone penitentiary where long ago Chepa had awaited deportation. Antonio said nothing bad to her about the incident. He just went to the man in charge of the penitentiary, who happened to be a *patrón* for whom Chepa washed, and Chepa was released after one night; but Carmen remained incarcerated for a month. Even one night in the penitentiary brought a flood of sad memories; Chepa could never pass that forbidding edifice, she said, without remembering bad things and feeling afraid.

Antonio developed heart trouble and for the last month of his life was quite ill. They called a Dr. Nava (not a *curandero*) who administered injections and prescribed pills "that calmed him" but did not make him well; he died in 1948. His favorite sister, Josefa, arranged for the necessary four *madrinas*, one of whom was Venena Yocupisio, whose two children he had baptized. He was buried by women only, as all the men who might have served as *padrinos* were working away from Hermosillo. Chepa washed his body, and two of his nephews dressed him in his best clothes; the Yaqui burial robe was not used. The *velorio* was carried out in Josefa's home with a Yaqui *maestro*, four *cantoras*, and the immediate family. None of his many nieces and nephews attended, which Chepa always held as another black mark against them. Chepa and the sisters hired a hearse and a car for the trip to the *panteón*.

The *novena* and the *cumpleaño* were held at Chepa's house. She arranged for her *patronas* to supply the necessary food. Almira Valenzuela was especially generous because her husband ran a small grocery store, but all of the *patronas* were willing to contribute because they all knew Antonio who, upon many occasions, had accompanied Chepa when she went on her laundry business and they all remembered him as "such a fine talker."

Antonio's grave, which Chepa took me to see, is mounded up with earth in the Mayo or Yaqui style. Its cross, now somewhat dilapidated, contrasted with the cement slabs, tombstones, statues, and artificial flowers of most of the other graves in the *panteón*.

After Antonio's death, Chepa continued her life as a washerwoman. She was able to support herself adequately until about 1963, when her hands became so stiff she could not wash. Life thereafter became progressively harder. Since she received no money from social security or any other governmental source, she was dependent on her old *patronas*, a small food allotment from a church welfare society, and a few friends and relatives. As her *patronas* died, she had fewer and fewer sources of money and food. One of her two remaining *patronas* during the last years of her life was Angela Terelli. Angela (a Yaqui, according to Chepa) was taken in by the Terelli family when she was a little girl and given their name. As their natural daughter, Luisa, never married, Angela ended up with the family house and money after Luisa's death. Chepa called on Angela Terelli every week or two and received a few pesos (never more than ten, and usually only three to five) as well as small amounts of beans, flour, and other staples. Ema Bustamonte, the only other *patrona* alive and resident in Hermosillo, supplied Chepa with much the same resources. Almira Valenzuela was more generous, but near the end of Chepa's life doña Almira lived in Nogales or in Mexico City with her children most of the time. Every two weeks the church welfare society, operating out of a small Catholic school, supplied Chepa with approximately a kilo of beans, a small sack of coffee, a bar of yellow soap, and another small item or two.

About 1958 a woman named Juana Gómez moved into the compound immediately across the street from Chepa. Juana was a classic example of the "penny capitalist." Her various money-making schemes seemed endless. She bought kerosene by the barrel and sold it by the cupful for a significant profit; she had the neighborhood monopoly on firewood, which she sold by the stick; she boarded men who came for their midday meal; she rented cots to men; she had a sewing machine on which she could make salable items, and so on. Juana presented herself to me as Chepa's good angel. She allowed Chepa to sit in her compound (which was cooler and less dusty than Chepa's own house), fed her occasionally, and gave her firewood and kerosene. Chepa paid for her neighbor's kindness, however. Within eight years, Chepa had signed over to Juana a small plot of land just to the west of her house. Juana immediately built a one-room brick rent house there. In 1969, Chepa signed over her poor carrizo house to Juana and began to worry about how soon Juana would throw her out. While I have no way of knowing exactly how Juana treated Chepa in my absence, I feel that on the whole, Chepa did not make a bad deal, although their relationship alienated Chepa's few remaining Yaqui ties. Chepa certainly felt freer to go to Juana's house than to any other, and she told me several times, when Juana was not present, that for the past few years Juana had done more for her than any of her relatives had.

When Victoria Soto died in 1967, her daughter, Mariana, continued to do a number of important things for Chepa. Unfortunately, Mariana and Juana Gómez detested each other and neither would help Chepa when the other was involved. It was Mariana who came to Chepa's aid during one serious illness, when she was unable to walk and was thus unable to acquire food or water. Mariana took her to a hospital (free for poor people in those days), but the doctor had to be paid, and Mariana provided the money. Chepa was in the hospital for five months.

Mariana repeatedly asked Chepa to live with her (and her sister and the sister's extended family) just up the hill. Their house, a plastered adobe, had running water, a sometimes functioning toilet, a shower room, and a bottled-gas cook stove. Chepa refused because, according to Mariana, she was "too independent." If Juana had thrown her out, however, Chepa said she would have asked Mariana for the land on which to build another carrizo house, thus maintaining her independence.

In addition to the help given by Juana and Mariana, Chepa could rely upon one or two other old friendship and kinship ties. Luis Wickoi and his wife, Catalina, occasionally gave her a meal. Rosalio Moisés, whom she had tended as a child, sent her money with some regularity for eighteen years. When Rosalio died in 1969, Chepa's living standard dropped. There were times of real hunger. She viewed her situation as hopeless and was ready to die "when God wills."

In the summer of 1970, Chepa accompanied me to Potam, where she stayed with Dominga Ramírez, a half-sister of Rosalio Moisés. Dominga pressed her to move to Potam and live with her, arguing that Chepa would not be any hungrier and she would be among Yaquis. For a day or two, Chepa was strongly tempted, even agreeing to the plan. She felt she would die soon, and there was no one in Hermosillo to give her the Yaqui funeral she desired. She predicted she would be bundled into a nameless pauper's grave. If she died in Potam, she would surely have a *velorio* and probably a *novena*, and be buried in front of the church among Yaquis. However, she soon changed her mind. She reasoned that by remaining in

Hermosillo, she would still have access to the *patronas* who gave her small amounts of cash. If she were in Potam, she would have absolutely no income, and therefore no small luxuries, like cigarettes. She smoked about a package of strong, cheap Mexican cigarettes a day when she had them, regarding smoking as the greatest pleasure left to her at her age.

Another factor in Chepa's decision to return to Hermosillo was her cat. For several years, she had owned a beat-up yellow and white tomcat, an oddity that everyone joked about. Dogs were common in Yaqui homes and in the lower-class *barrio* in Hermosillo, but a cat was rare. She shared whatever food she had with her cat. Chepa was on a near starvation diet and particularly craved meat, which was almost nonexistent in her fare. When she did get meat, half of it was fed to her cat. When Chepa went with us to Potam for several weeks in 1970, her main concern was for her cat. Juana promised to feed him, but Chepa was doubtful. The day we returned to Hermosillo the cat did not show up. Chepa assumed that it had been killed, and her depression was deep. When the cat came home the next day, she cheered up enormously, feeding him liberal quantities of the meat I had bought her.

In the fall of 1970, Chepa's health worsened, although she was able to attend the annual San Francisco fiesta in Magdalena. Upon her return, she became bedridden and Juana moved her over to her house, ostensibly to care for her. Two quite different stories about her final illness and death have been told by the various people involved, and there was a great deal of bitterness on both sides. The facts are that Chepa remained at Juana's until December 1, when Luis Wickoi (Micaela's grandson) came to move her to his house, where she remained until her death on December 21, 1970. Juana alleged that she had cared for Chepa as though she were her own mother, buying her medicine and feeding her. She attributed Luis Wickoi's sudden interest in Chepa to the fact that he wanted to inherit Chepa's house and steal all her possessions; she stressed the fact that Chepa died in their hands, not hers. Luis Wickoi, on the other hand, said that Chepa sent an urgent, secret message by the shopowner's son, asking him to remove her from Juana's care because Juana was killing her.

He said that when he arrived, Chepa put her arms around his neck and tearfully begged him to save her. He immediately carried her in his arms to his house. His wife, Catalina, told me how Chepa's frail body was black and blue from the blows Juana had delivered with sticks of firewood, how dirty, ragged, and virtually starved she was. Chepa told them that Juana deliberately mixed up her medicines and withheld food in the hope that she would die sooner so Juana could get complete control of all her property.

Chepa asked Luis to go to her house and bring some of her more treasured possessions. He reported that none of the things she specifically wanted were there and the house had been looted. The Wickoi family implied that Juana was responsible, while Juana said they had stripped the house.

On December 20, Chepa entered her final *agonía*. At midnight, Catalina took her to the doctor in Villa Seri who had been attending her, but he was at the hospital, so they returned home without seeing him and Chepa died in the early morning. The *velorio* held in Luis Wickoi's house was attended only by four adults—Victoria Soto's daughter, Mariana, a niece (a daughter of one of Chepa's half-sisters), and the Wickoi family. Luis paid for the funeral mass and burial. As Chepa had foreseen, her death was devoid of any Yaqui ritual. She would have been greatly saddened by the death of her beloved cat, which was viciously knifed about a week later.

Dominga Ramirez was a positive, happy, beautiful woman with a well-developed sense of humor. Her life had its quota of hardships and social and physical pressures, but her story is basically one of pressures successfully met. Dual enculturation in Yaqui and Mexican life ways permitted her to operate successfully in a variety of cultural contexts. Her life demonstrates the slow climb to a position of knowledge, respect, and authority that is possible in Yaqui society.

A half-sister of Rosalio Moisés and Antonia Valenzuela, Dominga, began her life at La Colorada Mine. Like Chepa Moreno, she was deported to Yucatán, but as a young child with her mother. She matured during the Revolutionary years, finally marrying a Yaqui attached to a Yaqui battalion in Mexico City. Again like Chepa Moreno, she saw a great deal of Mexico with the armies. Her husband took her and their child to his family home in Potam when he was released from the army. Dominga's somewhat negative reactions to the confined life dominated by her mother-in-law illustrate the stress that can occur when mother-in-law and daughter-in-law live in the same household. The family fled to the Sierra with other Potam residents in the 1926 Yaqui uprising, surrendering to the Mexicans after a few weeks of hardship and inactivity. Taken to Guaymas, her husband elected to be deported without her and their two children, thereby terminating their marriage.

For the rest of her life, Dominga lived at Cocorit, Potam, and a rancheria on Potam lands. She is the only one of the women whose life stories are given here who spent her adult years in the Yaqui Valley.

154

DOMINGA RAMÍREZ

Over the next several years, she had two affairs and contracted two more formal alliances that resulted in five more living children. Of her seven surviving children, Dominga personally raised only the last three. One of the others was claimed by his paternal grandmother and Dominga's own mother raised three. During the seven years spent at the rancheria Palo Parado with the man who fathered her last three children, she was closely confined to the drudgery of her household. Much of her adult life aside from that domestic interlude was oriented away from household affairs, as she was involved in a series of jobs and peddling. Dominga's mother provided stability within the household during these times and acted as the dominant figure in the extended family. Upon her mother's death, Dominga assumed the role of household and family head and, for the rest of her life, devoted her attention to these matters. In her turn, she was given grandchildren and other relatives to raise.

Dominga was the best informant of all the women I worked with; if we had spent a longer time together, a full-length biography could have resulted. I was fortunate enough to encounter her first in Tucson, where she was visiting her half-sister, Antonia Valenzuela, with whom I was working at the time. I had expected to get in touch with Dominga in Potam, but the Tucson meeting was a doubly effective introduction. Thereafter, I was in her company in Tucson, Magdalena, and Hermosillo; in many Potam households; attending fiestas in Potam and Rahum; visiting her relatives in Torim, Vicam Switch, Esperanza, and El Papolote; and on trips to Obregón,

155

Guaymas, Cochorit beach, Empalme, and the east side of the Bacatete Mountains. These encounters allowed me to see her in many varied situations and to evaluate a wide range of reactions to her. Her Tucson relatives tended to regard her as something of a wicked old woman whose forthright behavior could be an embarrassment. Otherwise, she seems to have been unusually respected as an older woman who "knew" and who was deeply committed to upholding the network of obligations related to the kinship, ritual kin, hospitality, and ceremonial systems. Dominga did not always occupy a respected role, nor was she earlier considered to "know." Her progression to this state was a long, hard road.

More people invested positive affective emotions in Dominga than can be said for any other woman in this study, as is seen in the behavior of her descendants at the time of her death. Her sons took the unusual step of taking her coffin from the burial padrinos and carrying it on their own shoulders to the graveyard. Every son, daughter, daughter-in-law, and grandchild is said to have cried openly. I was assured that this unusual open demonstration of their grief was a true measure of the esteem they felt for her.

In terms of her own emotional bonds, Dominga's attachment to her mother was the strongest she experienced. Her mother was a "hard" woman, and she certainly raised all the children in her care the "hard" way. Dominga, whose extrovert, happy personality was manifest early, stood up to her mother, thereby gaining preferential treatment. The mother's differential treatment of the two children in her care in Yucatán is a study in the effects resulting in part from their reactions. Aside from her mother, Dominga's closest emotional bonds were to some of her sons and perhaps to two female friends.

My relationship to Dominga was fairly egalitarian, involving a lot of joking. She treated me more as she treated younger female relatives, a mode of interaction that contrasted with the more formal respect relationships maintained with her sons. Dominga was accustomed to talking freely with a wide range of outsiders. I have seen her strike up conversations with strangers in situations in which many other Yaqui women would not dream of doing so. I was only one more outsider in a long sequence.

Dominga had few material resources to manipulate for prestige and status. What she did manipulate as a resource was information. As an elder, she had a substantial reservoir of this commodity, but her real *genius lay in garnering contemporary news and gossip. She worked at this activity, and time after time she had the latest word before anyone else in the group of related households. In keeping with her confirmed role as a seeker of information, she was interested in me, setting out to discover all she could.*

Dominga's memory was good, and her perception of the past seemed to be accurate insofar as her accounts could be checked. She arranged for people who could authenticate her stories to talk to me and otherwise channeled a constant stream of people to my door. Selectivity was more obviously a factor with Dominga than with other informants—more obvious because she provided so many other people who added details, who asked if she had told me a particular story, or who corrected her. The areas in which she deliberately clouded the account dealt with the number and identity of her consorts—three were lost for two field seasons—and her administration of harsh punishment to her children. Once these points were clarified, she talked freely about them, although she said she was ashamed of her actions in those areas. Some questions remained unsolved. There were many last names she might have used: Preciado (her mother's maiden name), Leyba (her stepfather's name), Palos or Valenzuela (from her father), Romero (her legal married name), or the names of any of her many consorts. She was most widely known as Dominga Ramírez, however, and I never discovered why she used Ramírez. She was more adamant than any other informant about refusing payment. Others also refused, but she verbalized her position more clearly.

Like Chepa Moreno, Dominga took me in hand, instructing me forcefully in correct behavior, especially when we were visiting other households—telling me who to shake hands with, where to sit, and what I should talk about with a particular person. She was the only informant who tried to teach me the Yaqui language. I was not a good pupil, but she persisted, constantly repeating Yaqui words and phrases when talking to me. She was inordinately pleased when I began to recognize a few words and respond appropriately. She also regularly corrected my Spanish.

Dominga was born at La Colorada mine about 1898 or 1899, the daughter of Miguel Palos and Augustina Preciado. She was, therefore, a half-sister of Rosalio Moisés and Antonia Valenzuela through their mutual father, and she called Chepa Moreno, her father's cousin, a *prima hermana*.

Both her father's and mother's families pertained to Torim pueblo. Two Preciado brothers worked in the mine: Francisco, who later became a rather prominent captain in the Yaqui army and figured in some negotiations between the Yaquis and the Mexicans, and Gregorio. The three oldest sons of Gregorio and his legal wife, Charla, also worked in the mine. Augustina, their fourth child, was between twenty and thirty years of age when she contracted her alliance with Miguel Palos. Two younger Preciado children, Leonardo and Concepción, were much closer to Dominga's age.

Dominga firmly believed that Augustina and Miguel married properly in the church at San José de Pima and that she was a legitimate child. In the light of other information, however, this seems unlikely. Miguel Palos is said by other descendants to have married Cecelia Hurtado in the church at Torim in the late 1880s. Cecelia was living with Miguel in La Colorada when Dominga was born. Divorce was unknown for the Yaquis at that time. Indeed, it seems doubtful that Miguel even established formal residence in the Preciado household where Augustina lived.

Dominga remembered little of her life in La Colorada, although she recalled a few things "like a dream." Her personal memories merge into the stories Augustina and others later told her, and because she was told about La Colorada so often, she had a fairly clear idea about relatives who lived there, major events, and the quality of their lives. The picture that emerged is remarkably similar to other accounts: life was secure and pleasant. Dominga particularly remembered that they lived in a nice house with pretty curtains. Augustina was a cook for "rich people," interrupting her normal employment for Dominga's birth, then returning to her job and leaving Dominga in the care of her mother, Charla Preciado. Only the men spoke very much Spanish. The women lived in the Yaqui way and only Yaqui was spoken at home. Augustina was described as dressing like an Indian and wearing her long hair, which reached to her knees, in braids.

The 1900 Mazocoba massacre disrupted the security of Yaquis everywhere in Sonora, including La Colorada. Many families left the mine. Among the first to go were Miguel Palos, his legal wife, and their youngest son, who moved to another mine. The Preciado family remained at the mine through several roundups of Yaquis for deportation, but they, too, were taken about 1904. On this occasion, the soldiers selected thirty or forty Yaquis, including Gregorio and Charla Preciado, their six children, and, of course, Dominga and Augustina's new baby, José. Dominga believed that Miguel Palos was also the father of her little brother, but that seems unlikely unless he had returned to La Colorada to visit Augustina.

The soldiers allowed the Yaquis only a few minutes to collect possessions before marching them to Torres, the nearest railroad station, whence they were shipped to Guaymas. Augustina was, by all accounts, an extremely vivacious, attractive woman, and she was quite willing to use her assets to get soldiers to help her carry her bundles and otherwise to get preferential treatment. Another woman, Lupe Moreno, who became annoyed at Augustina's behavior, began openly criticizing Augustina as a traitor and a loose woman. In the ensuing hair-pulling fight, Augustina soon got the upper hand and had to be restrained from throwing the woman off the moving train. Dominga remembered this incident vividly, saying, "How my mother fought—how she talked." She was sure she did not hear of the fight from Augustina in later years because fighting is bad.

In Guaymas, the Yaquis from La Colorada were held for several days in what is now the Palacio Municipal until a boatload of Yaquis was collected for shipment to San Blas. From there they were taken by train to Mexico City, where they were interned in a military *cuartel* until they were "bought" by *hacendados*.

Augustina; her younger sister, Concepción; Dominga, now four or five; and the baby, José, were "bought" for the Hacienda Tanihl in Yucatán. The other six members of the Preciado family were sent to an hacienda in Quintana Roo, where five of them died of starvation and the climate, as

Augustina learned years later when she encountered the sole survivor, Leonardo, in Mexico City during the Revolution.

Dominga's personal memory of Tanihl was much more complete than for her earlier years. At least thirty or more Yaqui and Mayo workers lived there, along with local Mayan *peones*. Lupe Moreno, who had fought with Augustina on the train to Guaymas, was among those "bought" for the Hacienda Tanihl; she was accompanied by her husband and several small children. The two former antagonists had by this time become friends, and they later became *comadres*. Among the other Sonoran Indians at Tanihl were Juan María Valenzuela (a *pascola* from Vicam); Nicolás Buitimea (also a Vicam *pascola*); José María Escalante (a Mayo *venado*, or deer dancer); Magdalena and Velorio Valenzuela (deported from Hermosillo); Juan and Juana Zúñiga of Vicam; Manuela Bartasal and her husband of Torim; María Jeca and her husband of Bacum; Feliciana Basolihtimea of Belem (deported as a lone woman); three Leyba (or Leyva) brothers deported from Ures (Luis, a bachelor; Ignacio and his wife, Manuela Flores; and Juan, his wife, Juana Yokehua, and their young son, Juan María); Adelina Caumea (a *curandera*), who lived with her husband, Santiago Caumea; Guadalupe Valenzuela and his sister, Carmen Valenzuela; José María Galavis (a *fariseo*); and José Suvai (a *maestro* of Potam), who lived with his Torim wife named María Buitimea.

Each family was assigned a small thatched house and issued hammocks. A household had to supply at least one adult field hand. Augustina either had no opportunity to join another household or elected not to do so. In any event, there was no man in their household; Augustina had to work in the henequen fields like a man, leaving the children to run the household. Work in the henequen fields was, at first, exceptionally hard on the workers' hands. Augustina's hands eventually hardened and thereafter she found the labor within her level of physical tolerance. The overseer kept telling her she should marry a local Mayan so that she could stop doing such hard labor, but she invariably answered that she would not consider marrying "one of those animals." Augustina's comments to the overseer and to her Mayan coworkers were repeated many times by Dominga, who would conclude: "How my mother told them!"

Concepción, who must have been about ten or perhaps a bit younger at the beginning of their Yucatecan sojourn, was given the tasks of grinding corn, preparing meals, washing, ironing, and so on. Said to have been sad, or *triste*, from the time of her birth, she became more introverted and passive. For whatever reason, she soon bore the brunt of Augustina's hostility and aggression. Augustina rapidly became a hard woman, although she had been easygoing in La Colorada, and most of the hardness was directed at Concepción, whom she now berated and beat regularly. Augustina's mistreatment of Concepción and the latter's passive acceptance of this treatment formed one of the longest and most detailed segments of Dominga's accounts of the Tanihl years. If Augustina's clothes were not washed, starched, and ironed just right, Concepción was beaten. If Concepción talked to other girls at the well, she was beaten. If the tortillas were too thick, she was beaten, and so on endlessly. Concepción became the household drudge.

That Dominga did not receive such constant harsh treatment was due, she believed, to the fact that if her mother yelled at her, she yelled back, but Dominga nonetheless was raised the "hard" Yaqui way. Being younger than Concepción, she had less responsibility. In the beginning her main task was to keep the fire going. Later she took over the corn grinding and enjoyed herself so much that she volunteered to grind for other Yaqui women. Decidedly an extrovert and a happy child, she had a great deal of freedom and was a welcome visitor in other households, unlike the sad Concepción.

The baby, José, had always been thin and sickly. Soon after arriving at Tanihl, Augustina arranged to have the Yaqui ceremony of placing rosaries held for him, selecting Magdalena and Velorio Valenzuela as godparents. His continued illness also prompted Augustina to make a vow, or *manda*, to a saint to place a habit on him. Adelina Caumea, the Yaqui *curandera*, unsuccessfully attempted the usual treatment for his ailment, *caída de la mollera* (characterized by a depressed, or "fallen," and pulsating fontanel, nausea, diarrhea, and fever). He died so quietly that Concepción and Dominga did not immediately notice. Concepción ran to the fields to tell Augustina, who, with the permission of the overseer, was allowed to return home. Augustina spent the rest of the day preparing for the *velorio* held that night. She selected the burial *padrinos*, who of course included José's *padrinos de rosario*; cooked chili con carne; and made the large Sonoran-style wheat tortillas. The *padrinos* dressed the body in the *mortaja*, or habit, that had been made as a result of the vow to the saint; placed a crepe paper crown embellished with paper flowers on his head; and put crepe paper flowers over his body, which lay on a small mat.

The *velorio*, held at the house of Magdalena and Velorio Valenzuela, began in the evening with the meal. Five Yaqui rosaries were placed on José's body. About midnight, the *pascolas* and deer dancer began performing. At dawn, the entire party walked some distance to a large cemetery outside the hacienda. Four *madrinas* performed the actual burial while Augustina, Dominga, and Concepción were sheltered behind the *panteón*. All of them made the sign of the cross at the grave before walking back to the hacienda. Augustina was glad that her son had a Yaqui burial with a *maestro*, *pascolas*, and a *venado*. Like the other workers, she had to return to the fields for a long day's work.

Tanihl lacked a store or commissary, although beans and corn were issued from the overseer's house. Workers made twenty-five centavos a day, paid every Saturday. The cash was spent at a store run by Señor Guzmán on a neighboring hacienda. Augustina refused to take either Concepción or Dominga to the store on Saturday evenings, a weekly disappointment, but she did return home with small amounts of food that, for at least a day, varied the inevitable diet of corn tortillas, beans, and *chiltipiquines* (small, hot chilis), the latter gathered by Concepción. Dominga remembered that they never had coffee, which cost too much, but they usually had chocolate, meat, and bread on Sundays, which was their day of rest, visiting, and such hospitality as could be provided.

Although no major Yaqui ceremonies could be performed, occasional household fiestas broke the monotony. Feliciana Basolihtimea, unusually deported as a lone woman, married Luis Leyba in the church at the nearby hacienda of Ulucman, which boasted a resident priest. The wedding fiesta held at Tanihl was, for Dominga, a memorable occasion, with the *pascolas*, the *venado*, and virtually all the Sonoran Indians involved. For once, food was abundant and varied.

The worst episode that occurred at Tanihl was Augustina's severe punishment by the overseer. Dominga did not remember what Augustina had done to receive the punishment. Knowing she was to be punished, Augustina ran away to a neighboring hacienda, only to be returned by a Yucatecan. For her double transgression, the overseer ordered that she be suspended from a tree by means of a rope passed beneath her arms, above a small smoldering fire, which burned her feet badly. She was then cut down and carried home to Concepción and Dominga, who cured her as best they could. Before her feet were healed properly, she had to hobble back to the fields. Although other workers were whipped for failure to perform their quota of work, Augustina escaped further punishment. Otherwise, Dominga remembered life at Tanihl as monotonous, especially the food, but not as particularly unpleasant or harsh. Unlike the situation at the Hacienda Nokak described by Chepa Moreno, a semblance of a Yaqui life way was maintained at Tanihl because of the large number of Yaquis and Mayos, the presence of several ceremonial specialists and a *curandera*, and the apparently moderate attitudes of the hacienda owners and overseers that allowed household fiestas to be held. Although Dominga learned Spanish, Yaqui continued to be used in the household and between Yaquis on the hacienda.

When the Mexican Revolution reached Yucatán, the "slaves" were freed. Dominga must have been about twelve by this time. The Tanihl workers walked to Mérida, where many were housed in a large *cuartel* called El Castillo. At this time, Federal Army forces controlled Yucatán. Many of the freed laborers were impressed into the Federal Army as soldiers. At least some were issued the black uniforms with red braid down the side, topped with high black hats with shiny black bills—a sight that impressed Dominga very much. One of her more memorable pantomimes portrayed the uniform and behavior of these Federal soldiers.

Augustina found a small house at El Castillo for the three of them and Nicolasa Bakasiari and her husband, Francisco Leyba, who had also come from Tanihl (there is a confusion of names here or elsewhere, as Francisco Leyba was one of the three Leyba brothers given different names earlier). Concepción continued in the role of household drudge, but now she had to grind more corn and help make the tortillas that Augustina peddled to soldiers living in El Castillo. Dominga accompanied Augustina on her rounds, clinging to her skirts. Augustina and Dominga found the freedom of movement, the give-and-take of the marketplace exciting. Once there was a tremendous roar of a crowd in the distance. Occasional cries of "Viva Madero" could be distinguished. When Dominga asked Augustina what was happening, Augustina silenced her by saying it was nothing of any significance—just "more propaganda."

With all of the freed Yaquis and Mayos from the many Yucatecan haciendas in Mérida, it was possible to assemble a full complement of ceremonial specialists. A full Fiesta de Gloria, or Easter ceremony, held at a ramada built outside of El Castillo was the first major Yaqui ceremony Dominga ever saw.

When their Yaqui soldier clientele moved to Valladolid with Federal troops for a few months, Augustina, Concepción, and Dominga went along, because their livelihood depended on selling food to Yaqui troops. They were back in Mérida, however, when the Revolutionary troops landed at Progreso. Women and children were locked up in La Mejorada *cuartel* during the battle of Mérida, which they could hear in the distance but had no way of knowing who was winning. When Yaqui soldiers released them, they streamed out of the *cuartel* to encounter jubilant Yaqui troops stripping off their Federal uniforms as they ran. At El Castillo, men and women rifled the Federal barracks, piling up all the Federal uniforms they could find for a great bonfire in the middle of the *cuartel*. The Revolutionary forces brought four Yaquis with them to aid in rallying the many Yaquis in Yucatán to the Revolutionary cause: Colonel Francisco Pájaro, Major Isikio Chávez, Captain José Bakasewa, and a *tambalero* (drummer), Luis N. León. That this forethought was successful is indicated in the fact that Dominga remembered their names.

At some point during their stay in Mérida, a Yaqui named Juan Montes asked Augustina if he could call on Concepción, permission Augustina immediately granted. To Concepción and Dominga, he seemed old. He was, however, eminently respectable because he was a lawyer's assistant, able to read and write. His calls were made less painful to Dominga by the bags of sweets he brought, but these were not enough to gain Concepción's favor. Soon he asked to marry Concepción, and again, Augustina granted permission, unmoved by Concepción's threat of killing herself. Juan, who was deeply religious, asked that Concepción receive religious instruction. Augustina found an old blind man to teach both girls catechism. After they related how he had put out the single candle and tried to catch them in the dark, Augustina transferred them to an old woman for instruction. On her wedding day in Progreso, Concepción told Juan Montes that she hated him.

Shortly thereafter, the movement of Yaquis out of Yucatán began. Dominga knew of a few who elected to stay, such as Guadalupe Valenzuela, who had married a Yucatecan Mayan at Tanihl, and his sister, Carmen, who married a Cuban in Mérida. Most, however, walked to Progreso to get passage to Veracruz. With Augustina and Dominga were the other members of their Mérida household—Nicolasa Bakasiari and her husband, Francisco Leyba—and others from Tanihl: Luis Leyba and his wife, Feliciana Basolihtimea, and Lupe Moreno and her family. Thus, Augustina and Lupe arrived in and left Yucatán together. Juan Montes was by this time in the Twenty-second Battalion of the Revolutionary forces and he and Concepción were on the same boat. Passengers were crowded below deck, and when that was full, onto the deck. The Tanihl group was thankful to be placed on deck, as they at least got fresh air. Meager amounts of food were served from the overworked ship's galley during the three-day trip. Javier Basopolemea, who died during the voyage, was wrapped up and dropped overboard without ceremony.

Upon arrival at Veracruz, they were marched directly to the Buena Vista station and entrained for Mexico City. A smallpox epidemic precluded a rest stop. The Twenty-second Battalion was assigned to Teresita Cuartel, so Augustina located a nearby house in order to establish the household near Juan Montes. Within hours she had Concepción grinding corn and they were back in the business of selling tortillas and other food to Yaqui soldiers.

One of Dominga's first memories of Mexico City was seeing an execution. She had been sent to Jalpan to have a bucket of *nixtamal* ground at a mill. Along the way she saw a crowd gathered at a cemetery. Three Zapatistas were blindfolded with handkerchiefs. One made the sign of the cross on the other two, then he stepped back in line and the order was given to six Carrancista soldiers to fire. An officer had to deliver the *golpe de gracia* (coup de grâce) to one who was "unable to die." Dominga was not disconcerted.

During their years in Mexico City they moved from the vicinity of one *cuartel* to another, following the movements of the Twenty-second Battalion and Juan Montes. After perhaps four years, they moved to a *cuartel* west of the Escuela de Tiro, and it was here their lives took a different turn. One day Augustina and Dominga were in the small Nocalpa market when a lieutenant colonel approached them. The lieutenant colonel, José María Leyba Cajeme, a nephew of the famous Yaqui leader of the same name, had been a miner at La Colorada, where he knew the Preciado family, including Augustina. He and his legal wife, Venina Yokehua, pertained to Cocorit and had married in the church there in the 1880s; he was therefore much older than Augustina. His entire family had escaped deportation and so had lived in Sonora throughout the intervening years. When General Álvaro Obregón raised Yaqui battalions in Sonora for the Revolutionary Army, Cajeme and his son joined. Venina elected to stay in Cocorit and their only daughter fled to Arizona.

At the chance encounter in the Nocalpa market, Cajeme gave Augustina a bag of money, saying *la güera* (the blonde), as Dominga was called, needed shoes. Augustina told him where she lived. Three days later soldiers came to take Augustina to Cajeme, leaving Dominga and Concepción alone. For three more days they were terrified; Dominga had never spent a night away from her mother. Food ran out, but without the impetus of Augustina's personality, they were unable to go to the market. Finally, Augustina came for Dominga. It is unclear what happened to Concepción, but she apparently remained where she was.

Dominga's life changed overnight. Cajeme was rich, living in a nice two-story house with servants. Milk delivered to the door was the most impressive sign of their new affluence. From a barefoot urchin darting through the marketplace, Dominga became a young lady in shoes and stockings with a hamper full of new dresses.

Augustina, freed from the constant need to work, began gambling again as she had done at La Colorada. Indeed, at La Colorada she had been regarded as a fast young woman because she went to the cantinas with Miguel Palos, played cards with men, and indulged in secular dancing. Cajeme disapproved of her gambling, so she tried to arrange to have her gambling visitors when he was absent. Dominga recalls that her mother played with skill, usually winning, often to the open disgust of her male opponents.

Cajeme was an officer in the Forty-second Battalion and soon they were on the move again, usually with the Twenty-second, so that Concepción seems to have been in the same places and perhaps was part of the movable household. Dominga mentioned brief postings in Puebla, San Martín Texmelucán, Toluca, Orizaba, Soledád, Veracruz, Atlixco, back to Mexico City, Xochimilco, Salazar, and Morelia. When Cajeme's son, Antonio, was killed at the battle of El Verde near San Martín Texmelucán, the household of which he had been a part was greatly saddened. Cajeme himself was shot in the leg at Morelia. In San Juan del Río, another Yaqui woman had a fair amount of success in capturing Cajeme's attentions, until Augustina precipitated and won a loud, public hair-pulling fight that greatly strengthened her position as Cajeme's woman.

Revolutionary activities moved northward as Carrancistas fought Pancho Villa's famous División del Norte. With some pride, Dominga commented that of course the Carrancistas won, because they had the Yaqui battalions, adding, "Pancho Villa was only valiant with the women." In Torreón, Yaquis and Mayos of the Twenty-second, Forty-second, Twentieth, and Thirty-fifth battalions put on a special performance for Generals Carranza and Obregón. Provisions were issued for the preparation of fiesta food by the Yaqui women. Just before the dignitaries arrived by train, the women were lined up and given flowers to throw as the generals walked to the ramada where Yaqui *matachines*, *pascolas*, and deer dancers performed. The fiesta was a great success.

These same battalions were present at the bloody battle of Saltillo, where the Carrancistas routed the Villistas. General Obregón ordered another fiesta in celebration of the victory. Fiesta food was again prepared in quantity and *pascolas*, *coyote*, and *naji* dancers performed. Dominga described the *naji* dancers as imitating birds, although the word *naji* means dragonfly. That was the only time she saw this dance performed.

In 1919, the Forty-second Battalion was stationed in Parral for almost a year. Because of their more settled life, and as befitted their status, Augustina sent Dominga to school. Dominga learned nothing, or so she asserted, because the teacher was deeply interested in a young man whose main claim to fame was that he was not a soldier. Since he was not allowed to call on her at home, he came to the school, carrying out his courtship before the fascinated eyes of the students. The teacher's temper deteriorated on the days he missed.

A major Fiesta de Gloria was held that year in Parral. Augustina made an *urnia*, a box about two and a half or three feet long, decorated with flowers and lace, that is used to hold the Christ figure on Good Friday after the Crucifixion. It was presented to the fiesta officials.

Concepción, a more tragic figure than ever, began to use the food money supplied by Juan Montes to go to cantinas, buy mescal, and regularly drink herself into oblivion. A daily routine began of looking for Concepción to bring her home. Juan Montes became more and more irate at his wife's behavior, finally, upon one occasion, taking his gun and threatening to kill her if he found her—which he failed to do. On another occasion, Dominga found her in a pigpen one morning about sunup. After Dominga managed to wake her up, Concepción went on a crying jag, saying she had been drinking with some men, who brought her to the pigpen and, after all had had intercourse with her, abandoned her where she lay. This was the final straw for Juan Montes, who left her to Augustina's mercies, thus ending their marriage. Augustina

once again assumed a hard, authoritarian role, confining Concepción to the house. Concepción was unable to escape, and
her drinking came to an abrupt halt.

Dominga saw Concepción smile only once after that. A
number of young women were visiting Concepción one afternoon. While they were talking and laughing, a rainstorm came
and went, almost unnoticed. When Augustina returned to find
the cots, which had been put out to sun in the morning,
soaking wet, she began to beat Concepción with a broomstick.
Never again was Concepción happy.

Dominga was by now an exceptionally beautiful girl, having
light-colored skin like her paternal grandmother and aunt.
Augustina and Cajeme decided it would be a good idea if
Dominga married Felipe Amarillas, a younger brother of General Amarillas. His family, eager to break up his incestuous
alliance with a cousin, agreed. Augustina behaved very differently with Dominga than she had with Concepción when
arranging her marriage. She decided to chaperone Dominga at
one of the soldiers' dances so the betrothed couple could meet
under favorable circumstances. Unfortunately, the scheme mis-
carried. Augustina sat on one side of Dominga, Felipe on the
other. Seating herself firmly on Felipe's other side, the *prima
hermana* with whom he had been living, openly upbraided him
for his fickleness and lack of attention, and made derogatory
comments about Dominga. Dominga refused to look at him,
speak to him, or dance with him, escaping to dance with
anyone else who asked her, all the while ignoring Augustina's
black looks. Augustina dropped the subject of marriage, Felipe
stayed with his *prima hermana*, and Dominga felt she had been
the belle of the ball.

From Parral, the Forty-second and associated battalions were
sent back to Mexico City. Cajeme rented a two-story house
with a balcony near the Cuartel Teresita. Dominga was much
more closely supervised and chaperoned than previously, and
was allowed out alone only to go to the private school in which
Augustina enrolled her. She wanted sophisticated dresses but
was made to wear girlish school clothes. Interested in men,
Dominga devised a number of ways of attracting their attention, the most effective being a regal pose on the balcony. A

man present at interviews in Potam in 1970 had been a fresh recruit with the Forty-second Battalion at that time; he recalled her stance on the balcony—while she carefully ignored the comments from below—as extremely enticing. Trips to and from school were made along routes most productive of male attention. A helpful *carbonera* (a girl who sold charcoal on the street) became Dominga's mailbox for admiring notes. Augustina, soon discovering that Dominga was receiving notes, instituted a daily search of her school books and person and administered a beating when she found incriminating bits of paper. Still, some of the notes survived and became Dominga's most cherished possessions. A Sergeant Félix held her attention until she found out that he had left a wife in Sonora. Then she looked with favor on a Mayo soldier, and finally noticed Anselmo Romero Matos.

Anselmo had joined the Forty-second Battalion in 1920 from his home pueblo of Potam. At that time he was about twenty or twenty-two years old, tall, and extremely good-looking. He, too, began passing notes through the *carbonera* and managed to speak to Dominga a few times. They arranged to run away. He met her after school and they went to a room he had arranged. Augustina and Cajeme were furious, of course, and Cajeme ordered soldiers to search for them. When they were found the following day, Augustina insisted they both be thrown in jail. Dominga, still in her school clothes and carrying her books, was put in a room with women and Anselmo was placed with the men. Later the authorities decided to place Dominga in a tiny solitary cell in order to remove her from the bad influence of the older, more experienced women. Dominga, however, cried so hysterically that they put her back where the other women could comfort her.

After a night and a day, Anselmo's "brother-in-law," Colonel Chávez, sent his assistant to obtain their release, and they were taken to his house. Colonel Chávez's consort was Anselmo's older sister, Isabel Romero. Isabel was a happy woman. Although neither she nor Colonel Chávez was legally married to someone else, they never bothered to get married. As a girl in Potam, Isabel had danced *pascola* so well that people threw pesos to her. Years later when Dominga returned to Potam, she was told about the happy Isabel. Not content with dancing *pascola*, Isabel had gone to Guaymas to attend the *yori* (non-Yaqui) secular dances, and it was there she met Colonel Chávez, with whom she soon ran away.

Isabel now took over, placing the culprits in separate rooms and lecturing them constantly. Feeling that the damage was done, she advocated marriage for the pair and arranged the ceremony in the cathedral a week later. Feliciana Uriarte, wife of a major in the Forty-second Battalion, was the wedding *madrina* and Lieutenant Antonio Yocupicio, a Mayo, was the *padrino*. Augustina and Cajeme ignored the wedding and forbade Concepción's attendance as well.

After their formal wedding, Dominga and Anselmo set up their own household. Dominga, who naturally did not return to school, was very enamored of her handsome husband. Augustina eventually thawed and in time became quite fond of Anselmo. About a year after their marriage, their first baby, Rosendo, was born at home with the aid of Augustina and a Yaqui *partera*. Dominga was fed pulque to stimulate milk production. Stressing that she never drank to get drunk like Concepción, she nonetheless admitted to enjoying pulque, especially with *mole*. She considered pulque more civilized than mescal or tequila.

Cajeme was, by this time, feeling old and useless. The Revolution was effectively over and he was suffering from a growth on his neck. Shortly after Rosendo's birth, he asked his old general, Obregón, now president of Mexico, to send him home to die. Obregón arranged for Cajeme's discharge, pension, and train fare to Cocorit, giving him papers to show where he had fought. When Cajeme, Augustina, and Concepción left for the north, Dominga was separated from her mother by real distance for the first time.

About 1923, two deaths occurred in the Romero family. Anselmo's brother, Teófilo Romero, was killed in a minor Revolutionary skirmish near Puebla, leaving two children from his alliance with a Mexican woman with whom he had lived in Mexico City. Shortly thereafter, Rosendo died of diarrhea at the age of about one year. The next year, a second son was born to Dominga and Anselmo in Mexico City. Named Anselmo after his father, he was healthy and happy. Dominga again dutifully consumed pulque. Eight months later, Anselmo was released from the army and given train tickets to the Río Yaqui. Dominga was happy at the prospect of being close to Augustina again.

Upon their arrival, Anselmo hired a team and wagon to take them and their possessions to his parents' home in Potam. Dominga's happiness continued through their homecoming and a trip to Cocorit to see Augustina, Cajeme, and Concepción. Soon, however, her life underwent a drastic change.

As an officer's "daughter" and later as a soldier's wife, she had led a rather privileged life. She had not washed clothes or ground corn since Cajeme found them in the Nocalpa market. Suddenly money was less plentiful, her clothes began to show wear, and, worse yet, she had to give away to other women in the household some of the dresses of which she was so proud. Her talents of dancing, talking brightly, and looking decorative were no longer appreciated. She was regarded as an uppity young woman. Freedom of movement vanished under the firm authority of her mother-in-law, who only spoke to her to give orders or to tell her what she had done wrong. Hard physical labor from sunup until sundown rapidly ruined her delicate hands, once her pride and joy.

Inasmuch as her domestic skills were poorly developed, she had to relearn how to grind corn for hours at a time, make acceptably thin corn tortillas (making the large wheat ones was a skill she did not yet possess), and so on. Her teacher was a sympathetic sister-in-law, María Jeca, a cousin of the María Jeca at Tanihl who had served as one of the baby José's burial *madrinas*. At two metates, side by side, Dominga and María knelt for hours. They also were the ones who carried water, carried hot *ollas* to the field to feed the men during periods of peak farm work, and walked to Oros to gather baskets of garbanzos in season, which were then carried home on their heads.

Anselmo at home was very different from Anselmo the soldier in Mexico City. He became hard, began to drink too much, and ignored Dominga. She believed that the influence of his mother, who disapproved of Dominga, caused him to act in this changed fashion. Once she decided he was going to beat her over some trivial incident, and, being fed up with her life of drudgery anyway, she impulsively ran away. Taking nothing in the way of food or clothes, and even leaving her prized Chinese earrings—the most lasting memento of more pleasant days—she walked to Torim to stay with Pancha González. Pancha was the last consort of José González, who had earlier been a consort of Cecelia Hurtado, the legal wife of Miguel Palos, Dominga's father. These relationships were not the reason she fled to Pancha, however; Pancha had been kind to her since her return to Potam. After one night, Dominga walked on to Cocorit—home to Augustina. Little Anselmo was already there because Augustina was curing him. For a month Dominga happily worked as a cook in a rich home and luxuriated in the more congenial atmosphere. Finally, Augustina asked her if she really believed Anselmo would beat her, and when she admitted that she did not think so, Augustina told her to return to Potam with little Anselmo.

Dominga told only one favorable story about her mother-in-law. The woman became terribly excited over the execution of a witch in Rahum. She was disappointed that she had not heard the news in time to attend the actual burning of the witch, named Rosa, who was said to have harmed many poor people, but she decided it was worth a trip to the scene anyway. She marshaled all the women and children in the household for the walk to Rahum; they arrived while the ashes were still warm.

The other exciting event that occurred during Dominga's sojourn in the Romero household, an event that sparked interest throughout the Río Yaqui and beyond, was the spectacular arrest and trial of General Mori. Mori was a Yaqui general who earlier in the century had been a leader of the Sierra Yaquis against the Mexicans. At the time of his arrest he lived in a nice two-story house in Pitahaya. The story goes that a substantial sum of money collected for the Torim church was placed in his keeping. Word spread widely and rapidly that he had stolen the money and hired two *albañiles* (construction workers) to build a subterranean vault for it on the black hill facing Pitahaya. Some said he then shot both *albañiles* to prevent their revealing the location of the vault, while others favored a version in which one *albañile* was killed but the other escaped. The escaped *albañile* has been reported to live in

Arizona, in Hermosillo, and elsewhere. Everyone has dreamed about finding this buried treasure; Dominga believed that it would be difficult to locate the vault itself because the black hill is so rocky but that it should be possible to find the hole where they mixed the concrete.

General Matus, apparently reacting to public pressure, sent Yaqui soldiers to arrest General Mori. His trial, held in Vicam before the governors of the eight pueblos, resulted in a public whipping, the stripping away of his Yaqui military rank (although some Yaquis and the *yoris* continued to call him general), and indefinite confinement in the Yaqui *guardia* at Potam. Dominga could not attend the trial, but day after day she saw him at the Potam *guardia* as she carried buckets of wheat to be ground. Mori's wife, an impressively fat woman with enormous gold earrings and fancy hair combs, moved to Potam to be near her husband, and Dominga observed her actions with interest.

Dominga's last child by Anselmo, named Milo, was born on September 5, 1926, as the harvest was underway. No *partera* was available, so the other women of the household assisted at the birth. On September 13, the five governors of the pueblo went from house to house, telling the people the Yaquis were again at war with the Mexicans and they should go to the Sierra. Potam was evacuated almost overnight. The governors instructed people to take only essentials. The Romero family hurriedly grabbed guns, knives, a few blankets and clothes, some food, and a bucket. Like many others, they walked off and abandoned their harvest in the storehouses, as well as all their personal possessions and their cattle and chickens. A few men took horses, but even the dogs were left behind. Former general Mori was taken along under heavy guard.

Poteños, as the people of Potam are called, gathered at Huapari, one of the closer Sierra concentrations of refugees. Yaquis from other pueblos assembled at other points deeper in the Sierra. Dominga remembered the three-day walk to Hua-pari and subsequent stay in a nightmarish haze. When the word came to leave, she was still in bed from childbirth, bleeding heavily, and extremely weak, perhaps because her diet had been limited to thin *atole*. The walk, carrying the week-old baby, Milo, and encouraging the little Anselmo, seemed unending. In Huapari there was nothing but a spring—no trees, no houses, no fort—nothing but rocks exposed to the blazing sun. Although Milo suffered a deep sunburn from lying on the rocks, he remained well and healthy and never cried. When it rained, Anselmo's old army cape was used to cover the children, but everyone else got wet, letting their clothes dry on them.

Food soon ran out. Men would then slip into Potam at night, rifling through the houses for provisions. The unprotected pueblo was being systematically stripped by the *yoris*, however, so the forays by Potam men met with less success each time. Dominga's treasured notes, passed through the *carbonera* in Mexico City, disappeared. She mourned their loss more than anything else. Men turned to hunting and for several weeks the meat they obtained was the mainstay of their refugees' diet.

The Huapari Yaquis saw no action against the Mexicans, and after two months the majority appear to have decided that the whole affair was futile. The few who still wanted to fight joined other groups deeper in the Sierra, but most, including the Romero family, went to Huarache, near Pitahaya, to surrender to Mexican soldiers. Finding all of the soldiers away, the group patiently awaited their return. Jurisdiction of the Yaqui soldiers over former general Mori stopped at this time. After being stripped of their guns, knives, and horses, they were shipped by train to Guaymas for internment at El Corralón. The provisions of lard, wheat, beans, coffee, and sugar issued to each family provided a welcome change of diet.

In addition to Anselmo, Dominga, and their two children, other members of the Romero family present at El Corralón included Anselmo's brother Ceno, his wife, María Jeca, and their daughter Magdalena; his sister Emilia and her Mayo husband, Maximiliano Rodríguez, and their daughter Julia; and Anselmo's great-grandmother, María Baehaewah, and her consort, old Miguel Obomea. Dominga did not mention her mother-in-law, whose whereabouts at this time and subsequent history are unknown.

As a result of the 1926–27 uprising, Yaquis were again deported, but not as laborers on southern haciendas. Some men were conscripted into the army and others were merely transported to another part of Mexico and turned loose. After only three days at El Corralón, the Yaquis were lined up to be marched to the waiting ship. Anselmo told Dominga that she was too much trouble and to take the children and go home to Augustina. Old Miguel Obomea, who had abandoned a large herd of cows and a rich harvest in Potam, told María Baehaewah that she would do better to stay alone than to try to accompany him. The two women stood together and watched the others go out of their lives. Those women and children not deported made ready for the trip to their new internment center at El Águila near Empalme.

Cajeme, Augustina, and Concepción had stayed in Cocorit during the uprising, but they got word of Dominga's movements. As soon as they heard that the Huapari group had been taken to Guaymas, they hurried there in search of her, arriving to find her perched on a wagon ready to leave for El Águila. Cajeme was able to "talk for" Dominga and secure her release and that of the two children. The soldiers refused to let him have old María, and they heard in a few weeks she had died of *tristeza* at El Águila. The saddened group went home to Cocorit.

Augustina became disturbed to learn that Milo had not been baptized, and it was decided to return to Guaymas so that old army friends could serve as his *padrinos*. They stayed with friends, General Luís Buitimea and his *yori* wife, Librada Ramírez. The baptism was performed secretly at their house because "the priests had been run out of the churches." During their visit, doña Librada was feverish and nervous, spending most of her time in a large tub afloat with freshly cut flowers, something that seemed to soothe her. From time to time she shouted, "Alleluia, yo creo" ("Hallelujah, I believe") from amid the flowers.

Doña Librada served as a godmother to many children. One of her godchildren was abandoned on her doorstep by his mother with a note saying that he was a gift from his parents. Although she was furious, she kept him. At the time of Milo's baptism, the child was perhaps five years old. Dominga especially remembered that doña Librada kept a little silver whistle with which to call him. After doña Librada died a year or two later, the boy's mother had to take him back.

The three days in Guaymas were a nostalgic success, a pleasant reminder of more gracious days when they, too, had lived in a two-story house with a balcony and had servants to cope with the details of living. The return to Cocorit was less auspicious. Cajeme's pension had supported the three in their modest adobe house. Dominga's coming strained the household resources. She got a job as a cook for one of the rich *yori* families. The usual pay was nine pesos a month and her own food. The *patrona* watched carefully to see that she took no food home, however. At harvest time, Dominga heard that better wages were paid for picking peas, so she worked at that, taking little Anselmo along to help.

Before too many months had passed, Dominga walking with a Sinaloan *yori* named Sévero Jiménez whose family was among the wealthier in Cocorit, which had a large *yori* population. Their relationship, which lasted for several years, had to be carried on in awkward places. Augustina refused to let them in the house since she disapproved of their relationship, constantly telling Dominga she should wait for Anselmo's return. Sévero's mother disapproved also, since she wanted him to marry the daughter of rich *yori* friends, a girl in whom he lost interest after meeting Dominga. Although they never lived together, he was generous, buying Dominga clothes and food for the household.

Dominga's first child by Sévero was born about 1928 or 1929. Sévero paid the *yori partera*, bought the necessary medicines, and, for the first time, came openly to Augustina's house. The child, named Ramón Jiménez, was baptized by *yori* neighbors selected by Dominga in the Mexican fashion, that is, by having a husband and wife serve as *padrinos*. Sévero's family refused to receive Dominga, but his mother, Librada Masillas, sent servants almost daily to bring her only grandson to visit. A second son, José María Jiménez, was born to Dominga and Sévero about 1930. Sévero again honorably accepted the responsibility of paying the expenses. For the first time, Dominga selected Yaqui *padrinos* and baptized the Yaqui way.

Some years previously, Cajeme's legal wife had died. Cajeme was therefore able to marry Augustina; as his legal wife, her position with regard to his military pension would be secure. The wedding took place shortly before Cajeme's death in October 1930. Augustina used all their money to provide a nice *velorio* and *novena*. To her surprise, the pension stopped. She spent a great deal of time and effort until her death trying to reactivate the pension she believed to be rightfully hers as the legal widow. She wrote to the president of the republic, and when a new president was inaugurated six years later, she wrote again. She wrote to the military authorities. She made a trip to Hermosillo and paid the governor five pesos to write on her behalf. Even after Augustina's death, Dominga kept the little box of Cajeme's papers in the firm belief that some day the pension would be paid. She hoped to go to Mexico City to arrange these affairs personally.

Shortly after Cajeme's death, Rosalio Moisés returned from Arizona to live in Torim. Within a few days he came to Cocorit in search of Augustina and Dominga. He was, of course, Dominga's half-brother, being a legal son of Dominga's father. Dominga had seldom seen Augustina cry, even at Cajeme's death. Now she cried openly, repeating over and over, "How I liked Miguel Palos." Rosalio seemed very rich and he bought food for them. An Aunt Chepa, whose relationship to Miguel Palos is unclear, was included in the festivities, and both Aunt Chepa and Dominga returned to Torim with Rosalio for a visit. An embarrassing moment occurred in Torim when several men sitting in front of a little shop said in Yaqui, "There go some sons of *yori* whores," believing that the trio could not understand *la lengua* (the language). Rosalio bought *pan virote* (a large, flat, round bread) as a special treat and they all stayed with Manuel González, Rosalio's half-brother through his mother. Rosalio gave them money for the return to Cocorit.

Cajeme's death was the beginning of renewed hardship and bad luck. The youngest baby, José María, died of burns suffered when he fell into the fire from a stool where Dominga had placed him. Augustina's attempt to cure him by pouring writing ink over the burns was unsuccessful. Now they were often hungry. Augustina and Concepción took in washing and looked after the children while Dominga returned to her nine-peso-a-month job as cook. Sévero had lost interest in Dominga and his support ended. Sévero never did marry a rich *yori*, and in later years the Jiménez family lost their fortune, becoming indistinguishable from the other poor people, right down to their huaraches. Only Dominga and the baby, Ramón, got enough to eat—Dominga at work and Ramón because of his daily visits to his paternal grandmother.

About 1932, Ignacio Leyba, a distant relative of Cajeme's, came to pay his respects to Augustina. He lingered in appreciation of Dominga, still a beautiful woman, and soon they were walking together. Augustina again talked seriously to Dominga, asking her to wait for Anselmo and saying that Dominga was turning into a "woman of the streets." By this time, however, Dominga had heard that Anselmo had formed on alliance on the boat trip from Guaymas to Mazatlán with a Mayo woman named Lena Yocupicio and that they were still living together in the Thirty-fifth Battalion, to which Anselmo had been assigned. Augustina's strictures, therefore, carried little weight and Dominga continued to see Ignacio Leyba. He proved to be considerably less satisfactory than Sévero from every point of view. He lied to Dominga, saying she was his only woman, when in fact he had a *novia*, whom he married in church the same day Dominga gave birth to his child. When he came to see her and the baby, Guillermo Leyba, he denied he was married. Dominga turned her face to the wall, telling him wearily to go to his wife. He never returned, nor did he offer her a centavo.

Cocorit now seemed a poor place. Hearing that women were needed as cooks for crews of men working on the Potam irrigation ditches, Dominga moved to the house of Fermín Cajeme, one of Cajeme's nephews, in Potam, taking only the still nursing Guillermo. She got the job in the open-air kitchen perched upon the bank of a canal. As usual, the passing men admired her beauty. Jesús Suárez drove his large herd of cows across the canal at this point every day. In no time at all he noticed Dominga and soon they were walking together. When he asked her to live with him on his rancheria at Palo Parado, she accepted.

Jesús Suárez and his legal wife, Magdalena Valencia, both Mayos from Huatabampo, had a fine house and five children in Obregón. He, among others, had acquired land in Potam territory as a reward for aiding the Mayo Yocupicio in his

successful campaign for the governorship. At the time Dominga met him, he spent more time in Potam and Palo Parado
than in Obregón. He was a well-remembered and controversial
figure in the 1970s, and many people other than Dominga
discussed him. All of the descriptions stressed his large, fat,
sleek appearance, his obvious wealth, as seen in the enormous
amounts of cash he habitually carried and his large herd of
cows, and the impressive number of women he had at various
times and in various circumstances.

In the beginning, Dominga was enamored of him, proud of
the splendid figure he cut, pleased at the presents he brought
her, enchanted with his charm, and appreciative of his skill as
a lover. That he refused to allow any of her children other than
Guillermo to live with them was unimportant since the others
were accustomed to living with Augustina. Her happiness,
however, was short-lived. The gifts stopped, he kept her a
virtual prisoner at the Palo Parado rancheria, and her life
became a routine of drudgery that made the days in the
Romero household under the authoritarian regime of her
mother-in-law seem pleasant by comparison. Worst of all, his
interest in women soon reasserted itself. At first he merely
stayed away overnight. Later he brought women to the house,
paying them with the cheese Dominga had made, while she
was relegated to a corner of the floor in their one-room house.
For a few years he maintained another woman, a Mayo named
Teresa Yocupicio, in a house in Potam, dividing his time
between his three houses and occasional other women. Sometimes he offered other men money to arrange assignations with
women he saw walking down the street.

Dominga believed Jesús used supernatural means "to tie
her" and "blind her eyes" to his faults: "Why else would I
have stayed with him?" A small figure of San Benito was his
love charm. When he lost his little *santo* a few years later, he
cursed its loss and thereafter had much less success.

The seven years with Jesús Suárez stood out as the worst of
Dominga's life. In spite of his wealth, he provided her with
barely enough provisions to maintain the household at a near-
starvation level, and he never gave her cash. Once she care-
lessly left a wad of money in his pants pockets when they were
washed. Each bill, some so faded that their denomination was

no longer discernible, was carefully dried in the sun. Her fear mounted as she imagined what he would do to her, but when he rode up on horseback and looked down on the ruined bills, he only called her a "stupid burro."

Augustina and Concepción could not earn enough with their laundry business to feed themselves and the children very well. Dominga needed to send them money from time to time but never had any cash, although Jesús left large amounts in a box kept in the rafters of the house. In later years she said she was a fool not to help herself, as one of Jesús's sons from Obregón did regularly, but it would have been wrong to steal, and besides she was afraid of Jesús. In order to get money for Augustina, she resorted to selling secretly a little lard, or sugar, or flour to her neighbors, sending the few coins she received by an acquaintance going to Cocorit.

Dominga was alone much of the time after the baby, Guillermo, was returned to Augustina in Cocorit at Jesús's request; Jesús was gone all day and often stayed elsewhere at night. With a small household, the housework and cooking were not too onerous, although—since there was no mill in Palo Parado—she had to grind wheat on a metate, a task she had never enjoyed, and Jesús was particular about the way his clothes were washed and ironed. The chore which occupied most of her time was making cheese from the milk produced by the large herd of cows. She once commented that when she thought of Palo Parado, she thought of cheese.

One of the more unpleasant aspects of life with Jesús was that he failed to treat her with any respect or dignity in front of the women he brought home or the men he brought to the house for card playing and drinking. For example, Juan Tava of Vicam came to the house one night at a time when Dominga was in an advanced state of pregnancy. For no apparent reason, Jesús began beating her with a stick. She fought back but was no match for Jesús. The fight ended with Jesús throwing Dominga into a corner and telling her to sleep on the floor, which she did. Juan's wife told me that story, which Dominga then said was true.

Augustina was luckier. As old as she was, don Miguel Molino asked her to live with him, an offer she quickly accepted. She sold the house inherited from Cajeme in Cocorit for a few pesos and moved with Dominga's children to Potam. The fate of Concepción, such a prominent and tragic figure in the stories of Dominga's earlier life, is unknown. Her presence in the Cocorit household was mentioned, but she fades from the accounts after Augustina moved to Potam.

Anselmo and Milo were old enough to work in don Miguel's fields in Rahum (he pertained to that pueblo). Although the boys had to walk several miles each day, often going without lunch, their lives were somewhat more secure. Augustina allowed Anselmo and Milo to walk to Palo Parado to see Dominga once, but the visit was never repeated because Jesús considered it a good joke to get them both drunk on tequila. This incident confirmed Augustina's view that Jesús was a thoroughly bad man, not a proper model for boys she was raising the "hard" way. Ramón was kidnaped by his father's brother to be returned to his doting grandmother, doña Librada, in Cocorit, and no one ever went to reclaim him.

Much of the time, Dominga was alone and lonely in the house at Palo Parado with her mountains of cheese. Jesús forbade her to leave the rancheria. Although she disobeyed him to the extent of visiting with nearby neighbors, most of whom were Mayos awarded land by Governor Yocupicio, she was afraid to go farther. During these seven years she attended no fiestas, went to Potam to stay with Augustina for the birth of her two Suárez sons, and went to Cocorit so that Guillermo's baptismal godparents could place Yaqui rosaries on him in the Yaqui rite. Since Guillermo was the only child baptized in the Yaqui way, he was the only one to undergo this ritual. Otherwise, her universe was Palo Parado.

The first Suárez baby was named Jesús. Augustina, who acted as *partera*, selected Teófila N. León and Cipriano Castro, both Mayos, as his baptismal *padrinos*. Baptism was in the Mexican style. Had it been possible, the Yaquis in Cocorit who had baptized Guillermo would have fulfilled their *manda* to baptize three babies for Dominga. Augustina also selected the *padrinos* for Dominga's second Suárez son, Lázaro.

Being confined to Palo Parado did not allow Dominga to escape the attentions of Jesús's sister, Pancha. This woman seems to have been the most objectionable person Dominga ever knew. When Pancha came to Palo Parado, she expected to be waited on in style and treated Dominga as a servant. She delighted in passing along the latest gossip on Jesús's amorous escapades, dwelling at length on the superior attractions of Teresa Yocupicio, who was kept in a far greater state of affluence by Jesús than that allotted to Dominga. Pancha would ask Jesús in front of Dominga, "Why do you live with this poor Indian girl? Why don't you get a nice *blanca*?" Pancha was also responsible for Anselmo's worst beating. Seeing him on the street one day, she autocratically told him to help her take some chickens to market in Guaymas. Assuming that he should obey his "aunt," he dutifully went along. When he returned home to Augustina, he was given a memorable beating with a long leather mule whip for going without permission.

Although Jesús wished to have no responsibility for Dominga's older children, he nonetheless objected to Augustina's raising them the "hard" Yaqui way and making all the decisions about their lives without consulting Dominga: "Your mother presumes too much." His most overt disapproval came when Augustina arranged Anselmo's marriage to Carmen Saila in 1940 without consulting either Dominga or Anselmo. Jesús argued that Anselmo was too young to marry (he was sixteen), he needed time to get experience as a man, and even if he had to marry, it was a pity he had to marry an unattractive, older woman. Dominga told him not to cause trouble. The boys had been raised by Augustina and were "in her hands." Besides, Augustina would do exactly as she pleased, just as she always had. The wedding was held in the Guaymas cathedral. Dominga was not asked to attend.

Augustina had chosen Carmen after a great deal of thought because the young woman had been properly raised the "hard" way, was deeply religious, spoke only Yaqui, showed the proper respect for her elders, and was known to be a hard worker. She was, in short, an ideal traditional daughter-in-law. Anselmo and Carmen established their household on don Miguel's Rahum lands. Once married, Anselmo could begin fulfilling the vow Augustina had made for him as a child to be a *fariseo*, something very dear to Augustina's heart.

The same year (1940), Dominga left Jesús Suárez, running away with her two sons to Augustina. She said that she had finally had enough and she wanted to live in Potam where her children could go to school. Jesús was delighted to get rid of Dominga, as he was unusually enamored of a sixteen-year-old girl named Angela, who was said to be a half-wit but very sweet and pretty. He built the girl a nice two-story house and provided her with everything she asked for. This affair was unlike any of his previous affairs or alliances in that he was intensely emotionally involved. Other women temporarily ceased to interest him. His previous affairs had been of such gargantuan proportions and had achieved such notoriety that the entire community watched this one with great interest.

After all that she had suffered at his hands, Dominga felt strongly about Jesús, and most of what she felt was hatred. The old fascination was not entirely gone, however, and she prayed that Angela's two-story house would fall down. Her prayers were answered during a rainstorm—unfortunately while little Jesús and Lázaro were visiting their father. Dominga was ashamed for having wished such a dreadful thing and asked God to forgive her; at the same time she gave thanks to God that no one had been hurt. Although Angela became Dominga's champion with Jesús, telling him he had treated her badly and should be supporting his children, he never gave Dominga or their children a single centavo. Angela occasionally brought Dominga a bucket of masa out of pity.

Pregnant with her last child when she left Jesús, Dominga gave birth to her only daughter, Julia, with Augustina again serving as midwife. The household now consisted of don Miguel, Augustina, Milo, Guillermo, Dominga, and the three Suárez children. Dominga decided that the best way to contribute to the family income was to become a peddler, inasmuch as the people of Potam were not rich enough to need cooks or washerwomen. While Augustina continued to run the expanded household firmly and capably, Dominga joined other women who took things to sell in Guaymas on an old truck owned by an Arab named Ismael. His red sweater matched his red truck, and he would smilingly say in his rudimentary Spanish, "Yo rojo, carro rojo" ("I red, car red").

Normally it took two days to get a load ready, so as a rule Dominga went to Guaymas every third day. *Petates* bought for a peso apiece in Potam sold for $2.50 to $3.00 in Guaymas. If she could collect two or three dozen *petates*, her profits could be as much as 90 pesos, but they rarely were. Eggs, squash, corn, beans, live chickens, and little pigs were also taken for resale. The truck collected the women and their produce early in the morning, delivering them to the downtown market in Guaymas. If they were lucky, everything sold at the market. Otherwise, they would have to walk from door to door, trying to sell what they had brought before the truck left in the late afternoon.

Although she found the life tiring and told several stories about walking the streets with heavy loads, too poor to eat, and the disappointments of the days she did not sell everything, she enjoyed the freedom from household drudgery (especially cheese making), and she found the marketplace far more stimulating than the lonely rancheria in Palo Parado. One of the larger operators among the peddlers, a fat woman named Tila, began having Dominga do her washing, ordinarily paying her not in cash but in other things such as circus tickets. Dominga was pleased to attend any public diversion. Peddling was suspended each year after the harvest because the women spent several weeks gleaning the crops traditionally left "for the pueblo," a task called *pepinando*. Baskets of garbanzos, beans, corn, wheat, or vegetables were gathered for use by the family or for sale.

This way of life continued for several years, during which time Dominga was absent from the household most days. Her only major household chore was hauling buckets and buckets of water for Augustina. In spite of the money she earned and the crops produced on don Miguel's land, the family resources were strained to the limit to feed so many people. Not infrequently they had only one meal a day and the children went to bed hungry. Clothes for the children were an eternal problem, and their failure to attend school was attributed to their outgrown and tattered clothing. None of her children learned to read and write in school, although after Anselmo married, he taught himself from books sent by Rosalio Moisés.

Don Miguel Molino died in 1944, leaving his Rahum lands to Anselmo and Milo, and the Potam house and large lot to Augustina. His death caused the family fortunes to deteriorate and a time of real hardship ensued, comparable to the years in Cocorit following Cajeme's death. Augustina felt she could no longer run the household and raise the children without help, so she asked Dominga to stay at home. Dominga readily agreed because the trips to Guaymas left her in a constant state of exhaustion, especially after the food supply diminished. Anselmo had to go deeply in debt to a shopkeeper named Adolfo León in order to buy seed for planting and other essentials for the farm work. Much of the proceeds of the harvest went to pay off this debt. Dominga remembered walking to the fields and watching Anselmo, thin as a rail, work all day without a bite to eat. Augustina, of course, continued to arrange everyone's lives, making a vow when little Lázaro was sick that he would serve as a *fariseo*, curing Dominga's and Anselmo's children when they were sick, and raising all the children the "hard" way. She served as a *madrina* to *chapayekas* (one of the categories of the *fariseo* ceremonial society) every Lenten season and baptized many children.

Dominga's old fascination with Jesús Suárez finally disappeared during these two or three years of hardship. She repeatedly described how he walked down the road, pockets bulging with bills and jingling with coins, ignoring his starving children as he passed. Nor did she escape the maliciousness of his sister, Pancha, who "talked badly" about Dominga, spreading gossip and verbally assaulting her when they met. The ultimate indignity occurred in 1946 when Pancha appeared before the village council to accuse Dominga and Isabel Flores (Pancha's own daughter) of sending anonymous letters containing *cosas cochinas* (bad things). She requested that the two accused women be jailed in Guaymas. They were placed in the Potam *guardia* under guard, apparently scheduled to be moved to Guaymas. Augustina asked a man to accompany her to Vicam, where she talked to General Guerrero, the head of the Mexican military detachment in the Río Yaqui. The fact that she was Cajeme's widow seems to have carried some weight, and after she explained that Pancha was a bad woman, the general ordered Dominga and Isabel released.

Milo Romero, Dominga's second-oldest living son, was very different from his older brother. Anselmo was hard-working, obedient, serious, deeply religious, never played around with women or drank, and worked at becoming literate. His family was growing satisfactorily. Milo also worked hard on the Rahum lands, but he enjoyed drinking and fast horses, and he was walking with Candelaria Ríos. About the time of don Miguel's death, he brought Candelaria home to live with him. Augustina, as sensitive to his easygoing charm as anyone else, did not entirely approve of the couple's refusal to marry in the church, nor did she approve of Candelaria, who was not in the least like the well-trained, traditional bride chosen for Anselmo.

Candelaria described her life as being completely dominated by Augustina. Whereas she had expected to continue going to dances and elsewhere with Milo, she found she had to stay at home and do the work Augustina assigned her. Although Dominga was actually her mother-in-law, it was Augustina who filled the role; and a hard mother-in-law she was. Their first two children were claimed by Augustina, and Candelaria recalled her frustration at having no control over her own children. Both of these children died, and Candelaria said pointedly, "They died in Augustina's hands, not mine." Dominga stood up for, fought for, and talked for Candelaria to Augustina, Milo, and anyone else who criticized her, with the result that Candelaria and Dominga established a warm relationship that lasted until Dominga's death. In fact, Candelaria said that the only reason she lived with Milo for so many years was because of Dominga.

Jesús and Francisca Valencia lived across the road from Augustina's house. One day in 1946 when she was alone in her house, Francisca had one of her recurring seizures (perhaps epilepsy) and fell into the *pretil* (fireplace). It was believed that if she had been found immediately, she could have been cured. She died, however, of massive burns that same night. Dominga attended her friend's *velorio* and *novena*. A few days later, Jesús came to ask Dominga to live with him, saying that they both had many small children and an alliance would be mutually beneficial. Dominga refused on the grounds that it would be wrong to live together so soon after Francisca's death. Augustina agreed that such a precipitate arrangement would be improper.

Augustina's death in 1947 was deeply felt by Dominga and all of the grandchildren she had raised, especially Anselmo. It was as though the family's foundation had been removed. Dominga became the acknowledged head of the household and family, a position she filled until her death. But she acted very differently from the traditional Augustina. Her personality simply did not allow her to assume a stern, authoritarian role toward her daughters-in-law, for example, but she did feel it was her responsibility to continue Augustina's "hard" regime of child training. She did this with less recourse to the whip that had been Augustina's badge of authority, however.

Shortly after Augustina's death, the *cumpleaño* for Francisca Valencia's death was held. The next week, Jesús Valencia sent two of his children across the road with a bucket of masa and the request that Dominga make tortillas. In accepting this charge, she accepted his offer to live together, and he immediately moved his family to the house that was now Dominga's.

Jesús Valencia was the best of all Dominga's men. He seldom drank and he was a hard worker. The gold earrings she wore for the rest of her life were a present from him. With such a large household—and there must have been nearly twenty people living there as a result of the two combined families—life was not easy. Dominga had only her daughter-in-law, Candelaria, as an adult female helper. Food and other things were neither abundant nor luxuriant, but there was enough to eat and most of the children had at least one presentable set of clothes. Jesús was a good provider, walking as far as Huirivis to cut firewood. The next seven years with Jesús were the most comfortable of Dominga's life in the Río Yaqui.

Unfortunately, Dominga found Jesús rather dull. She felt mildly guilty that she could not become enamored of such a good man who was so obviously enamored of her. Nor did her children respect him or behave properly toward him, something Dominga regarded as "a pity." Her own life involved

constant hard work with few frivolous compensations, and she
sometimes became sad and punished the children more severely than previously. Occasionally she whipped one of the
boys for disobedience, but she was strictest with her daughter,
Julia. One day Julia had not ground her quota of corn, and
Dominga reacted by beating her and tying her to the metate for
the remainder of the day. This was not a story Dominga volunteered. Other women, including Julia, supplied the details. A
neighbor who saw the crumpled Julia on the floor went in and
untied her, telling Dominga that was no way to treat her
daughter.

The fortunes of Jesús Suárez were reversed in the late 1940s.
His Palo Parado crops were less successful and he could no
longer attract women. He owned two houses near the Potam
church, one of which had long been occupied by his shrewish
sisters. Now he was forced to live with them in order to have a
woman to cook for him, since he did not wish to return to his
wife in Obregón, nor did she want him, and Angela had long
since shown him the door. His financial ruin occurred when he
lost his large herd of cows. The herd had been driven from
Potam to Agua Caliente by cowboys in his employment. A few
days later, he sent his (and Dominga's) son Lázaro to Agua
Caliente with a substantial sum of cash tied in a red bandana to
be delivered to Nicho, the head vaquero. Lázaro did as he was
told and returned. Jesús Suárez then rode to Agua Caliente to
check on his herd. Nicho said, "Your cows? What cows? What
are you talking about? See—these cows all carry my brand.
You don't have any papers to prove they are yours." There
was nothing he could do, or he did nothing, and Nicho kept
the money as well. Jesús Suárez returned to Potam a poor
man.

Now he wandered around Potam in old clothes, no longer
sleek and fat with pockets full of money. His sisters did not
take good care of him, and at times he had to beg for food.
Dominga's most often retold story concerned his coming to her
kitchen window and asking for a tortilla. She was frequently
standing in the same kitchen as she related this episode, and
she would act out how she silently handed him the tortillas
wrapped in paper. In 1953 he got sick. He sold one of his

houses for a few pesos but still lacked money to be cured. His final illness was spent lying on a petate on the floor listening to his sisters fight. Pancha told him she was going to bury him in a cow lot. Knowing that he was seldom fed, Julia, who had always liked her father, took him a plate of beans and a few tortillas. After hungrily gulping his food, he asked his son, Jesús, also on good terms with him, to buy him a soda. Soon his body became bloated and he died that night. It was said that he died alone. "Dios lo castigó" ("God punished him"), Dominga observed.

Jesús's sisters refused to dress the body for burial, sending in the middle of the night for Dominga's son, Milo Romero, who in turn called his half-brother, Jesús Suárez. Together they washed and dressed the body, finding under his arm two hundred pesos, which they brought home to Dominga. She, however, delivered the money to Manuel Suárez, the only one of old Jesús's legitimate children who had ever been nice to her. Young Jesús selected the burial *padrinos*. Since old Jesús had been a blue *fiestero* in Potam, the current blue *fiesteros* were notified. They tied a blue ribbon around his wrist and attended the *velorio*. Although none of his family had helped him when he was sick, the *velorio* was well attended by his wife, their legitimate children, his sisters, and other relatives. Dominga, however, remembered that the last food he received on this earth came from her kitchen. In reviewing the men in her life, she said, "The good times with Jesús were the best," adding quickly that bad times with him were the worst.

Shortly after Jesús Suárez's death, the thirteen-year-old Julia ran away to live with Cayetano Amado in Oros, and Milo moved his consort and children to the rancheria where he worked as a vaquero. Dominga was, therefore, left with no other females in the house when Jesús Valencia became ill. He became more paralyzed every day until, by the time he died a month later, he was unable to move. Dominga walked for miles seeking a *curandero* who could cure this kind of illness, but they all said nothing could be done. Dominga buried old Jesús properly with a nice *velorio* and *novena*. The Valencia children left Dominga's household, returning to their father's house across the road. Without the support Jesús Valencia had so generously provided, Dominga's life once again became hard, and her remaining children often went hungry.

The final phase of Dominga's life began in the latter half of the 1950s. She formed no more alliances with men, but settled into her role as mainstay and pivot of her family. For an interval, her household dwindled to herself and her three youngest sons. Jesús and Lázaro were away from home as much as they were there; having inherited a share of old Jesús's Palo Parado lands, they preferred to stay there when they were working in the fields. At other times they were walking with girls or drinking or attending dances.

Only Guillermo stayed close to Dominga. He worked on the Suárez lands for his half-brothers or hired out to other men when he could get a job. Even as a child he had been sad and "crazy," and as he grew older, he became worse. New moon was a particularly bad time; he became highly disturbed then. At one point the local doctor had him committed to the asylum in Hermosillo, but Dominga felt that the enforced association with really crazy people only made him worse, and she arranged to have him brought home again. One of Dominga's deepest regrets was that Guillermo had inherited no land. If he had had land, perhaps he would have been less crazy, and whether this was so or not, he would have lived more comfortably.

Slowly, Dominga's household again increased in size. The runaway Julia gave Dominga her first baby born in Oros because she left Cayetano to go to Bataconsica and work as a maid. In later years she gave Dominga two more babies when she left their father to go to Guaymas. Dominga's half-brother in Torim, Rosalio Moisés, also gave her his son to raise when he left Sonora for the United States. When Jesús formed an alliance, he brought his bride home to Dominga's house. Dominga remarked that she ended up like Augustina, raising other people's children.

When the Ejido system was inaugurated for the Yaqui tribe, it was no longer necessary for Anselmo to live on his Rahum lands, because the new system of farming involved Yaqui *sociedades*, or cooperatives, contracting with the Banco Ejidal for seed, irrigation water, fertilizer, and labor. Anselmo therefore built a small adobe house on a corner of Dominga's large lot for his family, by this time consisting of six children.

Anselmo, who had not lived near Dominga since he was a small child, rapidly became the most important person in her life. After his wife, Carmen, left him for another man, giving him her last illegitimate baby as a parting gift, Anselmo had one or two bad years. His oldest daughter, who should have taken over the household, elected to go with her mother, leaving him with five of his own children and the baby, for whom he had to cook and wash. It was Dominga who came to his aid, dividing her time between the two adjacent households.

Dominga had never particularly liked Carmen and was not sorry to see her go. Nor did she seriously object to the way in which Anselmo restructured his life, for Dominga was always tolerant of the transgressions of the young. At the age of thirty-six, Anselmo began walking with a thirteen-year-old Mayo girl named Refugia Moroyoki. When she became pregnant, he formally asked her parents for permission to live with her. His new alliance with a young, modern girl symbolized his changed life style. He approved of her modern clothes and in fact insisted that she not wear old-style skirts and blouses. Spanish was decreed to be the language of his household. Formerly a deeply religious man, he stopped dancing as a *fariseo* and decided that the Yaqui religion with its expensive ceremonies that encouraged drunkenness was one of the causes for the plight of his people.

Dominga felt it was a pity that the children of the new alliance did not learn to speak Yaqui properly. She was not happy that Anselmo turned his back on religion, refusing to accept that he could become an unbeliever. While she was not delighted with her new daughter-in-law, she nonetheless admitted that the young Refugia did very well at running such a large household.

Anselmo was definitely happier, and his fortunes steadily improved. He was appointed secretary of Potam, his lands prospered, and he obtained a position with the Banco Ejidal overseeing the newly formed Yaqui Cattle Cooperative. He became the most important and affluent of Dominga's sons.

Never one to drink his life away, he could nevertheless hold his liquor as a man should. Although certain relatives said he had become a *yori* and was getting rich through deals he could arrange as secretary of Potam and an employee of the Banco Ejidal, Dominga defended him fiercely, pointing out how good he was to her, how he got his brother a job, and how many people he supported. When he began going with other women, Dominga just said that he was acting like a man.

By the mid-1960s, there were four related households on Dominga's lot. Guillermo had established his own home, and Julia, who had returned from Guaymas with her current consort, lived in the fourth. Dominga was therefore living in the middle of a large network of her descendants. She developed a pattern of daily visits in each household, the only adult of the family to do so. Lázaro, the only one of her sons who lived elsewhere in Potam, visited her every afternoon, as did Manuel Suárez when he was in town. Milo, who lived outside of Potam, invariably called on Dominga when he came to the pueblo. She thus received more family news than anyone else. She also maintained more *compadre* relationships and visited in more households than did any other members of her family, with the result that she was a primary source of external news as well. News, gossip, and information were the main scarce resources she was able to manipulate, and she did so consciously and deliberately. Although she could not read or write, she was an inveterate user of the postal service, dictating letters and having replies read to her, thereby extending her informational resources.

Sharing was a way of life to Dominga. Everything, down to the food on her plate, was shared. Children stood by her as she ate, knowing she would pop choice morsels into their mouths. Grandchildren in need of school supplies or clothes sought her aid, if she had anything to give, or her support for their need when they approached their father. Visitors would be given a parting gift if possible. No one who shares on this scale can accumulate much in the way of possessions.

The quality of the hospitality offered and received was of supreme importance to Dominga, forming one of the subjects she talked about most. It was inconceivable to her that any acceptable visitor in her house would receive less than the best she had to offer. Since the younger women of the family held different, and, in Dominga's opinion, lower standards, she would be disturbed for days if someone called on her while she was absent, knowing the visitor had not been properly received.

Conversational abilities were greatly appreciated and admired by Dominga. "How I talked," "how he talked," "he really knows how to talk," or "she never could talk well" punctuated her inevitable rehash of every visiting session.

In none of these life stories does the joking and humor of Yaqui life show through. Even happy women like Dominga were matter-of-fact about their past, tending to stress tragedy and hardship as more memorable, more worth telling about. The story of Dominga would be incomplete without noting these prominent components of her personality and behavior. She was a superb mimic, giving classic portrayals of a rich, fat, swaggering Jesús Suárez; a stiff-backed school teacher in Vicam; or a duded-up vaquero in tight blue jeans. Her stories, often acted out, could reduce an audience to tears of laughter.

Most of the relationships she assiduously maintained were with relatives and *compadres*. One or two friendships with women her own age that lasted throughout her Potam years seemed to have been unusually significant, being surpassed only by Dominga's emotional commitment to Augustina and her own sons. The Castro sisters in particular offered Dominga an oasis from hardship and drudgery. She felt free to visit them regularly, always assured of a respectful reception and high standards of hospitality. They knew enough about each other's lives after forty-odd years to be sympathetic about drunken husbands, lazy daughters-in-law, and other mutual problems, but they were sufficiently distant to be noncompetitive and relatively uninvolved in any particular dilemma, an ideal combination. Dominga said that when things got unbearable at home, she could go to the Castro household and temporarily change her world.

Throughout most of her life, Dominga claimed to have been ignorant of Yaqui religion, an ignorance that must have been relative, because Augustina was deeply involved in religious

observances. Nonetheless, Dominga saw no public Yaqui rituals until the Revolution, and most of the ones she attended
for many years she viewed as exciting but essentially secular
events. Fiestas were fun, but she felt the Yaqui religion was
"dumb." In the last fifteen or twenty years of her life, these
attitudes changed. As her son Anselmo put it, she not only
believed, she lived the Yaqui religion. Her extensive *compadre*
network was built during these years as she baptized children,
placed rosaries, and served as a death *madrina*. Although Augustina made religious vows for sick children, Dominga never
did, preferring more pragmatic means of curing. At the end of
her life, she was called upon to serve in the *fiestero* system, first
as an assistant to a blue *fiestera* of Potam and then as a blue
fiestera of Rahum. When she was told in 1971 that she had
terminal cancer, her biggest worry was that she would not live
to complete her vow as a *fiestera*.

Now that death was imminent, she turned her attention to
dying with the enthusiasm that characterized her approach to
life. She reviewed her life, especially trying to recall all the
places she had left hair, for a person must, after death, collect
all the hair he or she has lost. She decided she would only
have to go to the *pretils*, because she always carefully burned
her hair.

Anselmo insisted that Dominga move to his house because
he thought Jesús was not taking good care of her. By Christmas of 1971, she was bedridden. On New Year's Eve, while
her several sons were out getting drunk, she called two of her
daughters-in-law to her side to plan her *velorio* and funeral.
She named the people whom she wanted to serve as the burial
padrinos, including three women who had served in the same
capacity for Augustina. Over the next two weeks, these people
were summoned by family members to Dominga's bedside so
she could personally ask them to accept this charge. Next she
had the daughters-in-law make the religious habit she had
vowed to wear if she recovered. Then she sent for old Anselmo
Romero, her legal husband, and when he arrived, she asked
his pardon for living with other men since they parted in 1926.

Finally, she sent for all her children (including Ramón, who
had seldom seen her since he was a baby), their consorts,

children, and grandchildren. When they assembled, she talked to them, making each one promise to marry in the church before he or she died. She asked Milo to stop drinking because it made him fight and was bad for his family. Milo said sadly that he could not promise—he was too far gone—but he would try. She put all her children "in the hands of Anselmo, for he is good and he will help you." Anselmo accepted the mantle of family head.

Dominga died on January 20, 1972, surrounded by no fewer than fifty close family members. Her *madrinas* placed a white lace dress over the *habito* she had chosen to die in. The *velorio* was held in a specially built ramada at Anselmo's house. Several *ahijados* placed rosaries on her body. Her sons, openly crying, took the wooden coffin from the *padrinos* and carried it themselves, as a sign of their respect, to the cemetery in front of the church, where she was buried next to Augustina.

Antonia Valenzuela, in her adult life, represented a not uncommon Yaqui behavioral constellation, at least for older and middle-aged women, in that she was sad and silent, directing her attention almost exclusively toward her own household. Her introverted nature and passive role and the fact that her life was not dramatic made her the most difficult of the informants to translate onto the printed page. Because of a series of historical accidents, her life developed along very different lines from those of the other two informants who were born at La Colorada Mine (Chepa Moreno and Dominga Ramírez). She spent sixty-seven of her seventy-seven years in Arizona.

Tough and aggressive as a child, she apparently did not manifest the sad, passive, silent syndrome until her teens; it was firmly established by the time of her arranged marriage. Retrospective life history data, unfortunately, provide little basis for evaluating the scope of or reason for the behavioral changes attributed to Antonia.

As an adult, Antonia operated selectively in the Arizona Yaqui culture, considering her household to be her proper niche. She became a stay-at-home woman, leaving the physical limits of the household as seldom as possible. Here, she more than adequately fulfilled those aspects of the woman's role concerned with caring endlessly for her family. Most of her relatives described her as never one to gossip or talk badly, and as being a stable, discreet, dependable, and predictable woman with deeply internalized precepts of obligations. In later life, these qualities, plus her lack of mobility, encouraged relatives to seek her aid more often than they approached others of her economic status, and she invariably responded appropriately within the limits of her means.

ANTONIA VALENZUELA

Her own deepest emotional tie was to the grandmother who raised her, with slightly weaker bonds to her father and brother. For the husband of her arranged marriage, she felt little respect or affection; her relationship with her second husband involved respect but little affection. Although she said she loved her children when they were small, "as a mother does," it is difficult to judge the depth of her emotional investment. The children did not perceive her relationship with them as having a strong emotional dimension. All but one of her children left her care by the time they were twelve or fourteen years of age; four of her five daughters remained fairly independent of Antonia, with the result that any existing emotional bonds received scant reinforcement. Her son, however, returned repeatedly to Antonia during his adult years, creating the strongest attachment of her mature life. Her relationships with her grandchildren, especially the eight she raised, were considerably warmer than those with her own children at comparable ages.

Spanish did not come easily to Antonia, who was comfortable only when speaking the Yaqui language. Most of her life history data were collected during interviews at which some of her daughters and other relatives served as interpreters, usually adding substantial amounts of information. With some effort on both sides, Antonia and I could communicate directly, and her understanding of Spanish was good enough that I could repeat my version of the interpreted accounts and observe her reaction.

In previous years, Antonia had refused to serve as an informant for other anthropologists. The long relationship between my father and her brother was the only reason she agreed to work with me. Actually quite well informed on Yaqui culture and Yaqui affairs, she received little credit for being a knowledgeable elder because of her customary silence. Her willingness to cooperate surprised all who knew her— indeed, the word astounded is not too strong to express the widespread reaction. People came to the interview sessions just to hear her talk. A nephew who interacted very little with Antonia said that if he had realized she knew so much, he would have talked to her. A frequently repeated remark was "Never before have we heard her talk so much." Her daughters regularly attended our sessions, not only for the novelty of hearing a normally silent woman talk, but to find out about their mother's past. They said that if I had not come to talk to Antonia, she would have died without telling them anything. Antonia responded to such comments by saying no one had ever talked to her like this before or asked her about her past.

As an informant, Antonia took her responsibility seriously; she had great patience and commendable recall. Never did she initiate topics of conversation, but she responded fully to questions and to the points raised by her daughters. Like Dominga Ramírez, she refused direct payment, accepting gifts and reciprocating.

Four of Antonia's five daughters contributed their own life stories, as did a granddaughter. Two of the older daughters provided enough information for detailed life stories; information from the two youngest daughters and the granddaughter allowed only sketchier treatment. For purposes of this study, a single, combined interpretive narrative of these several women has been compiled in order to reduce the substantial amount of repetition.

All of Antonia's children spent their entire lives in Arizona. Their knowledge of Yaqui history was not extensive, being limited to rather vague information about the Yaqui wars, persecutions, and deportations that forced many Yaquis to flee Sonora for Arizona. The Sonoran background was remote, and famous Yaqui leaders and battles were either unfamiliar or were just names. To Antonia's children, Yaqui culture was Arizona Yaqui culture, and they had no detailed information about Yaqui civil organization, Yaqui law, or other institutional aspects of Yaqui culture not transplanted north of the border.

Their knowledge of Yaqui religion was adequate for their minimal involvement in the formal religious structure. More significant to at least some of the daughters were the less institutionalized super-

natural belief systems centering on curing and witchcraft, but also including animal lore, luck, and omens. The latter beliefs affected the behavior of three of the daughters in rather decisive ways, whereas Antonia, who was adequately informed on these subjects, did not pay much more attention to them than she did to institutional religion. Antonia believed in God and the saints and witches and omens, but she did not believe that she personally had ever been bewitched. On the other hand, two of her daughters believed they had been, and one of them used witchcraft as an explanation for events with some frequency.

While Antonia was a classic example of the "sad" behavioral constellation, none of her daughters or granddaughters was described as sad or passive, and none had a personality, role, or behavioral characteristics that lent themselves to the behavioral constellations defined earlier, being neither good nor bad, happy nor sad, but falling somewhere in the middle.

When I returned to Pascua in 1975 to check the content of the narratives, Antonia Valenzuela was dead. The manuscript was read, in Spanish translation, to the oldest daughter, Amelia, who had been a primary informant and who had been present at many of the sessions with her mother and sisters. Loreta, another primary informant, could not participate because her oldest son died the day we arrived. For part of the verification session, another sister, Manuela, who had not participated in the original life history project, was present.

By and large, they approved of the narrative, but one major discrepancy arose between data collected earlier and what was said, in 1975, to be "true." This concerned Antonia's second husband, Perfecto Valencia, and his affiliation with a Protestant church. My notes of the interview sessions of earlier years record Perfecto as a convert to the Pascua Protestant church, and this was seen by some of the women of the family and interpreted by myself as consistent with his world view. Only his youngest daughter, Ramona, then maintained that he was not a convert. In 1975, both Amelia and Manuela asserted that he was never a convert, and Manuela, especially, felt that she was an authority on the Protestant membership of Pascua because her mother-in-law was a moving force in that group. I have chosen to leave the narrative as written, mainly because the greatest relevance of whether he was or was not a convert arises in reference to his relationship with his oldest daughter, Martina, and she was unavailable for the checking of the narrative.

Manuela's reactions to the narrative were interesting in other ways. She was highly critical of data provided by all of her sisters except Amelia, being particularly negative about accounts of witchcraft, saying, "My sister is crazy to believe in such things" and "You can't believe anything she says." She was also critical of references to her own life, feeling that she would have told it differently, as I am sure she would, but she did not say that any of what is included was wrong.

The question of reliability seems more serious for this narrative, partly because it is a composite with several people's memories and interpretations involved. In addition, the fact that these women had worked on producing life histories was, by 1975, a subject of controversy among a few people. Amelia was extremely annoyed when she related how a cousin had been telling people the life history would be no good because Amelia and her sisters knew nothing, and furthermore, they were liars. The cousin, a ceremonial and political leader, was said by Amelia to know a lot about the Yaquis, "but he does not know what happened to me, and that is what I told you about."

Another man called on Amelia during one of the checking sessions, largely because he was curious about my presence. When he found out about the life histories, he said, "If you want Yaqui histories, I will take you to my uncle. Now he has a history. Amelia knows nothing. Her husband is a lifer in prison. You can't trust anything she says." These evaluations seem to me to reflect two things: factionalism, which in Yaqui society is real and deep (the life histories are but another piece of fuel for the flames of divisive issues), and the universal attitude that the only Yaqui history of any interest is that concerned with the Yaqui wars or other dramatic events, which are seen as falling largely in the domain of older men. I have made a special effort to crosscheck the information in this composite narrative and to indicate which informant's views are being presented when that seemed pertinent.

Antonia Valenzuela was born on May 3, 1893, according to the birth date on her U.S. Immigration card. Her memories of life at La Colorada Mine closely paralleled other accounts, although she provided somewhat different versions of household composition and other details. The most interesting discrepancy concerns the name and ancestry of her remarkable grandmother. Her brother, Rosalio Moisés, gave the grandmother's name as María Daumier Valencia Palos, specifically emphasizing her French ancestry. Antonia had never heard the name "Daumier" but said that María was fathered by a Spanish *patrón*, whence came María's striking light coloration that was passed on to her daughter, Camilda, and her granddaughter, Dominga Ramírez, but not to Antonia.

María was the dominant woman in the household at La Colorada Mine, capably directing the lives of the younger women (her daughter and daughter-in-law) and the several children. All the children in her care, including Antonia, said, "This is the woman who raised me," and all descriptions of María portray a happy, vivacious, gregarious, talkative, magnetic person who was a good *curandera*, a good Yaqui, and a good woman.

In La Colorada, the family had plenty of food and an abundance of nice clothes. The hard-working Yaqui miners and their families sustained a pleasant way of life. Antonia had to perform a few chores such as carrying water, but much of the time she played with other children. Antonia was repeatedly described as a *maldita* in her childhood because of her disobedience and fighting with other children. She seems to have been the only child punished regularly at La Colorada by María, and once her father, Miguel Palos, spanked her for tormenting a smaller child. Her mother, Cecelia Hurtado, never punished her and, in fact, seems to have had little to do with her.

When Antonia was perhaps seven, the 1900 Mazocoba massacre changed their lives. Miguel Palos, Cecelia, and their small baby moved to another mine; shortly thereafter Cecelia left Miguel for another man. Since Cecelia lived in Sonora until her death in 1950 and Antonia in Arizona, they were never in the same place and Antonia never saw her mother again. Other relatives also left the household for other mines. The remaining household members moved to Hermosillo. For perhaps five years, the family unit consisted of María Valencia Palos; her husband, Abelardo Cochemea; their daughter, Camilda, with her young daughter (it is believed that Camilda's husband had been killed by Mexican soldiers); Chepa Moreno (Abelardo's niece); Rosalio Moisés; and Antonia. Old Abelardo got a job at La Playita orchard, where they established the household in one of the several houses provided for workers.

Now everyone had to work to survive. María became a washerwoman, Camilda a tortilla peddler, and the children helped in both enterprises. Their standard of living dropped and it became a struggle to feed the large family on basic beans and tortillas. No longer were there canned jelly and other treats from the company store, and their fine dresses, silk *rebozos*, and shoes and socks gave way to the traditional cotton skirts and blouses, and huaraches. Under the more severe subsistence and social pressures, María turned into a "hard" woman, showing the happy aspects of her personality less often and severely punishing the children more frequently. As had earlier been the case, Antonia was punished more than the others.

Old Abelardo was consistently described by those who knew him as a sad, passive, silent, hard-working man who did not drink or attend fiestas. Rosalio Moisés said Abelardo was a nonbeliever in the Yaqui religion, and he doubted that Abelardo even believed in God. Antonia (and Chepa Moreno) agreed that he did not participate in any religious ritual, but they strongly defended him as a believer. Antonia could not remember hearing old Abelardo talk except to other men who came to visit.

For the women and children, the daily routine was soon established. María rose first, making the fire and beginning to prepare breakfast. Antonia and Chepa washed the *nixtamal* María had put to soak the night before and then ground it into masa. Camilda, María, and Chepa made several dozen tortillas and taught Antonia the art. Her first efforts were thick, crooked tortillas reserved for family use. Breakfast about 9:00 a.m. was as substantial as resources permitted, running to *chicharrones* with frijoles, *atole*, tomatoes with green chilis, fresh tortillas, and coffee when possible, and tortillas and coffee during leaner times.

In midmorning, María turned to washing in the irrigation ditch, aided by those girls who remained at home. Every two or three days María walked to town to deliver clean clothes and pick up dirty ones. Camilda daily walked five miles from La Playita into one of the Hermosillo markets to peddle tortillas. One of the children had to accompany her, partly as a chaperone—because Camilda was an attractive young woman with an eye for men—and partly because a lone Yaqui woman was subject to insults and other indignities. The usual reaction to these insults was to ignore the unpleasantries and remove oneself from the scene. When Antonia went along, however, her reaction was less passive. Small Mexican boys seem to have delighted in calling out insults, a favorite one being "Yaquis eat horses." As an old woman, Antonia still got angry remembering such taunts. Unless restrained by Camilda or María when such comments were made, she whipped a slingshot and bag of rocks out of her blouse and retaliated. Her aim was extremely accurate.

One day Antonia accompanied Camilda to Parián market. A Mexican woman, apparently jealous of Camilda's striking good looks, a definite asset in selling tortillas to the soldiers who frequented the market, began a fight which, while heated, remained verbal. Antonia, however, located the woman's daughter and waded in with fists flying. Antonia remembered the successful subjugation of her foe with a great deal of satisfaction, even though she was beaten on the spot by Camilda for causing trouble and again by María when they returned home.

Upon occasion, both Chepa and Antonia would be sent into Hermosillo to carry messages, deliver washing, or for other reasons. Antonia remembered Chepa as exceedingly timid and fearful, always ready to cry. To reach Hermosillo, they had to pass through Ranchito, where gangs of Mexican boys inevitably waited to hurl rocks and insults at Yaqui girls. Chepa began crying before they reached Ranchito in anticipation of the worst. Chepa's show of fear made her an obvious target, while the stern-faced Antonia, slingshot at the ready, was molested much less often.

A number of stories, told by people who knew Antonia as a
child and verified by Antonia, stressed her tough, aggressive,
disobedient, unrepentant behavior. She never cried after receiving severe beatings, and when asked if the punishment
had been justified, she always said no, which meant she was
punished again for the same offense. Chepa Moreno related
the time Antonia was told to look after Camilda's baby.
Antonia picked up the baby, looked it over carefully, announced it was *muy prieta* (very dark), and dropped it on the
floor. Although she was beaten with a leather whip, she
showed no sign of regret or repentance.

Chepa also told of the time María ordered Antonia to go with
Chepa on the burro to sell tortillas. Antonia refused, where-
upon María put Antonia bodily on the burro, tying the two
girls together with a rope. Antonia began fighting Chepa, the
burro bolted downhill, the girls fell off, and Antonia cut her
hand badly on an ax strapped to the burro. The rope loosened
and Antonia ran off into the brush to hide. After several hours
they located her—weak from the loss of blood. María first beat
her with a whip and then took her on burroback to a rancheria
near Magdalena so that Augustina Preciado could cure her.
This reference to Augustina Preciado is at odds with the
information concerning her whereabouts obtained from her
daughter, Dominga Ramíriz, but Chepa and Antonia independently identified Augustina as the *curandera*. Following
their three-day stay with Augustina, they attended the fiesta of
San Francisco in Magdalena, the whole trip being remembered
as the happiest time of the Hermosillo years, and the only time
Antonia was allowed to attend a fiesta.

Antonia's aggressiveness and bravery did not extend to the
Mexican soldiers who came to take Yaquis away for execution
or deportation. She did not mind seeing soldiers in the markets
or on the streets, and the tortilla clientele consisted mostly of
soldiers. But when they came to La Playita or were known to
be searching for Yaquis, Antonia was terrified. María directed
the children to hide in trees, the *monte* (brush), the fields, or
even the irrigation ditch when soldiers approached the house.
Antonia vividly remembered her fear that the soldiers would
find her and take her away, or that she would return to the

house to find that they had taken other members of the household.

Many of their acquaintances were arrested and deported, among them a famous *curandero* living in Ranchito named José Juan Bakasewa, to whom María had regularly taken Antonia for the curing of repeated seizures. Antonia had, from infancy, experienced periods of unconsciousness lasting from a few moments to two hours, sometimes accompanied by jerking movements. José Juan Bakasewa prepared medicine of herbs and *agua de tierra* (dirt water); after he was deported, María made the medicine.

Finally the long-feared day arrived. Soldiers came for Abelardo Cochemea, taking him under heavy guard to a *cuartel* in Hermosillo. María frantically and unsuccessfully visited all of their *patrones*, seeking their intervention to obtain his release. Antonia never saw Abelardo again because she was not allowed to accompany María and Camilda to the *cuartel* to take him food. They, however, were present when three or four weeks later he was marched to the train, never to be heard of again.

Once more the quality of their lives deteriorated, and, for Antonia, the next year or two were the hardest of her life in terms of physical deprivation. Without a man to work in the orange orchard, they could no longer occupy the worker's house at La Playita. María rented a small house in Ranchito and she and Camilda now had to provide all the livelihood; they redoubled their efforts at washing and tortilla peddling. Chepa by this time had been deported with her husband, so she was no longer available to help. Antonia washed clothes and ground corn from sunup to sundown. Food was scarce and they were often hungry, except at harvest time, when María took Antonia to glean leftover crops in the surrounding fields. Although they had to walk for miles carrying heavy sacks, they temporarily had enough to eat.

Aside from memories of hunger, continuous hard work, harsh punishment, and tattered clothes, Antonia related one other event from the period of their residence in Ranchito. She was shown a miniature metate and some tiny dishes that she was told had been left by the Surem, the dwarf-sized ancestors of the Yaquis. Because of this event, the story of the Surem assumed reality and importance to Antonia, and to those who scoffed at the legend, she said that she knew it was true for she had personally seen their small utensils.

Since the mines were visited regularly by soldiers looking for Yaquis, it became unsafe for Antonia's father, Miguel Palos, to work as a miner. After Cecelia left him, he joined the Sierra Yaqui soldiers, serving under General Sibalaume for several years and taking part in a number of battles against the Mexicans. Upon several occasions he visited the household at La Playita when he came to Hermosillo to get supplies, guns, and ammunition. It was because of Miguel's activities that old Abelardo was deported. Shortly after that event, Miguel fled to Arizona. Several months later, he sent for María and the rest of the family. By this time María had formed an alliance with a man, who escorted them on the trip. The United States Immigration officials must not have understood the name Antonia; they recorded her name as Gertrude Valenzuela. Once entered into official documents, it became her legal name. For some years, the household centered in the house Miguel Palos built in the Tucson Yaqui *barrio* of Barrio Anita. The household composition was much the same as it had been in Ranchito, with the exception of Miguel's periodic visits from the Arizona mines where he worked.

Allowed to attend school briefly, Antonia recalled the freedom of walking to school unattended, the respite from constant hard work at home, and the nice teachers as among the more pleasant experiences in her life. When María and Miguel decided that she was too old to be allowed to go to school, she protested their decision in her usual forthright manner, only to be told that girls should remain at home. What good would it do to learn how to read and write or to speak English?

Many Yaquis, among them Miguel and Rosalio, moved to Sasco when the smelter opened. María did not want to leave her house in Barrio Anita, and so Antonia was sent to Sasco to keep house for her father and brother. There Miguel found Tomás Muina (or Molina), an old Torim friend with whom he had served in the Sierra under General Sibalaume. Tomás, his wife, Carlota (a *cantora*), and several grown sons, some with families, lived in a large house. Tomás and Miguel decided that it would be a good idea if Antonia married one of Tomás's sons, an idea approved by Carlota and María, who made the actual plans without consulting Antonia. María selected the wedding *padrinos* and planned the whole affair.

Ignacio Villegas, as he was called at that time, was a large, dark, stocky man several years older than Antonia who had lived with a woman in Sonora, by whom he had two children before leaving her in Imuris to join his parents and brothers in Arizona. Since he had never been married in the church, he was free to marry Antonia. Antonia was sad to marry Ignacio, but after all, one had to do what the *mayores* (elders) said. The marriage in the big Tucson cathedral was followed by a large fiesta with *pascolas* at María's Barrio Anita house. Antonia seems to have been neutral and resigned, but María had the time of her life, even dancing as a *pascola* while men stuffed money in her dress.

It is unclear when Antonia ceased to be outspoken, forthright, and aggressive. The last story involving such behavior concerned her disappointment over being forced to leave school. Certainly by the time of her marriage she was generally regarded as sad, silent, and passive. From that time on, she was concerned almost exclusively with caring for her family. From all descriptions, she worked hard all day, every day. Hours and even days might pass without her speaking. She preferred not to leave her house and she made no comments during the life history interviews suggesting that she desired more freedom, wanted to have a good time, or in any way would have preferred an alternative life style. For whatever reasons and through whatever developmental stages, she firmly internalized those aspects of the woman's role centering on family care and maintenance.

Everyone except María returned to Sasco the morning after the wedding fiesta. Now Antonia lived in the large household presided over by her mother-in-law, Carlota. It is not clear if Antonia was the only younger woman, or merely the youngest daughter-in-law. In any event, Antonia seems to have taken over most of the household work under Carlota's direction. Carlota was very different from Antonia, a nonstop talker and extrovert, visiting freely in relatives' and *compadres'* homes, often staying with her children for weeks at a time. She was frequently called away to perform her duties as a *cantora* and many people asked her to baptize babies. Carlota's basic orientation was, therefore, external to the household, so that she was delighted to have a stay-at-home daughter-in-law. She was not an oppressive mother-in-law, although she did not hesitate to give directions or berate Antonia, but mostly she simply left Antonia to manage.

Tomás Muina was ordinarily a silent man whose main preoccupation was to return to Sonora and fight the Mexicans again. He reminded Antonia of old Abelardo Cochemea in Hermosillo, who was animated only when talking to other Yaqui men about fighting. Usually Tomás ignored Carlota's constant visiting and absence from the household, but when he got drunk, he would want to beat her, telling her she ought to stay home. Whenever this happened, Carlota would leave the house and walk rapidly down the street, staying just out of his reach, while he tried to hit her, yelling that she was a bad woman to "walk" so much. After one of these one-sided fights, Antonia reproached them both saying: "Why do you do this? You are moth *mayores.* You should not do this." Following each outburst, Carlota would stay home a few days, but soon she would be off on another visit.

Ignacio (or Nacho) Villegas was considered by the *mayores* to be a good husband because he was older, he was a good provider, and he could read and write in Spanish, having attended school in Hermosillo. Antonia soon discovered he had a violent temper (he was *muy corajudo*). Guns were a prominent part of his personal property and he usually carried a large pistol. He could hold his liquor; and while he drank substantial amounts, he was never characterized as a drunkard, because he held his job. Card playing with smelter coworkers in the local cantina filled his spare time. Associating with him little, except in bed, Antonia developed no great fondness for her husband.

Antonia was soon pregnant, a fact that occasioned no public comment. When she felt the time was near for the baby to be born, she got on the train alone and went to María in Barrio

Anita. Antonia said she never discussed her pregnancy or approaching delivery with Nacho or anyone else. María "knew" when she saw Antonia that the baby was due. Being a *curandera* and a *partera*, María fed her toasted tortillas and *atole* and gave her a medicinal drink. For the birth, María had Antonia hold onto a post in a squatting position until the baby was born—dead. María made the sign of the cross on the baby's forehead and said the words of baptism. Then she placed the afterbirth in a small *olla* and buried it far away from the house so that lightning would not strike the house, since lightning will strike where it is buried. Antonia was too weak and ill to be directly involved in the burial of her baby. María asked Juan Buanamea Ronquillo, who lived next door, to make a small wooden coffin. His wife, Lucía Cervantes, carried the baby to the cemetery, dug the little grave, and buried the baby. No *madrinas* or *padrinos* were selected, no ritual was carried out, and the baby was not named. Lucía Cervantes was not a relative or a *comadre* of María or Antonia. Rather, Juan Buanamea Ronquillo was a miner who had worked with Miguel Palos at La Colorada and more recently at the Arizona mines of Amole and Silver Bell. The two men had been card-playing and drinking friends for more than twenty years.

Minimal mention was made of the dead baby upon Antonia's return to Sasco. In due time, Antonia became pregnant again, and again she returned to María for the birth. The baby, born April 9, 1912, was named Amelia Villegas, because Villegas was the last name that Nacho was using at the time. María pierced the baby's ears, arranged for Carmen Matus to serve as Amelia's *madrina de pila*, and selected the *maestro* to perform the baptism. Much the same procedure was followed for the birth of Antonia's next baby, Nicolás Villegas, who was born in 1914.

One evening in 1916, Nacho was playing cards in the cantina when a man came in with a prostitute from one of the local houses. Another man asked Nacho if he could borrow his gun because he wanted to shoot the prostitute. Nacho's refusal precipitated a fight that rapidly expanded into a brawl, spilling out into the street. In the confusion of several drawn pistols and knives, Nacho shot the woman, whom he said he had never seen before, in the eye. Knowing that he would be arrested if he were caught, he left that night on foot for Sonora. For the next two years he remained in Imuris, where he had lived with his previous woman and their two children. Antonia did not know, nor did she apparently care, whether he returned to that woman or lived with his sister, who also resided in Imuris.

Nacho had been gone only a few days (or weeks) when Antonia gave birth to another daughter, Manuela. This time she did not go to María, but remained in Sasco; Carlota helped at the birth. Manuela was named Muina (or Molina) because Nacho decided it would be wise, after the shooting, to cease using his mother's name of Villegas and assume the name several of his brothers already used.

At the time Manuela was born, no Yaqui *maestro* lived in Sasco. She was therefore baptized by a Catholic priest in the tent that served as a church for his visits. Antonia described the makeshift altar made of a table covered with a white cloth on which stood a statue of the Virgin Mary and over which hung a crucifix. Lino Tecu, a well-known *pascola*, and Locaria Valencia were chosen by Carlota as the baptismal *padrinos*.

After this event, Antonia decided to move to Barrio Anita with her three children in preference to remaining with her in-laws. Although Miguel and Rosalio sent some money from Sasco to María, there was not enough to support the household adequately. María washed for Tucson Mexican *patronas* at their houses, while Antonia stayed at home to care for her children. The following two years were lean ones. Amelia Villega's first memories are of her great-grandmother, María, whose happy personality made a deep impression on her. Amelia contrasted Antonia's passivity and sadness with María's vivacity, concluding that María "won" over Antonia ("María siempre le ganó a Antonia").

When Nacho returned from Sonora, he went first to his parents' home in Sasco, where he learned that the smelter was closing and no jobs were available. He had left Imuris with his sister, Luisa, and her family, who, however, went directly to Chandler, Arizona, because her husband wanted to work on farms rather than in a mine or at a smelter. Nacho and his

father decided to move the rest of the family to Chandler and
to use Tomás Muina's large black car to peddle goods to Yaquis
and Mexicans living on farms and ranches. After packing
everything, they went to Tucson to pick up Antonia and the
children, going on to join Luisa in Chandler.

The family fortunes did rather well for a while. Nacho,
Antonia, and their children became the peddlers, living in and
around the car, moving frequently from place to place. Nacho
also bought a wagon and horses so he could get work harvest-
ing wheat. He then bought two lots in Chandler which became
the central base for their own immediate family and those
members of Nacho's kin group who were with them at the
time. Two large tents served as their dwellings. They always
intended to build a house but never did.

The real family core, however, was located in Luisa's household. Her husband, Juan María González (also called Juan María
Wapo) got a job on the Allen farm, where houses were
provided for workers. It was there that Tomás Muina, now too
old to work, and Carlota lived, and this was the gathering spot
for Nacho and his full and half-brothers, several of whom
worked for Mr. Allen and had their own houses on his farm.
The main occasion for leaving the Chandler area during these
years was the Easter ceremony in Guadalupe near Phoenix,
where Carlota now served as a *cantora*.

Amelia Villegas provided more information than did Antonia
about the Chandler years. Amelia felt that Chandler was
home—where she grew up. One of her stories dealt with an
afternoon when she was about seven, soon after the family
began its mobile existence in the black car. Nacho was working
on a farm and it is not clear where Antonia was, but Amelia
and Nicolás had been left alone at the car. Seeing a cow, they
felt a great desire to drink milk. Amelia, being older and
braver, said, "I wonder if the cow would hurt us if we tried to
get some milk?" Walking to the cow, they began petting her,
slowly moving back toward the udder—Amelia on one side
and Nicolás on the other—and finally beginning to suck the
teats. The cow would move a few steps and stop, and they
would catch up and drink some more. After Nicolás bit the
cow badly, she refused to let them suck any more. They

suddenly decided they would be beaten if anyone found out what they had done; the wisest course seemed to be to hide the cow, which they accomplished by leading her some distance away to a clump of bushes. Antonia did not know about this escapade for many years. The farmer, in searching for his cow, asked if they had seen her. They of course said no.

Another time, Nicolás and Amelia were left alone at the car beside a field of chilis. Knowing they should not gather something without permission, they gathered a sackful, talking to each other all the while about the beating they would receive. As they expected, their father beat them, but they kept the chilis.

Antonia again went to Carlota rather than to María for the birth of her daughter, Loreta Muina, in 1918, and once more Carlota, who was not a *partera*, officiated at the birth, bathed the baby in oil, buried the afterbirth properly, and arranged the baptism. While Antonia was having the baby and recuperating with Carlota, Luisa's daughter, Loreta, was sent to care for Antonia's household. Amelia Villegas recalled Loreta as a pleasant caretaker who taught her how to embroider on that occasion.

In December 1918 a friend brought the sad news that María and Miguel had died the week before. Antonia immediately took the train to Tucson, sitting in the station until morning, when she took a taxi to the Barrio Anita house. She was told they had died from witchcraft and had been buried in the same grave, "so they would always be together." Antonia and her brother felt that the deaths of these two dynamic people who had molded their lives marked the end of an era. Since Camilda had died about the time of Antonia's marriage, none of the people who were adults in their childhood household remained alive.

After the *novena*, Antonia returned to Chandler. She and her children traveled to Tucson to attend the joint *cumpleaño* for María and Miguel, a fiesta that depleted the resources of immediate family members. Rosalio went to the city dump to scavenge food thrown away by the rich people of Tucson in order to feed his own and Antonia's family following the fiesta.

Life in and around Chandler continued to be rather mobile, but wherever they were during the week, Saturdays were special because everyone went to town. Women and children went by wagon and the men on horseback. Children were given spending money according to age, when enough money was available, and as soon as they arrived, the children scattered to find friends and to buy ice cream and sodas. Antonia and the other women bought the week's provisions, and the men visited on street corners and went to the cantinas, where they stayed till late. Antonia's children were perpetually disappointed that she did not tarry long enough to allow them to go to the movies like other children. An annual carnival was the highlight of the year for the children.

None of Antonia's children attended school regularly or seriously. Often they were too far from town and too mobile to permit school attendance. Even during one year of unusual stability when they lived in the two tents in Chandler and were sent off to school each morning, their school experience was more memorable for the fights they had than for what they learned, and neither Nicolás nor Amelia learned to read or write. The more conscientious Manuela regularly attended school, but Nicolás and Amelia became experts at leaving for school and arriving home at the proper time, having spent the intervening hours swimming or playing with some pigs in a field. Manuela was a tattletale, telling Antonia, "Mamá, ellos hicieron 'play hooky' " ("Mama, they played hooky"). At the time, Antonia seemed not to understand the phrase "play hooky," or at least she took no action. During the life history interviews, however, she said that she knew they were missing school. Amelia's stubbornness and independence were manifest even in school, and a frequently retold story concerned Amelia's trying "to teach the teacher." The teacher came to Amelia's desk, sat down by her, and said, "Let's read here." Amelia put her finger on another part of the page, saying, "No, let's read here."

One of Amelia's Mexican girl friends in the Chandler school told Amelia that her stepfather and mother were bad, beating her all the time. The two girls worked out a scheme whereby the girl was to live with Amelia. On the appointed day, Amelia took the girl home to Antonia, cut her hip-length hair, and dressed her in one of Amelia's dresses as a disguise. That evening the stepfather came in a wagon looking for his run-away stepdaughter. Antonia silently indicated her hiding place. Nicolás and Amelia were furious at Antonia for her betrayal. The girl later said she was beaten worse than ever. Amelia kept the shorn hair, braiding it into her own long hair to create knee-length braids that lasted until she got into a hair-pulling fight at school and the extra hair went flying.

At one point Amelia became quite ill and ran a high fever for some weeks. Carlota could not cure her, nor could *curanderos*. One of the results of this illness was that Amelia lost her dark body hair, previously so embarrassing that she had spent hours sitting alone in the brush, attempting to rub it off with rough stones. Unfortunately, the hair on her head also thinned so that she never again had the long, thick, beautiful braids that she considered her only asset in terms of looks.

The woman Nacho had left in Imuris died about 1919 or 1920, and the two grown children wanted to join their father. One of Nacho's brothers went to get them. The daughter, Francisca, took an immediate dislike to Antonia, although the son was very pleasant. He went to California, never to be heard of again. Antonia became seriously ill during Francisca's stay—an illness her daughters attributed to Francisca's witch-craft, an art they believed she had learned from her mother, who was said to have been a bad witch. Antonia did not accept this diagnosis and made no effort to be cured for witch-caused illness, but she was pleased when Francisca decided to live with her grandmother, Carlota.

In 1921, Tomás Muina and Carlota heard from Sonoran rela-tives that it was safe to return to the Río Yaqui villages. Amid great excitement they prepared to go home. Tomás Muina sold the big black car and bought a smaller one for the trip. They tried to talk the entire family into returning, but only one unmarried son and and their granddaughter, Francisca, elected to go. Nacho and his other siblings decided that jobs were better in Arizona.

Those Muina family members in the Chandler area went to Guadalupe near Phoenix for the Easter ceremony in 1922 or 1923, as was usual. Some Yaqui men, deciding Nacho was a *torocoyori*, or Yaqui traitor, attacked him with chains as he stood in his wagon. The fight caused the horses to bolt and Nacho was thrown to the ground with the wagon seat landing on top of him. Since the fight had attracted an audience, the men ran off without harming him further. For a few weeks his side was sore, but he was not seriously concerned. A tumor or lump gradually formed, which he treated daily by bathing it in hot water. As the ailment worsened, he consulted *curanderos*, who rubbed the lump and gave him medicine. He even consulted a doctor, but he had more faith in the *curanderos*. Eventually the lump got so large that Nacho decided it needed to be cut open. He broke a glass bottle, sharpened a fragment to a razor-sharp edge, and instructed his brother to open the tumor, which the brother reluctantly did after "baking" the lump with hot towels. A small bowlful of pus, the consistency of masa, drained out. Thereafter the lump was as hard as a rock with the texture of a cow's horn.

Carlota, who had become ill, returned from Cocorit to consult *curanderos* she knew and trusted. For perhaps a year, she went with Nacho to be cured, but then she died at Luisa's house. Her children, including Nacho, who was still able to work most of the time, took her body in its wooden coffin to Guadalupe by wagon, holding the *velorio* at the home of Carlota's *prima hermana*. After the burial, the large Muina family returned to Chandler and their jobs for a week, again making the trip to the cousin's Guadalupe house for the *novena*. They wrote to Tomás Muina, but he did not attempt to come. He did, however, come for Carlota's *cumpleaño*, held the following year at Luisa's house on the Allen farm. As soon as it was over, he returned to Cocorit, saying he was an old man and wanted to die on Yaqui soil.

Loreta Muina remembered little of her father, Nacho, but one incident made a deep impression. Loreta must have been about four or five when Sahual Wickiit (Yellow Bird) came on horseback one Sunday afternoon to see Nacho at their tent home in Candler. Nacho was sick and unable to work, but still walking. The men went out under a tree to talk and drink beer; for some time the mood was relaxed and friendly. Sahual wanted to borrow something or perhaps was just going to take it. Nacho suddenly got furious, telling the man to leave or he would kill him, and went after his pistol in the tent. Nacho's brother grabbed him and pinned his arms to his body until Sahual rode away. This story was used to illustrate Nacho's *corajudo* temperament. All of Nacho's children recalled him as a hard man with a quick temper, ready to whip them with a mule whip for any transgression. Amelia and Nicolás, always described as disobedient, independent, stubborn *malditos*, received much more punishment than the younger girls. Nicolás was apparently beaten almost daily for miscellaneous misdemeanors, as well as for stealing chickens and eggs, which, however, were kept for family use.

Nacho had not been able to work since about the time of Carlota's death. For a year or two he could walk, but without his wages the family was hard up. Regretfully, Nacho began to sell the horses, the wagon, and finally the two lots in Chandler. They moved in with Luisa, who had been helping them as much as she could. Finally, Nacho decided to go to Tucson to see better-known *curanderos*. Amelia, now thirteen, was delegated to go with him and care for him in his half-brother's Barrio Libre house. The brother, Ramón León, sent for a famous Mexican *curandero* from Nogales, who gave him medicine but explained that the illness was far advanced and Nacho's fate was in the hands of God. Other curers said the same. After three months Amelia sent word that Nacho was dying. Antonia and the other children went to his side and three days later he died.

Ramón León decided that Nacho should be buried in the same grave with María and Miguel, "que no se pierdan" (so that they would be together). Antonia objected because she did not want the husband for whom she felt scant affection or respect placed "for eternity" with her beloved grandmother and father. Ramón's plan prevailed, and they opened the old double grave and buried Nacho on top of Miguel, erecting a cross with three crosspieces to signify the triple burial.

Antonia and the four children returned to Luisa's house, where the large household was supported by Luisa's husband. Nacho's *cumpleaño*, held by that household, was a large fiesta with *maestros* and *cantoras* from Guadalupe, *pascolas*, a deer dancer, and *matachines*. All of Nacho's brothers and many other relatives attended. After the *cumpleaño*, which exhausted the family's resources, Antonia felt that she could not continue to live with Luisa because there were simply too many for one man to support. Her brother, Rosalio, wrote that women could get work in Tucson Mexican houses, so she decided to move to Pascua, taking Loreta and Nicolás with her.

Amelia and Manuela refused to accompany Antonia to Pascua, electing to stay with Luisa, who, with her husband and daughters, had always been of more emotional significance to these two girls than their own parents or younger sister, Loreta. Luisa was active where Antonia was passive, happy where Antonia was sad. Amelia again used the same phrase she had used in discussing her grandmother, María, saying, "Luisa won over Antonia." Luisa helped all who came, was a warm, outgoing woman, and after Carlota's death, she was undoubtedly the focal point of the far-flung Muina family. In retrospect, Amelia's only criticism was that Luisa was not strict enough, allowing her to run around and stay out late. Luisa's oldest daughter, Carmen (a product of Luisa's formal marriage to a man in Sonora who was killed by the Mexicans), was the one unpleasant aspect of life in Luisa's house. Carmen was a *corajuda*, fighting with everyone. Her husband had long since left her, and even the calm, kind Luisa lost her temper over her daughter's behavior. Since Carmen was as old as Antonia, she felt it her right to discipline Amelia and Manuela and beat them with a whip upon the slightest excuse. Nicolás left Antonia to return to Luisa and Amelia in Chandler when he was perhaps thirteen. Before long he moved on, joining his Muina uncles on farm jobs in the Chandler and Phoenix areas. Amelia and Manuela remained in the household until 1929, helping to nurse Luisa through her final illness in 1928, and staying on to help prepare her *cumpleaño*. Their duty to Luisa fulfilled, they moved to Tucson, away from Carmen's unbearable temper.

Meanwhile, Antonia with the other two children (until Nicolás left her) had joined Rosalio's household in Pascua. For a few months she worked in Mexican homes washing and cleaning while Rosalio's wife, Loreta Sánchez, cared for the children of the two families in their one-room house. For the first time in her life, Antonia had no older, dominant woman or hard husband to direct her behavior. She exercised her freedom by discarding the traditional skirt and blouse, adopting instead one-piece cotton dresses with full, gathered, shorter skirts. *Rebozos* were replaced by handkerchiefs tied over her hair. She retained this style of dress until she died, noting that if Nacho had lived, she could not have done so.

Hearing that better pay was available for cotton pickers around Phoenix, the family closed the little house in Pascua and moved to Scottsdale, where everyone, including the children, worked long hours in the hot fields. Not since she was a child in Hermosillo had Antonia worked so hard. She disliked the aches and pains that came from dragging heavy sacks and bending over all day, as well as the fact that she could not stay clean. It saddened her to see her children working like men, although Nicolás at least could pick more cotton than she could, and between them, they earned more than Rosalio and Loreta. When cotton picking was over, they returned to Pascua and Antonia resumed working for Mexican women.

Antonia emerged briefly from her characteristic passivity when a woman named doña Josefa González began talking badly about her and her children, saying they had "become Mexicans" ("Ellos se hicieron Mexicanos"), for the children publicly spoke Spanish and not Yaqui, and Antonia wore modern dress. Although all the children were bilingual in Yaqui and Spanish, Yaqui was spoken at home, for Antonia spoke almost no Spanish. Upset by the gossip, Antonia went to doña Josefa's house and confronted her directly: "Doña Josefa, we are Yaquis and my children speak Yaqui." Doña Josefa, however, continued to hiss and whisper when she passed their house, and she talked badly about them for many years, eventually causing further confrontations and trouble.

Antonia's remarriage provided doña Josefa's next occasion for gossip. Perfecto Valencia was a bachelor of about thirty, who lived next door to Rosalio's household with his older sister, Juana Valencia. He was the youngest of five children born to Juan María Castro and Juana Valencia in Sonora. Juan María was killed about 1902 by Mexican soldiers at the ranch Milpitas near Guaymas where he was working. Juana Valencia was another remarkable Yaqui woman, a dominant figure who held her large family together. Deciding it was dangerous to be a Yaqui in Sonora, she marshaled her five children, some grown and married with their own children, and moved them all to Tucson, where they joined the household of her uncle in what is now known as Blue Moon, but was then an unnamed collection of adobe houses surrounded by *monte*. Juana was a member of the numerous Wahuechia family and an aunt of the famous Yaqui leader Tetabiate, or Juan Maldonado. Juana never took another man, but with the help of the young Perfecto supported herself by peddling tortillas. She insisted that he go to school, and as a result he spoke English and could read and write. When Perfecto, who had never lived with a woman, married Antonia in a civil ceremony, doña Josefa was foremost among the people who talked against the marriage. It was said that it was wrong for Perfecto to marry a widow, and since Antonia had already been married in the church, she did not need to marry again. Perfecto, who moved in with Antonia, did not get along with Rosalio. Rosalio, as sad as Antonia, simply escaped to a hole in the ground, a kind of cellar, where he could avoid everyone. Antonia, of course, immediately stopped working because Perfecto had a good job.

Antonia's single participation in the ceremonial system occurred in 1927 when her sister-in-law, Loreta, insisted that she wear the crown and carry the saints during *Semana Santa* (Holy Week). Loreta held no formal ceremonial *carga*, but throughout her adult life she participated in every public fiesta as a *fiestera*, baptized an incredible number of babies, and assisted at numerous household fiestas. Antonia did not share Loreta's enthusiasm for or deep involvement in Yaqui religion. She remembered feeling ashamed when wearing the crown because she did not know what she was supposed to do, and she said she would never be involved in religious ceremonies again.

Antonia's first child fathered by Perfecto was born in 1928 with Loreta Sánchez attendance. Antonia did not recover rapidly and was unable to nurse the baby, Martina, but had to give her powdered milk provided by charity. The seizures and periods of unconsciousness Antonia had experienced since infancy ceased at this time and she never had another one. Tension between Rosalio and Perfecto had seriously affected the mood of the entire household. One day Perfecto's sister, Loreta Valencia, said, "Rosalio doesn't like you. You had better come live with me." They moved the next day, and for perhaps two years their headquarters was in that sister's household, although they spent much of the time on the farms and ranches where Perfecto worked.

Loreta Valencia had earlier been married in Guaymas to Antonio Cota, who fathered her only two children. After Antonio was killed by the Mexicans, she formed an alliance with Chico Valenzuela, a *pascola* dancer, often called Mazo-bue-oo (big fat deer), who moved to Arizona with her. Both were remembered by Antonia's Muina daughters, Amelia, Manuela, and Loreta, as very good people.

After her last child, Ramona, was born in Loreta Valencia's house in 1930, Antonia was again seriously ill for several months. During her illness, friction developed between the two sets of adults over the behavior of Antonia's children and responsibility for their care. Perfecto therefore bought a lot next to his sister Juana's house and they moved there. Still too ill to run the household, Antonia sent for her oldest daughter, Amelia, who took charge of the household, nursed Antonia, and cared for Martina and Ramona for several months. In her late thirties, Antonia finally had her own home, instead of one shared by other members of an extended family or one in which another woman held the stellar or dominant position.

While Amelia was staying with Antonia, the feud with doña Josefa González broke out again—this time over fighting at school between children of the two families. Doña Josefa and a neighbor stopped at Antonia's gate, yelling out that Antonia should raise her children better, enlarging on the old theme that Antonia was not a good Yaqui and was not raising her children the Yaqui way. Antonia, flanked by the impressively large Amelia, responded that doña Josefa should look to her own badly raised daughters before criticizing others.

During the next several years, Antonia's Muina and Villegas daughters developed close ties to two of Antonia's *primos hermanos*, Viviana and Simón Valenzuela, and joined their households. Viviana, the oldest child of Antonia's aunt Camilda, was born at La Colorada. Viviana did not remember her father, who was killed by Mexicans when she was a baby, and there is some confusion about his name; however, informants are agreed that he was Camilda's legal husband and that they were married in the church. Simón, a product of an affair Camilda managed to have in spite of María's close supervision, was born at La Playita in Hermosillo. Camilda chose the name Valenzuela, sometimes used by her brother, Miguel Palos, in order to obscure the identity of her lover, whose wife was one of her friends. Viviana and Simón grew up in the same household as Antonia, and like her, they were raised by the remarkable María.

Viviana's three babies died in infancy and her husband, Juan Castro, died in the smallpox epidemic of 1921; thereafter, she joined her brother Simón in his Barrio Libre house. She began walking with Bernaldo Maldonado, by whom in 1925 she had a son that she named Pedro Valencia, choosing the last name from that of her grandmother, María Valencia Palos. Eventually she moved to Pascua to live with Bernaldo Maldonado; although she also named her second son Valencia, the last three sons carried their father's name. Viviana was a good woman, but sad and silent like Antonia. Nevertheless, Antonia's daughters found her household more compatible than Antonia's because Viviana was less passive and because they disliked Perfecto, whom they regarded as hard and humorless. In any event, he had made it quite clear when he married Antonia that he felt no responsibility for her Muina children.

Simón's first consort was Pancha Wahuechia, a member of the large Wahuechia family to which Perfecto belonged through his mother. Pancha became Antonia's *comadre* when Loreta Valencia, who officiated at the birth of Antonia's last child, asked Pancha to be Ramona's *madrina de pila*. The Muina girls felt free to join this household because of Simón's relationship to Antonia, but Pancha was the real attraction. Whereas Simón was sad like Antonia, Rosalio, and Viviana, Pancha was happy, talkative, enjoyed a good time, and presided over a pleasant household.

The personal accounts of Amelia, Loreta, and Antonia provide somewhat contradictory versions of exactly when each of the three Muina girls lived with Viviana and when they lived with Simón, but both households were in close contact and there was a great deal of interaction between them. Amelia and Manuela joined Viviana's household when they left Chandler in 1929. It appears that Manuela at least had moved to Simón's household by 1930 or 1931, and it was there that Loreta went when she left Antonia shortly after Ramona's birth. After Amelia nursed Antonia back to health, Viviana called formally on Antonia to ask to borrow Amelia to help in her household in the section house at Rillito, where she was temporarily living with her consort.

One of Amelia's more vivid memories concerns the only time she got drunk. Simón gave home-brewed beer to Amelia and Manuela—just to see how they would act. They thought it was awful-tasting soda pop. Simón was vastly amused by their behavior. In desperation they sought Viviana, who was cooking for a *velorio* at a *comadre*'s house; she took care of them. Amelia recalled feeling ashamed as she sat tilting at half-mast in her chair, feeling upon her the disapproving eyes of all the people attending the *velorio*. Viviana later told Simón his joke was not funny.

The young Loreta attended school far more faithfully than had Amelia or Nicolás, although for one year she played hooky regularly, spending her days in a junkyard, until Antonia discovered what she was doing and enlisted Simón Valenzuela's aid to stop this behavior. Nonetheless, she learned some English and how to read and write. When she began preparing for her confirmation at Santa Rosa Church, she entered a period of deep emotional response to Catholicism, regularly attending mass, praying, making the Stations of the Cross, and attending catechism lessons. Joaquina García, a wealthy Mexican woman who acted as a patron of the Santa Rosa Church, asked to serve as Loreta's confirmation godmother, providing a white dress and veil for the occasion (which Antonia did not attend), and later hosting a party for the confirmed girls that Loreta remembered as one of the nicest events of her life. Thereafter, doña Joaquina took a personal interest in Loreta, having her to lunch on school days, giving her clothes, and lecturing her constantly on the importance of not running off with a boy but continuing her education.

Despite doña Joaquina's lectures, Loreta was soon married to Nestór Paderes, who formed part of Loreta Valencia's large household. Nestór, the son of Severa Valencia (another of Perfecto's sisters) and Manuel Paderes, a Mayo, had been Ramona's baptismal *padrino*. Nestór and Loreta Muina did not become *novios* until she had moved to Simón's household shortly after Ramona's birth; it would have been improper to "talk" to Nestór while they lived under the same roof. Loreta felt little fondness for Antonia, nor did she enjoy the evident strain between her mother and Loreta Valencia. Antonia did not attract Loreta's primary allegiance any more than she had that of Amelia, Nicolás, and Manuela. Loreta said, "Antonia did not raise me. I was raised by the two Loretas," referring to Loreta Sánchez and Loreta Valencia. The strongest emotional bond of her lifetime was to Loreta Valencia.

Another reason for Loreta's leaving the household was her dislike of Perfecto. Perfecto disapproved of Nestór and Loreta's association, apparently feeling that Nestór was too young to consider a marriage or alliance, but that the pretty, independent, thirteen-year-old Loreta should be safely married as soon as possible. His unsuccessful attempt to arrange a marriage for her with a much older man appears to have been the final stimulus to Loreta's leaving the parental household. She refused to marry "an old drunk," as she called the man. Antonia again stepped out of her normally silent, passive role to defend Loreta. After Loreta threatened to run away with Nestór at the age of fourteen, Antonia went to Severa Valencia to arrange the marriage, feeling it was preferable for Loreta to marry properly in the church.

Since this was the first marriage for one of the Muina siblings, Amelia and Manuela took a great interest in the preparations. Perfecto refused to contribute much toward the event, so Amelia went to work, saving all her money to finance the wedding and buying the material and making Loreta's

wedding dress. She made the mistake of giving the rest of the
money to Nestór for the fiesta. Loreta moved back to Antonia's
household just before the wedding in order to be married from
her mother's house.

The long-planned wedding had to be postponed when
Nestór failed to arrive on the appointed day. When he did
show up, he had spent the money intended for the fiesta.
Loreta's wedding, held a week late in the Sacred Family
Church, was attended only by the marriage *padrinos* and there
was no fiesta. The wedding was as sad as if the couple had
been living together rather than having been proper *novios*.
They thanked the *padrinos*, who might at least have offered them
a cup of chocolate, and went prosaically to live in Loreta Valencia's large, crowded household. Loreta was barely fifteen at
the time of her marriage in 1935.

Manuela was the second of Antonia's children to marry, and
she, too, selected a young man from the extended Wahuechia
family, Luis Lara, a grandson of Perfecto's sister, Juana Valencia. This time Perfecto felt he could afford a wedding fiesta, so
in 1936, Manuela married in better style, returning to Antonia
just before the wedding as Loreta had done.

Antonia's daily life revolved around her own household, as
always. Where they lived depended on Perfecto's place of
employment. Until World War II he worked on various farms
and ranches or for the Southern Pacific Railroad. The house in
Pascua that served as their central base was occupied by Loreta
and Nestór while they temporarily lived elsewhere. After
Manuela's marriage, Amelia sometimes accompanied Antonia
and Perfecto, working in the fields like a man, while at other
times she stayed with Loreta and Nestór, Viviana, or Simón
Valenzuela. Martina was often left with Loreta Valencia when
Antonia and Perfecto worked out of town, with the result that
she said she was raised by Loreta Valencia, and yet another of
Antonia's children gave her primary allegiance to another
woman.

Perfecto was extremely fond of his youngest child, Ramona.
Although he agreed to leaving Martina in Pascua while the
family lived on farms and ranches or in railroad section houses,
he refused to leave Ramona. From the time she could toddle,

he took her with him to the fields, talking to her constantly. Puzzled by her imaginative behavior, which was first manifest when she was quite young, he nonetheless defended her staunchly against all accusations of lying and theft. One of the things she did repeatedly was to approach strange Yaquis and Mexicans in town, telling them Antonia and Perfecto were not her parents, but that she was an orphan they beat and starved. In spite of Perfecto's consistent championing of Ramona, Antonia and her older daughters believed that he knew Ramona really did these things and felt it was a sickness for which she was not responsible. Perhaps because he felt she was not responsible for her actions he kept her with him all the time. In any event, they were inseparable, with the result that Ramona grew up in the fields rather than in the house with Antonia, seldom attending school for more than a few days or weeks at a time. Ramona, therefore, did not learn much English or how to read and write. Her only emotional investments were in her father, whom she adored, and in Nestór Paderes, who was her *padrino*, her brother-in-law, and her cousin.

About 1940, Amelia became involved in an accident which she felt could have caused her great harm. Perfecto, Amelia, and Nocilás were working full time on the Allen farm near Marana. Their combined wages provided an unusually affluent period for the household. A number of other Yaquis and Mexicans also lived in the workers' houses. A Mexican woman from Texas who had moved into a house across the canal with her family began acting just like doña Josefa González in Pascua, talking badly about Antonia's family, whispering and hissing as she passed their house, and spreading malicious gossip. Amelia became increasingly upset. She described how *coraje* built up inside her for months until she had to explode. As the woman walked by one morning, Amelia stopped her, telling her the family did not like the ugly rumors or the woman's behavior. When the woman remained very polite, saying she had not meant any harm, Amelia became suspicious and braced herself against being bewitched or being beaten up. The suspense gradually built up over the next several weeks. Finally, the woman came to the door to ask if Amelia knew where chickens could be bought, and if Amelia would serve as her guide. Amelia felt the day of reckoning was at hand and that this was just an excuse to separate her from the protection of her family so the Mexicans could beat her up. To have refused would have caused more trouble. Amelia spent every second of the trip planning how to defend herself. When no disaster occurred, she was relieved but almost disappointed. She felt that the trouble between the two families stemmed from jealousy over relative affluence and fights between children.

Perfecto joined the army during World War II, as did Nicolás. Without a man in the household, the family could not remain at the Allen farm, so the women and children returned to Pascua. Antonia ran the house while Amelia and Ramona joined truckloads of laborers picked up daily by Mexican labor contractors for work in nearby cotton fields. Domestic work was available in Tucson, but Amelia always preferred outdoor work. In Perfecto's three-year absence, none of Antonia's unmarried daughters were as closely supervised as Loreta had been when she was a young girl living in Perfecto's household, because while he was usually lenient toward young children, he punished girls severely for talking to or walking with boys. Ramona, Martina, and the much older Amelia took advantage of his absence to meet men and go to dances and movies. Both Ramona and Amelia managed to go out on trucks with the men they eventually married or lived with. Antonia made no effort to curtail their behavior, or, if she did, it was not effective.

The family's final encounter with doña Josefa González occurred in 1945. Doña Josefa had never ceased talking badly about Antonia and her family, but now she began spreading rumors about Amelia, saying she walked with this man and that. As had happened when she confronted the Mexican woman on the Allen farm, Amelia again felt herself "filling up with *coraje*." Knowing doña Josefa's daily routine, she waited for her in the street, forcibly stopping her when she passed. Amelia told her that the time had come to repeat all those ugly stories to her face that doña Josefa told other people. At first doña Josefa hedged, saying that perhaps she was too talkative, an *habladora*, but she meant no harm. Amelia rejected this

interpretation and the argument became more heated, attracting a considerable crowd. Doña Josefa finally accused Amelia
of stealing her *novio*, and Amelia hotly denied walking with
him ("Who would want an old man like him?") or with any
other men ("All these people know I stay home"). Amelia hit
the older woman hard across the face, saying that if doña Josefa
were younger, she would really beat her. There was never any
more trouble with doña Josefa, who in fact tried in later years
to become friendly. Amelia felt it was "crazy" to talk badly and
make trouble and then make friendly overtures. The end of
doña Josefa's gossip was attributed by Antonia and all the
members of her family to the public confrontation that convinced "the people" that the rumors were false.

Ramona first met her *novio*, Chico Flores, at Richey School in
Pascua during one of Ramona's short and infrequent periods of
school attendance. His father abandoned the family before
Chico's birth and his mother died when he was a baby, leaving
him in the care of his great-aunt and *madrina de pila*, doña
Simona Soto. Even as a child he was chronically afflicted with
asthma and bronchitis and needed medicine and curing all the
time. During one of his more serious illnesses, doña Simona
made a vow he would become a *matachine*, and he began to
fulfill the vow at the age of fifteen. He had to begin working
when he was twelve because the household needed the money, but work in the dusty cotton fields aggravated his respira-
tory ailments so that he alternated between working and being
sick. He also gave priority to his duties as a *matachine*, so that
he often worked very little.

When Perfecto returned from the army, Ramona was walking with Chico. They particularly enjoyed going to the Pasadita
dance hall, which was very popular with young Pascuans at
that time. Perfecto was unable to make her behave properly,
but he waited up for her, beating her with his belt, or, if he
went to bed before she got home, he would beat her the next
morning before she even got out of bed. Perhaps Ramona got
pregnant, or perhaps not. Chico asked Perfecto for permission
to live with Ramona, and, bowing to the inevitable, Perfecto
agreed. Chico moved in and their first baby was soon born.
Perfecto's nephew, Antonio Cota Valenzuela (Loreta Valencia's

son and one of Chico's drinking cohorts), asked Chico if he could baptize the baby the Yaqui way, which meant that he would baptize the next two babies as well. Chico agreed. Antonio selected his aunt as the *madrina*, and together they baptized Ramona's and Chico's three children, born in 1946, 1948, and 1950.

Soon after Ramona's first baby was born, Antonia had her only serious fight with Perfecto. She claimed not to remember the cause, but the fight was sufficiently serious that she left him and joined her daughter Loreta for several weeks. When he came to get her, she silently returned.

In 1947, Amelia began seeing more of Joey Castillo, whom she had met on the trucks during the war. At this time Amelia was living partly in Simón Valenzuela's household, as she had on and off for nearly twenty years, and sometimes she stayed with Antonia. Neither Antonia nor Pancha Wahuechia approved of Joey, who was widely regarded as a bad *viciado* man. Pancha tried to undermine Joey's position by introducing Amelia to other men, even trying to arrange her marriage to a Barrio Libre man, but Amelia continued seeing Joey.

José Castillo (called Joey Chato) was born in Hermosillo in 1910. His mother died when he was a toddler of two or three years, leaving Joey and a new baby to be cared for by their father, José Valencia. During the minor military activities of 1914, the father decided it was expedient to leave Sonora. He walked from Hermosillo to Tucson, carrying the baby and leading the young Joey. After he loaded up with ammunition, he prepared to return to Hermosillo. The four-year-old Joey, too tired to walk back, elected to stay with his father's sister, Gregoria Valencia. Thereafter, it was said, Joey grew up "like an orphan." When relations grew strained with his aunt, he moved to Carlos Quintana's household. The Quintanas were Mexicans living in Pascua, and there seem to have been no kin or *compadre* ties. Joey Chato said don Carlos Quintana raised him. Even as a child, Joey Chato was wild. At thirteen he ran away to Chandler, where two old *marijuanos*, relatives of his mother, introduced him to this vice. A rolling stone, he soon moved on to California, where for the next five years he worked for short periods on a series of farms.

Joey had gone with women from his early teens, but the first woman he lived with was a Mexican in Yuma by whom he had a son about 1928. After that he is said to have gone with, lived with, or had children by many women: Yaquis, Papagos, and Mexicans. His vices included drinking, being a *marijuano*, being bad with women, and fighting. In and out of jails and prisons in Arizona and California since he was about twenty on charges of assault, drunkenness, and marijuana usage and selling, he was, when Amelia first met him about 1944, recently out of the Arizona state penitentiary after serving three years for stabbing another Yaqui man during a drunken fight on a farm near Marana.

Everyone who knew Joey Chato agreed that he was exceptionally charming when not drunk or on marijuana, but when he was, he became "brave." Amelia was blinded by his charm and turned a deaf ear to everyone's pleas that she not talk to him. Antonia and Perfecto forbade her to see him and refused to receive him at the house. Amelia therefore arranged secret meetings with Joey, taking Pancha Wahuechia along as an unwilling chaperone. The courtship involved quite a lot of subterfuge because they could not tell either Antonia or Simón Valenzuela the truth. Simón was as disapproving of their association as were Antonia and Perfecto.

Matters came to a head in 1947. While Amelia was attending a fiesta celebrating the baptism of Viviana's last baby, Joey openly came looking for her—the first time he had done so. Antonia, furious that he would make such a public appearance, asked Amelia if she had been secretly walking with Joey. The thirty-six-year-old Amelia responded, "Yes, I am now *grande* [grown]." Antonia, repeating that Joey was a bad man, suggested that Amelia should leave town until the infatuation cooled. Amelia agreed to go to Phoenix and live with her aunt, Felipa Muina. She then found Joey and asked him to walk with her to Pancha Wahuechia's house, as it was too noisy to talk at the fiesta. There she told she was leaving for Phoenix as soon as she got her money from Antonia (who kept all the money for members of the household). Joey Chato said he would go with her if she wished. She agreed. He said, "You know what you are doing and if you want to go with me." Amelia went alone to get her money, allowing Antonia to believe she was leaving Joey, but later meeting him at the bus station so they could travel together to Phoenix.

Felipa Muina cried when she saw Amelia with Joey, saying that Amelia had always been good, and Joey was so bad. She predicted that Joey would never marry her, any more than he had married the countless other women with whom he had consorted. Joey became angry at Felipa's comments and told Amelia that they could not be happy in a house where their lovemaking was so public. After only a week or two, he decided to move to Florence and look for work. There, Joey told Amelia that although he had seduced lots of women, he had never married and he wanted to marry her. After their civil marriage, Amelia rather gleefully sent the news to Felipa and Antonia. She and Joey honeymooned in a cotton field near Coolidge, using piles of cotton for a bed—and a hot bed it made, Amelia recalled.

Their first six months were blissfully happy—the happiest time of Amelia's life—although they were often hungry and had no money. Once they bought a sheep, eating it as long as it lasted. Joey's bad habits reasserted themselves, however, and he started drinking heavily and using marijuana again. As always, he became violent when under the influence, and he would alternately beat Amelia and retreat into a morose silence for days. During drinking bouts, he became insanely jealous, accusing her of going with other men: "Go into the house. I want to beat you, you no-good whore." The beatings did not diminish even when she reached an advanced state of pregnancy.

They were living in a rented house near Scottsdale when Amelia began having labor pains. She went alone to a Mexican midwife in Phoenix, where the baby, Joey, Jr., was born. At first he was crooked, "as if he came from an egg," seemed to be blind, and was almost lifeless. With no food in the house, Amelia wondered if he could live. Joey finally got another job and then they could eat. One of Amelia's Muina cousins told her to coat the baby in cooking oil, wrap him like a tamale, and put him in a warm oven morning and night, a treatment Amelia believed saved his life. Their Mexican landlady took pity on Amelia, saying, "I will baptize your child. You don't have to walk the streets to find someone." The landlady's husband served as *padrino* in the Mexican style. The baby continued to have a series of severe illnesses which *curanderos* and doctors said were due to Amelia's severe malnutrition during pregnancy and inadequate food after birth. They moved to Tucson so that Amelia could take him to the welfare baby clinic.

During one of Joey, Jr.'s, illnesses in Pascua, a *fariseo* came to see how he was. This man was the stepfather of the *chapayeka* for whom Amelia had, in her youth, completed a three-year vow to serve as his *madrina de chapayeka*. The baby was, upon this occasion, believed to be dying. The often drunk *fariseo* was absolutely sober that day. He stood for a long time looking at the baby. Finally he said, "He will get well. I will pass on my *manda* to him. He will live to dance as a *fariseo*."

Early in their marriage Amelia discovered that Joey was something of a witch. He could have been a powerful one if he had not stayed drunk or on marijuana all the time. After having admitted his powers to Amelia, he delighted in scaring her with tales of things he controlled and things he had done. Much of his success with women, including Amelia, he attributed to love aids he possessed. He owned a *chone* (a scalp or a doll to which a scalp is attached that has super-natural powers), given to him by an old man on his deathbed who had said, "Joey, take this. It will protect you." Small—only two or three inches high—it could, like all *chones*, grow to a foot or more in length. *Chones* must be cared for; they come out at night to be combed. Joey told Amelia that Pimas around Sacaton have a lot of *chones* made from Apache scalps that must be old, because where would one obtain Apache scalps now? Many Piman *chones* roam loose because older men who knew how to command and control them have died and younger men have thrown them away, since *chones* are dangerous without this knowledge. Joey finally threw his away too.

In 1949 Joey and Amelia came to the farm near Eloy where Antonia and Perfecto were living with the news that better-paying jobs were available in California. Joey asked Perfecto to go there with him and Marcelo Muina (one of Amelia's many Muina cousins) in the latter's car. Perfecto quit his job and the men took Antonia and Amelia to Pascua, where they were left with Loreta Muina. A month or two later, Joey Chato sent money for Amelia and Joey, Jr., to join the California group. Refusing to let Amelia go alone, Antonia sent Martina with her.

In California, they all got well-paying jobs gathering tomatoes, plums, peaches, and pecans. When that work was finished, they started out to Merced, near Fresno, where Marcelo Muina's wife awaited them. Marcelo's car broke down at Los Baños and while they were waiting, Joey Chato found a bar he refused to leave. Marcelo decided to leave the broken-down car and Joey Chato with the bartender, and the others went by bus to Merced, arriving after midnight. The following two days Marcelo was drunk in a Merced cantina; and when he finally came home, they needed money, so everyone went to work gathering fruit again. It was the weekend before Marcelo returned to Los Baños to collect the car and Joey Chato.

The car was there but could not be repaired and had to be abandoned. Joey Chato, however, had disappeared. Marcelo looked for Joey for days and then every weekend for several weeks, going everywhere he thought Joey might be, even to San Francisco, where Joey had friends. Amelia asked everyone about him. Marcelo's wife, the only lighthearted member of the household, told Amelia that Joey had just run off with another woman. The only explanation seemed to be that Joey had drowned in one of the floods rampant at that time. Amelia forgot the bad times when he beat her and just remembered how nice he had been. She cried all the time, and years later when people mentioned California, she got sick. Martina gave Amelia money to return to Arizona and Antonia.

In Pascua, a major crisis had developed. Loreta Muina had run away from Nestór, abandoning her children. Loreta's account of her marriage and its abrupt termination stresses the hardships she endured, whereas her mother and sisters took a harder line, emphasizing her abandonment of her small children. In the beginning, she was infatuated with Nestór, although in retrospect she mentioned that Perfecto had pushed her into too early a marriage with his harsh treatment and attempted arranged marriage. Nestór was a good provider for several years. Within a year and a half of their marriage he had bought a house and lot in Pascua, thereby allowing Loreta to have her own house and run it her own way at the age of seventeen.

Through the period of having her first three children, Loreta was happy. Loreta Valencia, who had raised Loreta herself, and who was a good *partera*, assisted at these births. She had the younger Loreta give birth squatting in a doorway and holding onto a suspended rope to prevent contact with anything cold or metallic, which could cause harm, even death, to mother and child. She also insisted that Loreta strictly observe the forty-day *dieta* (regimen) with continued avoidance of metal (no sewing with needles, for example) and cold (no going barefooted), plus dietary and activity restrictions. The next three children were delivered by the mother-daughter *partera* team of Juana Valencia and Manuela Paderes. They favored a prone position for childbirth, which Loreta found less satisfactory.

All six of Loreta's children were properly baptized, some by Valencia relatives. Loreta Valencia "called" them, or claimed them, for the Pascua Mexican Baptist church, which they attended regularly, dressed in their best clothes, for several years. That these six children are said to have turned out well is attributed to their Baptist training. Because of this Protestant interlude (none remained Protestant), none of them went through the normal Yaqui and Catholic rites of the placing of rosaries or confirmation, and in later years certain difficulties with the Catholic church were encountered when they wanted to marry in the church.

Loreta's infatuation with Nestór had begun to cool by the time her last three children were born. Although he had started drinking heavily in his teens, for several years his drinking did not interfere with his working or with his providing for his family's livelihood. He gradually drank more and more and finally refused to turn over his paycheck to Loreta, who had to go to work in a laundry shortly before the birth of her sixth child in 1943. Since there was no other adult woman in the household, she left the younger children in the care of her oldest daughter, Gabriela (who was only eight when Loreta began work). Little Gabriela did the best she could, but she was in school and could not exercise adequate control. Except for Sunday school at the Baptist church, the children had very little supervision. Loreta's resentment over Nestór's failure to turn over his paychecks and the chronic household poverty filled her with bitterness. In the last five or six years of their marriage, they seldom slept together and Nestór was frequently absent. The pleasure she experienced with her first babies more and more often turned to irritation over their unruly behavior. Always tired, she felt that nothing pleasant happened any more. Her depression deepened when, at the age of thirteen, Gabriela ran away with a man. Loreta was sad to think that her daughter, who had done so well in school, would soon be having babies and working hard without ever having had a good time.

Loreta said that finally she just could not take any more. Perhaps if there had been another woman in the house to help control the children and share the work, she could have continued. One day she simply did not return home after her day's work; instead, she went home with a friend and laundry coworker. It is not clear whether she regarded this as a temporary or permanent step. Feelings of relief, freedom, and tranquility characterized the next several days. Whether Loreta intended to go back or not, the news that Nestór had gone with the woman he had been walking with for some time sealed her action. She returned to the household formerly presided over by Loreta Valencia to begin a new life. Both Loreta Valencia and Chico Mazo-bue-oo had died in 1937, leaving the house to Loreta Valencia's son, whose wife, Mariana Vacamea, was now in charge of the household. A sad, shy, stay-at-home like Antonia, she was Antonia's niece, the youngest child of Camilda and her last consort, Claudio Vacamea.

Antonia took over the care of Loreta's children. Since there was no money, she had to go to work picking cotton, going out daily on trucks from Pascua, which meant the chilren were left alone all day to run wild. She wrote to Perfecto, asking him to send Martina home to help because the distraught and pregnant Amelia was no help at all. Eventually, Martina arrived to help Antonia care for the children and Amelia, followed shortly by Perfecto. In spite of Perfecto's good union job, Antonia was not able to return to her favored role in the household because there were too many people to support. She shifted from the hated cotton fields to the less lucrative but more desirable job of cleaning and washing in Mexican homes.

Antonia and Perfecto elected to remain in Nestór's house and to sell their smaller house two blocks away. Ramona and Chico joined them, so the household now numbered thirteen. Both Loreta's five children left in her care and Ramona's children said that Antonia raised them, not their mothers. Antonia won the primary emotional allegiance of these grandchildren as she never had won that of her own children.

Perhaps four months after Amelia's return from California, Perfecto spoke to one of Joey Chato's Mexican drinking friends, who told him, "Why do you say Joey is lost when I saw him in the Fresno newspaper?" It turned out Joey had been arrested and jailed for six months for possession and sale of marijuana. Upon his release, he made his way to Tucson, walking for hours around the edge of the city before getting up enough nerve to confront Amelia. She was horrified by his thin, emaciated appearance. He told her he was very sick and at first put it down to the effects of jail and the California climate, but neither doctors nor *curanderos* helped. Amelia took him to a doctor who "removed a lot of water from his lungs." Then they went to see his old aunt Gregoria Valencia, who said he was bewitched, as she could tell from a certain look in his eye. Gregoria at once went to Nogales to get a famous *curandero* who specialized in witch-caused sickness. He pronounced Joey to be near death. He cured Joey by placing his hands on Joey's head, reciting, and bathing Joey's whole body in cologne from a bottle shaped like a little casket because witches cannot stand scents. Giving Joey the casket of cologne to be used daily and an aluminum medallion with a star on it for good luck, he left. When he returned five days later, Joey was much improved, eating normally for the first time in months. During his sickness, all food had tasted like grass and he could barely eat. This time the *curandero* said he knew why Joey was sick—a woman had buried his picture in the Nogales cemetery.

It was decided that the woman was Filomena Osuña. Half Mexican, half Tarascan, Filomena was roughly Amelia's age. Tattooing was said to cover her arms, legs, breasts, and abdomen. Amelia first encountered her shortly after the birth of Joey, Jr., when Filomena stopped her on the street and offered to cure Joey Chato of his running around and drinking for $100. A second time she came to Amelia's house, offering to cure Joey for just the jewelry Amelia was wearing. Amelia responded that Joey, who had paid a lot of money for the cross on a heavy chain, the bracelet, and the ring, would surely miss them immediately, and she would rather not have a man she had to use witchcraft to keep. At a third meeting, Filomena offered to cure Joey for nothing.

Amelia was of two minds about Filomena's reasons for offering to cure Joey. On the one hand, Filomena probably wanted Joey for herself because she always had a man, sometimes gigolos she brought from Mexico, using her witchcraft and love potions to keep them tied to her. In later years, Amelia saw her performing magic against a man who left her, using blackened candles turned upside down, reciting before a picture of the Virgin with a *caimán* (cayman, or alligator) at her feet, and calling out *maldiciones*, the dreadful things that would happen to her former lover. On the other hand, Filomena made her living by dispensing love medicines, one of which was *baso-pejol*, a root that is ground up and was locally known as a *bruja de amor*. So perhaps Filomena was just recruiting business. Amelia recalled all too clearly the effects of Filomena's curing another woman's husband. It was true that the man stopped running around with other women, drinking, and using marijuana, but it was also common knowledge that the woman became a promiscuous drunkard as long as she was under Filomena's influence. Filomena's failure to win Joey upon any of the earlier occasions was presumably the reason she bewitched him, using a picture stolen from her friend Gregoria, whom she visited regularly.

Joey's health was improving when Amelia gave birth to their second son, Alejandro, in Santa María Hospital. Unlike the first son, Alejandro was fat and healthy. As soon as Joey could work again, they moved into a rented house. For the first time Joey joined a union and worked as a concrete mixer. Although he still drank, used marijuana, and fought with his wife and his sons, Amelia was no longer as afraid of him as she had once been, and for several years they enjoyed a relatively stable life.

The only time Antonia served as a baptismal *madrina* was for Luz Contreras, who asked her to baptize three babies in the late 1940s and early 1950s. Luz was an old friend whose parents had been associated with María Valencia Palos, Miguel Palos, and other members of Antonia's family. Luz's grandparents were Luis Contreras, a long-time coworker of Miguel's, and Nicolasa Waibel, who had a rather colorful and dramatic life. After Luis was killed in a fight at the Silver Bell Mine, Nicolasa went with another man to Sasco. Miguel forbade Antonia to speak to her there because she worked as a maid in one of the red-light houses. Stories vary, but some say she killed the man she was living with. In any event, she left hurriedly for Sonora, where she lived with yet another man, whom she murdered. Her subsequent trial, one of the famous legal cases tried under Yaqui law, resulted in her own and her young son's execution in Vicam by a Yaqui firing squad. Mickey Contreras, her oldest son, lived with Antonia's grandmother, María Valencia Palos, from the time of his father's death at the Silver Bell Mine until María died. Later he married Ignacia Lolatcha, a daughter of Juan Pistola. Ignacia died at Luz's birth, Mickey went to California, and Luz was raised in Pascua by an old aunt, who arranged Luz's marriage to Victorio Valencia. Luz was one of the few people beyond the kin group with whom Antonia interacted, and until the 1960s, when Antonia ceased to leave her own home, Luz's house was the only one she would visit. When one of Luz's children died, Antonia was involved in her death rituals. The two surviving *ahijados* wore the *luto* (cord of mourning) for Antonia at her *cumpleaño* years later.

Antonia's attitudes toward religion and the supernatural were rather neutral. A private believer in God, the saints, witches, *suawakás* (beings from another world), and so on, she disliked Yaqui public ceremonies, never attended mass or confession, never believed herself the subject of witchcraft, and apparently paid little attention to omens. If there were Yaqui ceremonies in La Colorada, she did not mention them. In Hermosillo, she, like her grandfather, Abelardo, did not attend them. Only after the move to Arizona did she attend public Yaqui ceremonies, first with her grandmother, María, and later with the Muina family under the influence of her husband and mother-in-law. After their deaths, she assumed the crown in an Easter pageant to please her sister-in-law, after which she participated no more in religious observances. Her daughters told of trying to get her to attend as a spectator, and once in a while she acceded to their wishes, but each time she quickly became uncomfortable in the crowds, announced that the whole thing was foolish, and returned home.

Perfecto was apparently less passive in his rejection of Yaqui ceremonies and religion. His true attitudes are difficult to reconstruct because his surviving relatives held conflicting views of his position. Ramona, the daughter he adored, maintained that he was a believer but a nonparticipant like Antonia. Martina, Antonia, and some of Antonia's Muina daughters held that he was a convert to a Protestant sect and was actively opposed to Yaqui religion, Yaqui ceremonialism, and Catholicism as the causes of excessive drunkenness and the poverty of the Yaqui people. Perfecto was also impatient with other aspects of Yaqui culture, as was illustrated by the often repeated story about a white man stopping Perfecto to ask directions to the house of the Yaqui "chief." Perfecto responded, "No tengo chief! Aquí mando yo" ("I have no chief. Here I am in charge").

Various members of Perfecto's Wahuechia kin group were among the first converts to Protestantism. The Pascua Mexican Baptist church attracted Manuela Paderes (Juana Valencia's daughter) and Loreta Valencia, among others. In varying degrees, they influenced other family members; for example, Loreta Valencia "claimed" Loreta and Nestór's children for regular attendance. When the Assembly of God church group took over the building formerly occupied by the Mexican Baptist church, they took over much of the congregation as . well, mostly members of the Wahuechia family. Despite Ramona's protests that her father remained a Yaqui Catholic, other evidence favors his conversion to and active participation in the Assembly of God church. Martina also became a member, but Antonia was no more interested in that religion than in institutionalized Catholicism.

One morning in 1950, two months after the birth of Ramona's third child, the family woke up to a nightmare. Chico Flores had hanged himself in the back yard during the night, apparently in the depths of a depression following an unusually severe attack of asthma. Perfecto found him when he went outside to go to the outhouse about daylight. First he awakened Antonia, who had to tell Ramona and her two older children that their consort and father had taken his life. The oldest son was particularly affected because Chico had been an unusually affectionate father, playing with the boy for hours at a time, teaching him the *matachine* steps while beating the rhythm with spoons. Ramona continued to live in the household for another ten years, but responsibility for the three children fell to Antonia and Perfecto.

Martina had seldom lived with Antonia and Perfecto in her childhood, and it was not until she returned from California to help Antonia with Loreta's children that she was regularly in their household. By this time, she was quite independent, had an eighth-grade education, worked for her own money, and enjoyed a good time. Her independence was reflected in her trip to Hermosillo, alone, to see Antonia's mother, Cecelia Hurtado.

Martina found her grandmother a fascinating woman with a strong, positive, happy personality. Not since Martina lived with Loreta Valencia had she been in the company of a Yaqui woman who knew so much and who was so willing to impart her knowledge. Accounts of the Yaqui wars, family history and gossip, and Yaqui beliefs flowed in an unending stream from the vivacious seventy-five-year-old Cecelia. Martina marveled at her stamina and agility as she gracefully carried five-gallon cans of water on her head from the river to her house on the steep slopes of the Cerro de la Campana in the Barrio La Matanza and walked miles to collect and deliver laundry, for Cecelia, like Chepa Moreno, lived by washing. Hermosillo possessed other attractions for a slim, attractive Tucson Yaqui girl which Martina enjoyed in the company of Cecelia's daughter from her last alliance with a Mexican, and with the daughter's children. Martina dutifully called on Chepa Moreno, who lived just down the hill from Cecelia, but found her silent and rather dull.

For some years, Martina had been in active conflict with her father, who strongly disapproved of her regular attendance at dances, her failure to ask permission to leave the house, her drinking, and her running around with a group of Wahuechia Valencia *primas hermanas* who were as disrespectful of conventions and their parents as was Martina. Antonia could be ignored, but Perfecto lectured her constantly, forbade all the behavior she found enjoyable, and beat her regularly for her repeated disobedience. The situation worsened upon Martina's return from Hermosillo because she began dating a Mexican heroin addict, whom she met on a blind date arranged by one of her Wahuechia cousins. Juan (Johnny) Quintana, born in Pascua, a son of old Carlos Quintana who raised Joey Chato, was one of the first two men in Pascua to use heroin, taking up the habit after his return from the army in 1946. They obtained their heroin in Nogales. When Martina began using marijuana, her parents and siblings thought she was truly lost to the vices, and Loreta Muina prayed for her soul daily. For Martina, acknowledged as the best dancer in Pascua, the four years of walking with Johnny were happy ones, except for troubles at home, because they went dancing at least twice a week at the dance halls and attended numerous parties. Johnny's addiction did not bother Martina at that time; she laughed when Perfecto called him a *viciado*. Martina maintained that she was not really bad during these years and that she did not get credit for not doing the bad things she could have done, such as becoming a promiscuous *cantinera*.

Martina and Johnny married in the Catholic church in 1954, after she had given up marijuana and had asked Johnny to give up heroin. For perhaps a year, their lives continued to be a round of happy parties and dancing, even after Martina was obviously pregnant. By the time their son, Erasmus, was born, it was obvious that Johnny was making no effort to give up heroin. After a number of fights about his vice, Martina left him, stripping their rented house while Johnny was at work and returning to Antonia with all the possessions. Johnny came for her as soon as he discovered the empty house, but she refused to return, saying, "It is better if you take your road and I will take mine." Johnny stayed with his sister until he received his paycheck, which he took to Martina. Refusing the money she said, "Take it for your vices." Later that same night he returned with the promise to go off heroin, give up his addict friends, and be good to Martina and Erasmus.

As good as his word, Johnny never had another shot. Acute withdrawal symptoms lasted for a year and minor ones much longer. During working hours—and he worked every day—he had little trouble, but the nights were sheer torture. Sleep was impossible for both of them. Martina, who had promised her complete support in the effort, walked the floor with Johnny, prayed, gave him soothing orange leaf tea, and when he cried like a baby for the needle, she gave him massive doses of cough syrup for the codeine it contained. Johnny had to suffer to overcome his vice. When methadone programs were introduced twenty years later to help the increasing number of Pascua addicts, Johnny and Martina remarked that such a cure was really just substituting one vice for another; the only true road to atonement was suffering.

During this time Perfecto became a tower of strength for Martina. Their open warfare of many years' duration receded as he talked to her seriously for long hours about how to help Johnny defeat his vice and how to live a good life. Under his influence, she sought the Assembly of God minister and together they prayed fervently for Johnny's recovery. Soon she joined that church, Perfecto by her side. At the time of the life history interviews, Martina said that Perfecto was the only Yaqui man she ever respected, a good, hard-working man with no vices, who looked after his family. In retrospect, she felt that he had been right to punish her earlier because she was wild and her behavior did not serve God. Once the addiction was overcome, with the wholehearted support of both Johnny's and Martina's families, the couple spent several more happy years together.

Antonia's favorite child in her later years was, without a doubt, her son Nicolás. Although they were not particularly close when he was small, and he left Antonia's care at an early

age, as an adult he came to depend on Antonia for assistance.
Being more mobile than his sisters, he visited Antonia more
regularly. "How she fought for Nicolás," said his sisters repeatedly. His career was rather checkered. By virtue of being a
male, he had much more access to Yaqui knowledge as a child
through his Muina uncles and grandfather, who were well
informed on historical, military, and institutional matters.
What he picked up appeared to be rather incidental and he
disclaimed having any great knowledge. He began drinking
and using marijuana in his mid- or early teens, although these
vices were not debilitating until many years later. Once he
experimented with opium in the company of a Pascua Chinese
shopkeeper. His World War II army duty took him to Ger-
many; from there he sent Antonia pictures of the German girl
with whom he lived and their son.

Upon his return to Pascua, Nicolás began living with Olívia
Mendoza, a Papago girl from San Javier; their daughter was
named Sylvia. His deeper involvement in marijuana led to his
arrest in 1950 for selling it and a two-year sentence in the
Leavenworth federal penitentiary. Shortly after his return to
the Papago girl, they separated; Sylvia went to her Papago
grandmother after Olívia went to Phoenix with a Black. Antonia was very fond of this granddaughter, who visited her
respectfully until she was grown.

For several years Nicolás established a pattern of working at
short-term unskilled jobs on farms, sporadic periods of going
on welfare, heavy drinking with other Yaqui men, and brief
affairs that occurred mainly during drinking bouts. Much of
the time he stayed with Antonia and Perfecto, but he also
moved around a lot. His positive relationship with Antonia
was forged during these adult years when she served as his
refuge.

In 1954 he established an alliance with Chepa Moreno (not
the Chepa Moreno whose life story appears in this book) that,
although punctuated by frequent upheavals during which he
returned to Antonia, nonetheless lasted. Chepa Moreno's personal history before her alliance with Nicolás was complex.
Raised in Hermosillo where she was born in 1918, she had left
her mother and come to Arizona alone as a young woman.

Described as happy, gay, and dedicated to having a good time, she eventually married Jesús Soto in the church in 1938. Their two babies died and then Jesús sickened and died, some say of witchcraft. Chepa subsequently married José Frías in a civil ceremony. He, too, had previously been married, but his wife had been murdered by a Mexican with whom she had periodically slept and from whom she and José had stolen a substantial sum of money. José and Chepa had two children before he was sent to prison for running over a little girl while drunk.

Chepa had been going around with other men, including Nicolás, after she married José about 1943. While José was in prison, she had two children by other men. All her children were legally removed from her custody and placed in foster homes. Chepa later formed an alliance with Marcelo Moreno from Sonora, which was terminated when an aunt from Hermosillo came to visit and discovered in horror that Chepa and Marcelo were *primos hermanos*: "Why did you live with your cousin? You didn't know? May God pardon you." This story was often retold by informants to illustrate the importance of teaching children who their relatives are so that incest cannot inadvertently occur.

Chepa and her fifth baby were deported to Mexico about 1949 because she had no legal immigration status. From Hermosillo, stories of her promiscuous behavior over the next four years spread to Tucson. Leaving her daughter with her mother (who was then living with Joey Chato's father), she went to Nogales. Nicolás heard she was there and went for her, arranging papers for her legal entry into the United States in 1954. Chepa was regarded by Antonia and Nicolás's sisters as essentially a good woman. Her earlier promiscuity was attributed to the fact that she was one of those women who have to have a man. She upheld kin and ritual obligations, worked hard, and although she raised none of her own five children, she later raised five grandchildren. Toward Antonia and Nicolás's sisters she always behaved properly and respectfully, and although she and Nicolás fought often and violently, she made him a good consort and stopped walking with other men.

Nicolás began drinking more and working less, until welfare became their normal source of support. During drinking bouts he went with other women, one of whom was believed by Antonia and others to have attempted to win him with witchcraft, an attempt that led to his lengthy illness.

When Loreta Muina, who had been living near Chandler for several years, returned to Pascua in 1959, she resumed regular contact with Antonia. Following her abandonment of her husband and children in 1949, she had gone with Pedro Vacamea, Mariana Vacamea's younger half-brother, whom she had met in Loreta Valencia's old household. Mariana's father, Claudio Vacamea, had taken another woman after Camilda's death and fathered three more children. Pedro, earlier married in the church, had left his wife and children and was living alone but eating with Mariana when Loreta joined the household. After they began living together, they moved to Claudio's old house across the street from Mariana's until Pedro decided jobs were better around Coolidge. For the next several years, their primary home was at Green Acre Farm, where four of their six children were born. Like Nestór, Pedro drank a lot, but he gave Loreta his paycheck and was a pleasant person to live with. For a time she was happier than she had been in years. Other women again attracted him, and about 1953 or 1954 he abandoned Loreta and their children for a life in the cantinas of Phoenix, where he encountered Felipa Muina, Loreta's aunt, who had become a *cantinera*.

A woman named Catalina who lived at Green Acres wanted Loreta to leave Pedro and live with her son, Juan. Under the guise of caring for the children while Loreta worked in the fields, she talked against Pedro perpetually and arranged to have Juan talk to Loreta. Loreta, however, tried to ignore Juan and made an all-out effort to win Pedro from Felipa, going to Phoenix to get him. After a dramatic interlude, Pedro returned, only to leave for Phoenix and Felipa shortly after their fourth baby was born.

Pedro returned again to take Loreta and the children to Felipa's house because he wanted to work in Phoenix. Felipa was much ashamed of being involved with her niece's consort, and she avoided Loreta as much as possible by staying in the bars. Loreta said, "Pedro, I don't like living with Felipa. I believe that what people say about you and Felipa is true." He replied that she was crazy, but a few days later he announced that they would go to Chandler. This time Pedro lasted a month before returning to Felipa, using the money Loreta had given him to buy milk for the baby to pay his way. Loreta again went to Phoenix: "Look, Felipa, if you want Pedro, take him. Let there be an end to this." Felipa answered quietly, "No, Loreta, I will not go with men I know." Pedro chose Loreta and never again went with Felipa.

Loreta's relationships with Catalina and another Yaqui woman at Green Acres deteriorated as Catalina continued her campaign to get Loreta to leave Pedro for her son, Juan. Not only did she talk badly about Pedro to others, but she would talk about him in his presence as though he were not there, causing Pedro to exclaim, "She acts as if she were your mother."

Disruptions began when Catalina's friend, Magdalena Valencia, went to Pascua for a visit. Hearing that a famous *curandero* from the Río Yaqui was in town, she went to see him and asked how to run off people she did not like from Green Acres Farm. Since the *curandero* was curing Loreta Sánchez's uncle (Loreta Sánchez was Antonia's brother's former wife), Loreta Sánchez was told of this harmful request. Knowing that two of Antonia's children were at Green Acres—for Nicolás and Chepa Moreno were also there—Loreta warned Antonia. Shortly thereafter, Loreta Muina came to Pascua for a visit and Antonia asked her not to return. Feeling the whole thing was foolish, Loreta returned to Pedro. Within a few days she began to feel sad, and at night she heard three *chichihuales* (whispering sounds meaning someone is thinking about you). These can be either good or bad, and can, for example, mean that a dying person is thinking about you. In this case they were bad. Loreta not only heard them but felt them as they hit her in the face. Her body began to ache, and finding the enclosed space of the house intolerable, she wandered endlessly, pushing the youngest baby in a buggy. Her pains increased sharply as she neared Magdalena's house. It seemed as though flames were licking at her body, causing her to collapse until she regained enough strength to move away.

Other people were also affected. A Mexican woman who experienced similar symptoms when she neared Magdalena's house lost a child when he was caught in a mechanical cotton picker driven by his father. When Loreta's condition worsened, Pedro took her to the Coolidge hospital, where they said nothing was wrong with her. Several other desperate trips to a doctor with Loreta gasping for breath ended with the same diagnosis. Up to that point, Loreta said, she believed she was physically ill, but after the doctors said she was crazy, she knew it was witchcraft because doctors know nothing about that sort of illness.

Each night she dreamed that she was dead in a coffin in the Pascua San Ignacio Yaqui Church and many people came to look at her. One day a snake stuck its tongue out at her in her house, but when she blinked it was gone. One of her daughters also saw the snake and she, too, became ill. Pedro, in desperation, took Loreta and the four children to Mariana in Pascua, leaving the car there with Loreta and taking a bus back to his work. Loreta's restlessness continued and she spent a day with Amelia, moved to Antonia's, back to Mariana's, and so on. Sleep eluded her. Amelia remembered that when Loreta was with her, she awakened several times a night, asking, "Don't you hear the noises?" Amelia unsympathetically said it was a cat or a rat and went back to sleep. One night at Antonia's a bad spirit sat on the porch but did not enter.

Antonia and Mariana decided that Loreta should go to a Papago *curandera* in San Javier, Sra. Mendoza, who was Olívia's mother and Sylvia's grandmother. Viviana's oldest son was delegated to take her because she refused to drive herself, and since Loreta felt that, as a good woman, she could not go alone with a man, Amelia was also sent. Sra. Mendoza cured by reciting prayers in Spanish, using no medicines and not touching Loreta at all. The following day when Loreta was worse, Nacho Valencia and Amelia took her to Sra. Mendoza's old mother, who chanted in Papago while shaking a rattle. Like her daughter, she used no medicines. She told Loreta

something serious would happen that night but if Loreta
survived, the next day they would take her to a more powerful
curandero. To Loreta, it was clear that she was near death. As
predicted, she got much worse. Mariana gave her holy water to
drink.

The next morning Loreta had Mariana's son drive her to
Green Acres. On the way, at 11:45 a.m., she had a vision that
was a repetition of her dream about San Ignacio Church, but
this time she was awake. Pedro at first refused to leave his
work, but she frantically told him she was dying and he had to
care for the children. Back at Mariana's she had another attack
at midnight that felt like "her heart was leaving her body little
by little." Pedro dressed and took her to the older Mendoza
curandera, who was drunk on beer bought with the money
Loreta had given her the day before. Crying and saying, "You
poor thing, you are so sick," Sra. Mendoza went with them to
the old Papago *curandero*'s house, but he refused to open his
door because he could hear Sra. Mendoza's drunken cries.
Giving up on him, they dropped Sra. Mendoza at her house
and drove directly to a Barrio Libre Yaqui *curandero*, don
Román Sánchez. By this time it was about 3:00 a.m. Loreta
believed he knew they were coming because he was dressed,
the lights were on, and he seemed to be waiting for them. He
asked what they wanted, but "he already knew." She said, "I
am very ill." "How do you feel?" "I see things. I hear things. I
choke. My heart is leaving my body." She explained about the
chichihuales, the things that flew in her face, the animals and
butterflies that beat against the doors and windows at night,
and the snake in Green Acres. "I know I am not crazy, but no
one else does."

Silently, don Román went into the room where he kept his
saints to prepare a medicine of holy water and herbs, over
which he recited to his saints. After Loreta drank it, she felt
better, and he finally spoke, telling her to go home and he
would dream about her case that night. Exhausted, they
returned to Mariana's, where Pedro immediately went to sleep,
leaving Loreta sitting uneasily on a chair. Once again, grass-
hoppers, ants, and butterflies and small animals filled the
windows and doors, trying to get in.

The next morning, Mariana said that a large *bulto* had sat on the head of her bed but disappeared when she woke up. Loreta's baby had been put in the bed between Mariana and her husband when Loreta and Pedro left the house at midnight, and they believed the *bulto* was after the baby. Mariana's daughter told Loreta that a huge snake (a *vipora*) was on the top of her bed about the time Loreta was at don Román's. Obviously the witchcraft was so strong it was affecting others in Loreta's vicinity.

Don Román dreamed of three women who stood to one side. They asked, "Why are you curing this woman? You will get sick, too." He identified the women as Magdalena Valencia, Catalina More, and a Papago woman who once lived with Joey Chato. "Yes," he told them. "I am going to cure her." He gave Loreta two half-gallon jars of a dark green medicine, which, however, she did not take "because it looked like poison." On a subsequent visit he had her place her face in the smoke of burning chilis, which of course burned her skin.

Marcelo Muina, a cousin, took Loreta to Luz Muina (his sister-in-law) for curing, but Luz lived too close to the source of evil (Magdalena and Catalina). After Loreta heard birds on a telephone line begin to cackle like hens, she said, "Here I cannot be cured," and returned to Mariana's. Restlessly she moved to Pedro's sister in Marana and back to Pascua.

Pedro, his sister, and her Papago consort, the latter a *curandero* of some repute, next took Loreta to a famous Mexican husband and wife curing team in Sasabe, Sonora. The wife first checked Loreta and made a diagnosis, which was not divulged to Loreta, and gave her *romero* (rosemary) medicine. Three more times Loreta returned, bringing flowers which were used in the curing. The woman found the witchcraft so strong that she called upon her husband to help.

At the conclusion of this successful cure, they told Loreta that she had had bad things in her, but it was better if she did not know who had harmed her: "Forget what happened and think of the future with a clean heart. Never think badly of anyone." And they told her how to handle *chichihuales* in the future: talk to them in bad language and they will go away. Thereafter when she heard their *chi-chi-chi*, she muttered, "Cabrón, chingado, why are you following me? Go away!" and spat on the ground.

Loreta's illness provided the impetus to leave Green Acres for Pascua, where she and Pedro agan took over Claudio Vacamea's old house. Their last two babies, Loreta's eleventh and twelfth, were born in Tucson hospitals. Although the doctors urged her to have a hysterectomy, she refused because she would have to confess the fact to a priest, and that would be "ugly."

Although not regarded as sad, Loreta in some ways resembled Antonia, in that she had consistently devoted herself to her household and the care of children and grandchildren localized in her own household. She preferred not to work outside the house, although at times she was forced to, and she seldom visited in other households except for those of Mariana, whom she called upon daily; her mother; her sister, Amelia; and Simón Valenzuela. She has never set foot in some of her older daughters' homes. In other ways she was completely unlike Antonia. Whereas Antonia was normally passive, stepping outside her silent routine on only a few occasions, Loreta was extremely verbal, discoursing freely on family affairs and the ailments of Yaqui society. When a local newspaper ran a lengthy article on the poverty and social problems of Pascua, Loreta was one of their outspoken informants.

With Loreta's return to Pascua, all of Antonia's children were again living near her; and while her passivity did not change, it was at Antonia's house that family contacts were maintained. By about 1960 the economic pressures on Antonia's household were reduced as Ramona left to live with Pete Espinoza. Perfecto's union job in construction was now adequate to support the household, with Ramona's children old enough to get odd jobs, so Antonia at long last was able to stop working as a cleaning woman. She never again went to a store or downtown; her grandchildren and children ran her errands. Nor did she visit in any house except Martina's, next door, which she reached by going through the back yards. She did, however, make two trips to Sonora.

In 1960, Perfecto arranged to have his own and Antonia's immigration status regularized, and that year Antonia was able to return to Sonora for the first time since 1904. Sad that she had not been able to return before her mother Cecelia, died, she nonetheless enjoyed the trip so much that she stayed three months rather than the planned few days, visiting with Chepa Moreno, whom she had not seen in over fifty years; meeting her half-sister (Cecelia's daughter) for the first time; seeing another half-sister, Dominga Ramírez, in Potam; and attending the Día de San Juan in Vicam and the Virgen del Camino fiesta in Lomas de Bacum. These two fiestas seem to have been the only ones she ever enjoyed. Perfecto was angry she stayed so long. He made his own long-awaited trip to Sonora in 1963, and Antonia later attended the Día de San Francisco in Magdalena with her daughter Loreta.

Perfecto was struck on the head by a loaded bucket at a construction site in 1964. It was believed briefly that he was dead. As soon as he was able, he returned to work, although he could have retired on disability insurance. The family believed he got "blood sickness" from this accident that eventually led to his hospitalization. While in the hospital, he suffered a nervous breakdown and was transferred to the state mental hospital in Phoenix. Martina went to see him, reporting that he recognized her and could walk and care for himself. The family was therefore surprised when notified a week later that he had died. A social worker tried to get the family to agree to a pauper's burial for financial reasons, but Martina took control and arranged to have his body returned to Tucson. The *velorio* at Martina's house was the subject of family controversy because Martina, herself a Protestant, refused to allow a Yaqui *velorio* such as Ramona and other relatives wanted. A priest came, but there were no *pascolas* or *matachines*. Antonia agreed with Martina that Perfecto would not have wanted a Yaqui *velorio*.

Because she received regular social security checks as a result of Perfecto's union employment, Antonia had one of the more secure incomes in the extended family, and her own needs were modest. She kept her money stuck in her hosiery, her shoes, and the front of her dress, and whenever someone requested her aid, which Nicolás and her grandsons often did, she would fish out a dollar or two.

In the late 1960s, Antonia's third child, Manuela, lost her husband. Manuela had remained with Luis Lara from the time of their marriage in 1936, although within weeks of their fancy wedding, their relationship soured as Luis began drinking heavily and became insanely jealous of Manuela, even forbidding her to call on or receive her mother and sisters. During her infrequent shopping trips, she secretly went to see Antonia and Amelia until Luis accused her of seeing other men and beat her severely when he was drunk. It was something of a relief when he joined the army during World War II and Manuela could see Antonia and her sisters whenever she wished. The old life style resumed, however, when he returned. One baby girl died in 1946, but the other seven children lived to adulthood. In the late 1960s, Luis wandered off to California and was not heard from for some time. After several V.A. checks were returned unopened from his California address, the family began to look for him. Eventually his oldest daughter in Phoenix discovered that an unidentified drunk knifed to death in a Phoenix park and buried in an unmarked pauper's grave was her father.

Manuela had had enough of Pascua, where she had been so unhappy. Giving her house to a son, she moved into a modern apartment elsewhere in Tucson with a married daughter and cared for her small grandchildren, insisting that they grow up away from the drunkenness and violence of Pascua. She temporarily opted out of Yaqui society, although her identity as a Yaqui remained strong and she continued to visit her mother and sisters.

Ramona's alliance with Pete Espinoza went from bad to worse, and she called on Antonia for emotional and financial support almost daily in the late 1960s. Pete was not bad when Ramona first went with him, and he was exceptionally fond of their daughter, born in 1961. For several years he supported them well, but by the late 1960s, few positive things were said of him. He was no longer able to work, and the family was permanently on welfare. Ramona used the welfare allowance for food, rent, and clothing, leaving Pete to find his own money to support his numerous vices. He did this by making regular rounds of Ramona's sisters, Antonia, and others in the *barrio* asking for money, by collecting empty bottles and scrap iron to sell, and by selling marijuana. He even sold Ramona's saints.

Ramona was not particularly upset by his vices, because she drank, had used marijuana, and knew many heroin users. What bothered her most was the abuse she suffered from him in front of his companions in vice. Instead of indulging his vices elsewhere, he often brought men home. Fights not infrequently erupted when the men were drunk or on marijuana, and Pete often beat her, called her a whore, and accused her of sleeping with some man he had brought home to stay with them for a few days. As Pete sank deeper into the vices, his companions became more undesirable and violence increased. The Tucson police kept their house under surveillance, arresting Pete and others with monotonous regularity. His heroin involvement cost more money and caused further unpleasantness. Several serious fights and knifings occurred, and once Pete was seriously injured when some former friends caught him when he was drunk and thoroughly worked him over.

Eventually Pete became a solitary figure, hooked on heroin to the near exclusion of other vices. Physically he deteriorated rapidly as he refused to take his insulin shots (he was a diabetic), and he more or less stopped eating. Finally he sadly said the devil possessed his soul: "I want to receive the *Espíritu Santo* and be a good man, but I am hopelessly lost." A soul in deepest torment, he constantly relived his sins, talked to the devil, and sought death. But he believed that "the bad can't die; they must live and suffer," and how he suffered, knowing that hell and eternal damnation awaited. Once when Amelia asked him matter-of-factly if he was not afraid to die, he answered emotionally, "No tengo miedo de la muerte. Que me lleve a la chingado muy pronto" ("I am not afraid of dying. May I be sent to hell quickly").

Throughout these trials and tribulations, Antonia was, until her death, Ramona's only refuge. Ramona felt free to go to Antonia's for long hours, and Antonia fed them when necessary. Loreta, Manuela, and Martina had little respect for Ramona, whom they regarded as lazy, promiscuous, dishonest, and selfish: "Why should we help her when she has never helped anyone but herself?" Amelia received Ramona, as well as Pete, and, like Antonia, helped as best she could. Ramona's godfather, the only person in the world Ramona respected and loved besides her father, would, she believed, have helped her, but he lived in Eloy. There was no one else.

Amelia's own life had not gone smoothly for several years. In the late 1950s, Joey Chato and Amelia were arrested for selling marijuana. Maintaining that she knew nothing of the whole *cochinada* (filthy mess), Amelia was released. Joey, however, was sentenced to five years in the Florence state penitentiary. A hernia operation kept Amelia from working for some time. A period of real deprivation followed in which she literally dreamed of being able to buy her sons nice lunch boxes like other children had and fill them with good food every day—a dream that was never fulfilled. Instead, her hungry children were ridiculed at school and Amelia took in washing. Always something of a *corajuda*, she lost her temper more and more often under these conditions. She beat her children so severely and with so little cause that Antonia, after attempting to change her behavior by talking, finally informed the police, who gave her a stern lecture. When he was released on good behavior after serving four years of his sentence, Joey Chato resumed selling marijuana. Although a woman who was irate over Joey's introducing her son to the vice threatened to inform the police, she was persuaded not to.

One day in 1965 Joey simply left for California, vanishing from Amelia's life until 1967. A few days after she heard he was again in Phoenix, Marcelo Muina came to tell Amelia that young Eusavio Muina (a grandson of Nacho Muina's brother) had been shot and asked if she wanted to go with him to the *velorio* in Phoenix, as of course she did. They agreed to go early the next morning. Later that night, Nestór Paderes came to Amelia, asking if she had heard the news: "Tu Joey mató a Eusavio" ("Your Joey killed Eusavio"). Amelia felt sick.

In Phoenix, she found a battered Joey in jail. Amelia asked why he had done this dreadful thing. Joey replied that he believed he had lost his mind and gone crazy, continuing, "I believe they will have to kill me." Amelia hired a lawyer "to talk for Joey."

Amelia's story of the killing comes mostly from Joey, with additions from Muina relatives. Upon his return from California with several hundred dollars in his wallet, Joey encountered two of Amelia's cousins, Eusavio and Lucas Muina, who insisted that he drink with them and then stole his wallet after knocking him unconscious in the cantina toilet. At first Joey did not know who attacked him, but he found his empty wallet and papers in Eusavio's house. For several days the cousins successfully evaded Joey, but he found them and asked if they had taken his money. They denied it. Producing the evidence of his wallet, he demanded that they repay him because the money was for his family in Tucson. Lucas actually got a job, ostensibly to repay Joey, but no money was forthcoming and Lucas soon quit working. The next time Joey approached them, they beat him up, saying they would never pay him. From the floor, he told them, "Eso es lo que quisi oír. No me vas a pagar. Pero óigame bien. Con tu vida vas a pagar." ("That is what I wanted to hear. You are not going to pay me. But listen well. You will pay with your life.") They laughed.

A few days later when he found Eusavio and his wife sitting at a table in a cantina, he said, "Ahora vas a morir" ("Now you are going to die") and shot him dead. Lucas, who had been standing at the bar, wrestled the gun from Joey's hand. Joey struggled until the police arrived, getting more beat up when he resisted arrest. He later said he remembered walking into the bar, seeing Eusavio, and feeling an intense rage, but he remembered little of what happened thereafter. He was sentenced to life imprisonment in the state penitentiary in Florence. Should he die in prison, it is a matter of great concern to Joey that he be buried among Yaquis; he desperately hopes he will not be doomed to an eternity in prison ground. Except for one offense when he and other prisoners fought after getting drunk on home brew, he has done well in prison. Looking back over his sinful, vice-laden life, he decided to make amends by studying to become a *maestro*. He learned to recite and how to perform a *maestro*'s duties, so that if he should be released, he can serve his people. Amelia laughed and said that when that day comes, she will willingly eat *huacabaqui*, the fiesta stew. If Joey, Jr., takes up his inherited vow to be a *fariseo*, perhaps she will become a *cantora* and they will all attend fiestas all the time.

After Joey Chato went to prison, Amelia's life became more orderly. Joey, Jr., started working part time, and with the

welfare money and what Amelia received from washing and
ironing, they were no longer at a starvation level. It was almost
a relief to know where Joey Chato was, and to know that his
tempestuous presence would not be reintroduced into the
household. Joey, Jr., and Alejandro did not regret his absence,
for they had not respected him. Amelia devoted almost all of
her time and energy to caring for her two sons. It was said she
would do anything for them, and her deep attachment to them
became the subject of innumerable family jokes about her
"babies." Amelia rarely left her own house except to visit
Antonia.

Martina also experienced certain stress in her life during this
time. Her marriage had become embattled, with the result that
she moved to Antonia's house after each severe fight with
Johnny. Instead of acting "like the whites," attending social
parties together, they gravitated into the more normal Mexican
and Yaqui pattern of Johnny drinking with men and Martina
interacting more with women. Johnny had become a heavy
drinker, a state that did not affect his working daily on the
garbage truck, but which became a major point of contention at
home. Martina's poor housekeeping was another source of
conflict.

Some women—Antonia, Loreta, and Amelia, for example—
presented much the same appearance to the world day in and
day out. Amelia and Antonia pinned their hair up the same
way every morning, and all their dresses were of the same
general style. In contrast, Martina, whose dress size had
increased through the years, varied greatly in appearance. At
home and at work she favored white uniforms. For special
Assembly of God church events or her now rare attendance at
parties with Johnny, she wore heavy make-up, elaborate
dresses, a high hairdo, and perhaps gold shoes. When depressed, she left her hair uncombed and used no make-up at
all. Her appearance was an extremely sensitive indicator of her
mood and activity.

Martina's membership in a Protestant church did not reflect
a wholehearted acceptance of Protestant beliefs. She continued
to pray to her *Tata Dios* in much the same way as Amelia or
Loreta. It is unlikely that she appealed to the saints, but she
did not deny them. Judicious in accusations of witchcraft and,

like Antonia, believing she had never personally been the
subject of witch-caused harm, she nonetheless believed in
witches. Her rejection of Yaqui religion was based on other
considerations. Those relatives to whom she felt the closest
ties, the Wahuechia Valencias, consistently formed the core of
Protestant sects in Pascua. Her own conversion occurred during a period of great emotional stress that ended positively:
Johnny did, in fact, overcome his heroin addiction. Up to the
time of her conversion, there is no evidence that Martina had
an interest in social problems—indeed, her less than exemplary
behavior was devoted to having a good time. Conversion
marked the beginning of a shift in her basic attitudes and
interests in which the single most formative influence was her
father and his approach to life. By the late 1960s, when she was
about forty, her own position had become clearly defined. This
in itself is not an uncommon Yaqui pattern because knowledge, authority, and responsibility often come in maturity.
Like her father and others, she accepted the view that the
Yaqui ceremonial system encourages the vices and discourages
steady employment, and therefore contributes significantly to
Yaqui poverty. Religious officials did not provide adequate role
models for younger impressionable members of Yaqui society.
"Most *maestros* stay drunk all the time and many are homo-
sexuals," she said, citing examples. A Protestant affiliation
offered her the opportunity to believe in and act upon what
she regarded as the religious essentials.

Assembly of God membership was not the only badge of
Martina's approach to life. Her attitudes toward education,
employment, and the vices were others. Although completing
more grades before quitting school than any other of Antonia's
children, and learning reasonably good English, she deeply
regretted not having continued her education. At the age of
forty she began attending Pima College, working hard on her
homework every evening after work. Regarded as a fanatic
about her children's attendance and performance at school, she
was extremely pleased at Erasmus's receiving awards and a
scholarship and wanted him to attend the University of Arizona. To Martina, education was a fundamental steppingstone
to a more desirable life style.

If one must have education, one must also have a steady, well-paying job to achieve a better life. Among her siblings, Martina had goals in terms of employment which were unique in the late 1960s and early 1970s, although several members of the descending generation had similar attitudes. For many years she worked sporadically as a motel maid because she needed money for immediate purposes and because she found the environment more compatible than being stuck at home, but the work was only a variation on the traditional theme of domestic employment for Yaqui women. As a mature woman, she had the oppotunity to become a filing clerk in a community health clinic run by the university medical school, an opportunity that coincided with the full crystalization of her attitudes. The job became of value in itself: "Now I really *do* something." Since this clinic had enormous success in supplying medical services to Pascua residents, she regarded herself as "helping the people." Vices are the steel trap for unwary Yaquis, in Martina's view. She attempted to modify the behavior of her nephews by lecturing them on the evils of the vices, by withholding aid to those she knew were drinking too much or were using marijuana or heroin, and by helping to support those seeking a higher education. For example, she partially supported Ramona's oldest son during a year in a California college, but withdrew support and actively tried to change his behavior when he returned home a long-haired hippie with vices. So strongly did she feel about the high social costs of the vices that she resorted to reporting violence and property damage to the police. Although convinced that it would be in the best interests of Pascuans if drug pushers and users were reported to the police, she dared not do so for fear of retaliation. As one story demonstrates, the form of retaliation she feared most concerned her son, in whom her hopes and plans for the future were concentrated. In 1969, a group of her nephews drank all night, becoming quite drunk by early morning. Because they were annoyed with Martina over some of her moralistic lectures, they decided to knock down her mailbox, an action she observed and reported to the police. As a result, each received a visit from the police, which further irritated them. Two of the culprits came to her house to confront her, asking why she had reported them when her own husband and brother were worse. She quietly replied, "It was for your own good. You are young; Johnny is too old to change." The nephews' ultimate revenge came in threats to take Erasmus out and "make a man of him"—introduce him to wild girls, get him drunk, give him some marijuana, and maybe even shoot him up with heroin. As they were fully aware, they were verbalizing her most deep-seated fears.

Martina's widely known attitudes and religious affiliation have served to isolate her somewhat socially and have created friction with her relatives and her husband in a number of ways, as well as initiating frustrations for her personally. Johnny, who did not share her basic attitudes, resented the periodic social repercussions of Martina's behavior. They received many demands for assistance since their house was the largest in her own extended family, their combined income when both of them were working was one of the best in the *barrio*, they had a telephone, and their English was the best in the family. The moral judgments Martina exercised and the restrictions she placed on such aid were contrary to the basic obligation system. It may be said that she manipulated the system beyond acceptable limits. Furthermore, she gave precedence to improving the socioeconomic status of her nuclear family, something that she said would have been impossible if she met all requests for aid. Relatives particularly resented her non-Yaqui influence in family death ceremonies.

Martina's own frustration arose from her realistic perception of her ineffectiveness in instituting changes she regarded as desirable. When she refused aid to lazy, *viciado* nephews, they merely raided her kitchen when she was at work and got money from Antonia or Amelia. Realizing that she had to live in Pascua, for she had no intention of leaving Pascuan society as her older sister, Manuela, had done, she walked a fine line between doing what she believed was right and not antagonizing too many people. She consciously evaluated the probable effects of a particular course of action, as when she and Johnny bought a new car, something of a rarity in Pascua. Cars are a resource in the obligation and friendship systems—they are freely borrowed by relatives and friends and serve an integral function in social behavior, especially that of men who drive around drinking. The car of another informant's husband was borrowed regularly by no fewer than twenty people, for example. Martina knew that when they acquired the new car a rash of requests to borrow and ride in it would inevitably follow, as they did. Deciding in advance to accede to the minimal number of requests, she rather closely predicted the consequences of her policy and her margin of social safety.

In spite of the characteristics that made her somewhat atypical, Martina could not be called marginal or a dropout from Yaqui society. The concerns that caused her to maintain her Protestant affiliation were shared by Yaquis who continued to operate within the framework of Yaqui religion, as well as some who had moved into nonparticipation. Within the family, her positive responses to requests for aid weighed at least as heavily as her attempts to modify behavior. In many respects, she more closely approached the ideals of women's behavior than did others in her family. Large segments of her beliefs and behavior were shared with other Arizona Yaquis. She did not "walk in the houses," was circumspect and proper in her relations with men, and raised her own children. Without a doubt, she identified herself as a Yaqui, and she possessed one of the primary prerequisites of being identified as a Yaqui—she spoke *la lengua* fluently; but her universe centered in the con-temporary Pascua scene. Perhaps the only person who never criticized Martina was her mother, who felt that old Abelardo Cochemea might have approved of her attitudes toward re-ligion. Martina rather regretfully realized that her Protestant affiliation would probably preclude her becoming an agent of social change on a *barrio*-wide basis.

In the mid-1960s, Antonia was diagnosed as having cancer. After some radiation treatments, she refused to continue with the doctors, saying she would die when God willed. She spent her final years almost entirely within her household, caring for those relatives who happened to be there at any one time, tending her many plants, and watching boxing on television. Her children and grandchildren enjoyed watching her watch boxing because she got so excited, acting almost as though she were in the ring. Amelia once commented that the only time she was able to believe the stories about Antonia's aggressive behavior as a child was when she saw her mother reacting to boxing.

At the conclusion of my third interviewing season in 1970, Antonia told me she would not see me again, and gave me a pair of gold earrings and the wedding band Nacho had given her. Her daughters interpreted that as an omen. Shortly after I left, she entered her final illness, characteristically refusing medical care until she could no longer walk and care for the plants she loved. Her daughters finally insisted that she go to the hospital. A well-known Papago curer was taken to the hospital by a grandson to assess the seriousness of her condition and to perform such curing as is beyond the knowledge of doctors. After laying his hands on her head and reciting, he told the grandson, "She is very bad. But God in His mercy is great. Who knows? It is in the hands of God." A few days later, on August 4, 1970, she died quietly. The *velorio*, held at Martina's house, alienated those relatives who felt Antonia should have a Yaqui ritual with a ramada, *pascolas*, *matachines*, *maestros*, and *cantoras*. Instead, Antonia's body was laid out in Martina's living room. Everyone approved of the way she was dressed for burial in a pretty pink dress, her best gold earrings, and the dark glasses she had worn constantly for several years. Antonia's *ahijados* and a woman who had placed a habit on Antonia during an illness requested permission of Amelia, the oldest child, to place rosaries on her body. Although no Yaqui ceremonial specialists performed, the one and only ordained Yaqui priest, Father Felipe Rojas of Obregón, Sonora, who was visiting Arizona Yaqui communities at the time, attended and led the recitation. Antonia was buried next to Perfecto in the Good Hope Cemetery in a well-kept plot bordered by a cement wall. Antonia's name was added to the bronze double plaque. Only a short distance away in the same cemetery is the un-grassed, mounded-earth, Yaqui-style triple burial of María, Miguel, and Nacho. It is impossible to know which style of burial Antonia would have felt was more appropriate or better expressed her own evaluation of the sum total of her life. One suspects that if she had chosen, she would have wished to spend eternity near María, but it was characteristic of her silent, passive, take-what-comes life style that her burial ritual was dominated by her most decisive daughter, Martina.

The *novena*, like the *velorio*, was held at Martina's, again attracting many relatives of the normally fragmented kin group. One of Perfecto's Potam cousins made the long train and bus trip to attend. Those relatives who objected to the non-Yaqui-style observances of Antonia's *velorio* and *novena* planned and saved for her *cumpleaño*, which was held in August 1971 at Loreta Muina's house. Simón Valenzuela, who had been rebuffed when he offered to build a ramada for the *velorio*, cooperated with Nicolás, Antonia's younger brother from Barrio Libre, her sons-in-law, grandsons, and other relatives to build the ramada. Loreta and Pedro Vacamea assumed most of the expense and arranged to have *pascolas* from Guadalupe, a deer dancer and musicians from Vicam, *matachines* from two Tucson *barrios* and Marana, and a *maestro* and *cantoras* from Barrio Libre. Pedro's involvement was appropriate because he had assumed a position as a Pascua ceremonial leader following the loss of older ceremonial leaders who moved to the newly founded Pascua Nueva.

Martina, the most businesslike member of the family, arranged for Amelia to have Antonia's house. Although this action infuriated Ramona, everyone else agreed that the eldest should have it. Insofar as the siblings maintained contact on a common meeting ground and recognized a successor to Antonia, it was Amelia.

One could not call Antonia the head of the family because she offered no direction, made no decisions affecting the family as a whole, and was far too introverted and passive; but in her own quiet way she was the family anchor. Always there, always dependable and predictable, she exemplified those aspects of Yaqui values that stress individual autonomy. Regardless of what her descendants did in their own lives, she passed no moral judgments, she seldom attempted to change their behavior, and she gave aid to those who came to her.

Acknowledgments

In exploring the potentials of anthropological life histories or personal narratives, Clyde Kluckhohn and L. L. Langness provide the starting point. This particular study has its roots in my work with Rosalio Moisés. The research was largely supported by the Canada Council; the University of Calgary also provided assistance. Frances Roback and Laurie Nock each served as my assistant; both contributed to data collection as well as to other aspects of the research. John Molloy helped me formulate parts of the interpretive framework. Mrs. Dorothy Stockbridge of Cambridge, England, typed the first lengthy draft of the study, which Edward Spicer kindly read and thoughtfully criticized with his usual kindness and thoroughness. The final draft was typed and edited by Mrs. E. L. Wittig; Laura Nader read the final draft and offered useful criticism. Lesley Nicholls and Hildur Anderson assisted with details of manuscript revision. Barry MacDonnell drafted the maps and Anne Burkholder provided the sketches of the four women.

The list of Yaquis and others in Arizona, Sonora, and Texas who made me welcome, talked to me, extended hospitality, and otherwise assisted in the research is lengthy: Matilde González, Juan González, Crescensio Arenas, Júlian Arenas, Juana Choque, Consuela Zuñiga, Anita Espinoza, Fausto Espinoza, Matilde Espinoza, Francisco Murillo, Francisca Moroyoki, Epifania Moroyoki, Chata Guzmán, Magalena Wong, Catalina Wong, Josefa Alvarez, Francisco Contreras, Rufina Valencia, Julia Valencia, Anselmo Valencia, Cristina Valenzuela, Lupe Aguilar, Evangelina Valencia, Luz Valenzuela, Secundina Alvarez, Castula Valencia, Juana Frías, Carmen Frías, Maura Valenzuela, Francisco Ochoa, Philomena Ochoa, Manuel Valencia, Juana Bracamonte, and Ana Valencia. To these people, the Canada Council, and the University of Calgary, I take this opportunity to say thank you.